trate the difficulties of financing higher education at a time when funding is scarce.

Specific recommendations include: separate, well-defined functions for various institutions; specialized counseling, new programs in service and technical areas, and work-study opportunities; graduate teacher-training, systematic faculty self-evaluation, teaching clinics, and broader faculty recruitment; joint trustee, faculty, and student participation in decision-making; and increased public support for higher education.

Covering every aspect of the field, *Higher Education in America* will be a valuable help for all administrators, faculty, and students.

THE AUTHORS

ALGO D. HENDERSON is research educator at the Center for Research and Development in Higher Education, Berkeley. He has served as president of Antioch College, as a member of the President's Commission on Higher Education, and as founder and director of the Center for the Study of Higher Education, University of Michigan. He is the author of *The Innovative Spirit,* published by Jossey-Bass.

JEAN GLIDDEN HENDERSON has served as administrator at C. W. Post Center, Long Island University, and at Finch College, New York.

★★
★★★★★★★★★★★★★★★★★★★★★★★★★★★★★★★★★★★★★★★

Higher Education
in America

Problems, Priorities, and Prospects

★★
★★★★★★★★★★★★★★★★★★★★★★★★★★★★★★★★★★★★★★

****
****

Algo D. Henderson

Jean Glidden Henderson

****
****

★★
★★★★★★★★★★★★★★★★★★★★★★★★★★★★★★★★★★★★★★★

HIGHER
EDUCATION
IN
AMERICA

★★★★★★★★★★★★★★★★★★★★★★★★★★★★★★★★★★★★★★★
★★★★★★★★★★★★★★★★★★★★★★★★★★★★★★★★★★★★★★

Jossey-Bass Publishers
San Francisco · Washington · London · 1974

HIGHER EDUCATION IN AMERICA
Problems, Priorities, and Prospects
by Algo D. Henderson and Jean Glidden Henderson

JACKET DESIGN BY WILLI BAUM

FIRST EDITION

Code 7417

The
Jossey-Bass Series
in Higher Education

★★★
★★

Preface

★★
★★★

The literature on higher education—books, journal articles, and reports—is becoming extensive, but most of these items analyze a specific problem or area of concern. Such studies make important contributions to our knowledge, but they examine the trees and not the forest. When an economist attacks the problem of financing universities, he may provide insights into the economics of finance, but, in identifying the most feasible sources of income, he may overlook the social justification for educating people and the philosophical bases by which a nation chooses to spend more or less for colleges and universities than for highways.

We are critical of many of the solutions being proposed for the special problems of higher education because in the long run the proposals would distort the nature and the social role of colleges and universities. For this reason, we examine in this volume the whole of higher education. *Higher Education in America* provides an overview of the problems of higher education and examines the policies that prevail, with an emphasis on long-run trends and issues—those that affect what colleges and universities will be doing during the next decade. In it, we consider objectives, students, curriculum, teaching, research and services, intellectual and academic freedom, and the problems of leadership, participation in governance, multicampus systems, the role of the state, and who pays and how much can we afford to spend for higher education. We have drawn on the information and ideas provided by experts, and through a bibliography we open the way to specialized sources of knowledge. We have had to limit our discussions of problems, however, because of our desire to weave a synthesis on *the* problem of higher education. We have subordinated criticisms to a positive statement of our views.

For students who are preparing to become administrators, the book presents an orientation to current problems and to educational philosophy. For policy makers, including administrators and trustees, it provides an identification of trends and a discussion of policies for colleges and universities. For faculty and students, it helps to articulate academic concerns about some of the trends in higher education, and it informs them about alternatives.

Higher Education in America is a sequel to Algo Henderson's *Policies and Practices in Higher Education* (Harper and Row, 1960). In a few places, with permission from Harper and Row, we have used content from the earlier book; however, these portions have been thoroughly rewritten. The concept for the book grew out of a course on the problems of higher education developed originally by Algo Henderson and taught more recently by James L. Miller, Jr., at the Center for the Study of Higher Education, The University of Michigan. We are indebted to James Miller for providing constructive ideas for this book. We wish to express our appreciation also to the staff of the Center for Research and Development in Higher Education, University of California, Berkeley, for various types of assistance.

Berkeley, California   *Algo D. Henderson*
April 1974   *Jean Glidden Henderson*

Contents

xi

Higher Education
in America

Problems, Priorities, and Prospects

1

Background
for Change

The wave of growth experienced by colleges and universities during the past quarter century is cresting. It has left in its wake a multitude of problems. More than that, much of social policy toward higher education is being questioned.

During the postwar years, opportunity for education beyond the high school was extended. During the decade of the 1960s, education was racked by controversy, frustrations, and sometimes violence. And now, during the seventies, education is experiencing changes. The changes grow out of a reexamination of purposes, out of a realization that segments of the population have been bypassed as we have worked for equality of opportunity, out of a surge of experiments and innovations in programs, and as a result of a trend toward systems of institutions. We need a fresh sense of direction to guide colleges and universities in the midst of social change. This direction, in part, will be found by observing some trends of the past.

1

For two centuries after the founding of Harvard University in 1636, American education followed traditional patterns. It then began to develop a character of its own. Church-founded colleges, established by the several denominations to preserve and advance particular elements of culture, dotted the hills and plains. As the frontier of civilization moved westward, each of the states initiated a public university as the capstone of its public school system. The federally encouraged colleges of agriculture and mechanic arts, beginning a century ago, gave impetus to research, to occupational training, and to types of extension education that had been frowned on by the universities of Europe.

The age of science and industrialization had arrived, and the United States was quick to recognize the implications for higher education. Harvard's elective courses broke the standard pattern of four years of required classics, permitting rapid expansion of the curriculum and making room for the new sciences and the social sciences. Each knowledge area grew rapidly, bursting outward in concentric circles.

The beginning of this profound change occurred as the wave of democracy, spirited by Jefferson and brought to a head during the Jacksonian period, swept over the new nation. Alarmed by the extension of the ballot to illiterate persons, the educators—Horace Mann and his contemporaries—advocated universal literacy as the solution. And so, for the first time anywhere in the world, the compulsory study of reading, writing, and arithmetic by all children was advocated. This necessitated the establishment of public normal schools for the training of teachers. It also led to a recognition of the responsibility of the public and the use of tax revenues so that educational needs were adequately met.

Parents who had passed through four, six, or eight years of school wanted their children to have more. This created a demand to have the public school program extended upward. The frontier advanced so rapidly that the grammar schools and the private preparatory schools of the eastern coast did not take deep root in the Middle West. They were supplanted by the public school system, which came to include a full-fledged high school. The famous Kalamazoo court case (*Stuart* v. *School District*, 1874) established the legal right of a community to provide free education in a public high school. The reasoning of the court could well apply to today's controversy as to who should pay for higher education: "We suppose that it had always been understood in this state that education, not merely in the rudiments, but in an enlarged sense, was regarded as an important practical advantage to be supplied at their option to rich and poor alike, and not as something pertaining merely to culture and accomplishment to be brought as such within the reach of those whose accumulated wealth enabled them to pay for it."

Within a short generation this lusty infant, the high school, had far outgrown its parent, the preparatory school. The high school was free to the students. Many states advanced the compulsory attendance age and raised the minimum age for employment. These acts brought additional students into the high school. With each decade the secondary enrollments increased, especially following World War I. By 1950, attendance had become general and in some states not far from universal. With the additional numbers, the interests became more varied and the needs diversified. The preparatory school had limited its program to the college preparatory role; the public high school assumed additional functions. As a result, the high school curriculum became comprehensive. The appetite of the people for knowledge continued to grow. The generation that had graduated from high school wanted its children to attend college. Following World War II, the wave swept into the colleges.

During the nineteenth century, a basic pattern for higher education became clear. Private colleges, both church-related and independent, multiplied in numbers and flourished in an atmosphere of relative freedom from state supervision or interference. Parallel with them, however, each state—and with greater promptness and decisiveness, the newer states—founded a state university and state normal schools and colleges. Dissatisfaction with the traditional liberal arts colleges, and the almost total absence of professional schools except for theology and law, had led the president of Brown University, in 1850, to

lament that there were no institutions for agricultural, industrial, mechanical, and mercantile education. Shortly thereafter
the Morrill Act—first enacted in 1859 and vetoed by President
Buchanan but again passed in 1862 and signed by President
Lincoln—became the first significant move by the federal government to stimulate higher education. It offered land to each
of the states to encourage them to begin programs of education
and research in agriculture and the mechanic arts (Eddy, 1957).
Johns Hopkins and the University of Michigan presently set a
new pace for moving collegiate study to more advanced levels
by adapting to American needs the German model of graduate
study and research. Private ventures by the hundreds—mostly
profit-making—also were begun, to fill vocational training gaps
left vacant by the high school or to meet the needs of post-high
school students.

In view of the recent tendency of the public colleges to
increase tuition charges, it is interesting to note that the original
goal commonly sought by the states was extension of free education to the higher level. During the earlier years of the University of Michigan, for example, a student could study liberal arts,
law, or medicine with the payment of only a matriculation fee
of ten dollars.

Thus the seeds for a radically different system of higher
education in the United States had taken root during the nineteenth century; but most of the growth has occurred since the
turn of the century. At the beginning of the twentieth century,
most college students were from higher socioeconomic groups.
We were still being influenced by the classical tradition. Under
classical policy, a limited number of young people were educated at the university, where they were inculcated with the
cultural heritage. They then became the leaders in government
and the professions, assuring the society a cultured and presumably wise leadership. The remainder of the youth needed little
education or, at most, some vocational education for their
work. A variant from this pattern assumed that society benefited from enabling persons of privileged status to have some
leisure. Thus, the culturally educated became patrons of art,
music, architecture, education, and sports.

In 1900, only 4 percent of the appropriate age group attended college or university. The preparatory school curriculum and the college preparatory course in the high school were oriented to college attendance. The secondary curricula consisted of the substratum in a sequence of studies, the end objective of which was entrance into a prestige occupation. High school and college together constituted an escalator for the intellectually inclined youths. For those who had the money but not necessarily the brains, the ivy-clad campus still smacked a bit of the school for cultured gentlemen in the British tradition. Some 52 percent of the college graduates entered four professions: law, medicine, dentistry, and the ministry.

But the yeast of change was fermenting. The liberal arts curriculum was flowering, subject matter was being fragmented and becoming more specialized, professional schools had been launched, more were coming, and all of them were developing rapidly. Coincidentally, fresh reserves of youths, women as well as men, were pressing into the high schools and looking beyond. Some educators were calling for a broader perspective on higher education. David Starr Jordan, president of a private university (Stanford) that was to grow rapidly in prestige and size, proclaimed in 1903 that "the keynote of the modern university is its usefulness" and "every man that lives has a right to some form of higher education. A generous education . . . should be the right of every son and daughter of this republic" (p. 173). A few public universities were being required, as a matter of public policy, to admit any applicant who possessed a high school diploma.

Shortly after 1900, the idea of the public two-year college was introduced. The plan spread and by 1970 had become a major factor in giving youth—all youth, whether elite or not—the chance to get some college education.

The passing of the land frontier and the increase in the amount of capital required to initiate a business enterprise reduced the opportunities for ambitious youths in agriculture and business, and it became clear that the best route to opportunity in America was through education. Fresh knowledge, whether acquired through university research or through pragmatic experimentation on the farm or in the factory, does not lie idle in the United States. It is quickly disseminated and used. The earlier European practice was to pass much of the practical knowledge along by the apprenticeship system. In the United States the institutions of learning, which ignored precedents and were less concerned about prestige, have organized this knowledge and systematized instruction (Brubacher and Rudy, 1968). They have consistently related theory to practice and practical knowledge to general knowledge. The gain in effectiveness of our industry and agriculture is obvious. Professional schools such as agriculture and engineering, through research and education, have been true leavening influences in technological development and in producing an affluent society.

More recently, and especially under the impact of the technological growth that followed World War II, a new dimension has been added to the national policy for education. This is the need of a modern society to develop fully its human resources. In a way, this concept had been emerging earlier. Andrew D. White, in the formative years of Cornell University, had spoken of the genius and talent of citizens as the most precious of state treasures. And he asserted that it was a duty of society to itself to see that the stock of talent and genius in each generation had a chance for development, so that it could add to the world stock and aid in the world's work.

Although White thought of talent as a "state treasure," he was thinking of the students of highest ability. There has never been much difference of opinion in the United States about the desirability of making it possible, financially or otherwise, for the students of highest ability to attend and complete college. The recent thinking about the admission of youth to college, though certainly including the highest 4 percent to 10 percent, goes far beyond these limitations. Educators now advocate admitting the top 25 or 50 percent to selected programs, and they also advocate open admissions for any students with high school diplomas who wish general and vocational studies.

During the nineteenth century, women had to knock hard on the doors to get admitted to a college, but by 1970 they were generally accepted equally with men; however, some fields of study continued to be male oriented. It was only following 1970 that some professional schools and graduate departments began to admit women more freely. Educators also recognize that educational opportunity has been stacked in favor of the white majority; blacks and other minorities are just beginning to be considered part of the available human resources.

Some educators support the theory that a society should do what it can to encourage and assist *all* of its citizens to grow in knowledge and skills consistent with each one's abilities and interests. This introduces the controversial question as to what segment of the total job should be done by higher (or postsecondary) education, and here there are more pronounced differences of opinion. But the nature of higher education is still changing and its scope broadening materially. The central questions now are concerned with the roles of the institutions beyond the high school in developing human resources.

A radical change has taken place in the thinking of parents and their children about the types of occupations into which a college-educated man or woman may go. In contrast to the earlier goal of a prestige profession or teaching, the aims now cover a multitude of choices—professional, business, public, and social service. The four professions which in 1900 recruited 52 percent of the graduates now receive only a tiny percentage of them. This does not represent a shift of interest away from these professions—they are still essential and attractive as careers. But the number of persons in these occupations has grown only slightly in comparison with the number finding outlets in the many newer professions, in business, in institutions of many kinds, in governmental service, and in the skill levels of many technologies and administrative areas. Another radical change has taken place in the thinking of some young men and women who question whether they want to work on a job as employees of the establishment. They seek alternatives in finding security and the good life.

It makes good sense to couple occupational or specialized education with general education—or the reverse—and that is what most institutions do. To some extent they have always done so, as the vigorous growth of liberal education in this country shows. It is becoming clearer all the time that the knowledge needed by the average person in carrying out his responsibilities of citizenship is rapidly growing. Formerly, the citizen was concerned with his neighborhood and, in a measure, with events in Washington. Today his voice is needed in determining policies and events around the globe and on into space. The need for informed judgment by the electorate has become crucial.

With the passage of the decades, the American creed of educating people for the good life has become more meaningful. It is the distinctive feature of the American philosophy. Our aim is to open the door to the good life to everyone, and we have been discovering that the portion of the population that can profit by this type of study on the college level is much larger than had earlier been assumed. Perhaps our cultural growth has been retarded by diffusion—a contention difficult to prove—but if so, we have laid a more substantial foundation for further development, and our system provides a better chance of bringing to the top persons of creative talent and leadership capacity.

The newer concept of higher education is education for the many rather than for the few. To meet the needs of the many, the educational programs have been diversified and now comprise many and varied fields of interest with curricula of varying lengths. Thus the student, with constructive guidance, may emerge from his formal training at a point consistent with his interests and abilities, able to secure placement appropriate to his training. When large numbers of youth from all socioeconomic levels enter college, the number with intellectual ability sufficient to succeed in the higher levels of education is considerably enlarged.

Many persons of lesser intellectual abilities, but with other talents and diversified interests, attend college. This raises questions about the nature and quality of the programs to be offered. If each institution tries to do everything for everybody, the dilution may become serious. If educators emphasize quantity and legislators emphasize low unit costs, we may promote mass education rather than education of the masses. Extension of educational opportunity and the diversification of programs need not and should not mean a lowering of the quality of the programs or of student achievement. We need more, not less, competence in occupations and in civic affairs, and a continuously rising appreciation for and skill in living the good life.

The structure of higher education has also been changing. Heretofore, we have had universities, specialized and professional colleges (such as teachers' colleges and schools of agriculture and engineering), and liberal arts colleges. In recent decades we have been moving toward a new grouping that includes complex institutions (usually called universities), unitary colleges (such as liberal arts), and community (two-year) colleges. Accompanying this change is a need for area planning and overall coordination. At the state level, these moves are leading to the development of regional and statewide systems of colleges and universities.

Our ability to change in the future is supported by the many and varied innovations of the past. Public colleges to train teachers, to engage in applied research in agriculture and industry, and to open education beyond the secondary school for all persons were created, not in isolated cases but as nationwide movements. The classical pattern of curriculum was broken; graduate schools were launched and rapidly expanded the size and diversity of their programs; and as new professions emerged, the universities created the schools in which the personnel could be trained. Wisconsin encouraged the farm boys with cow dung on their boots to come to the university for short courses—and thus began our flourishing program of extension courses and continuing education.

The weaknesses of rote learning and of authoritarian indoctrinations were recognized early, and new methods of teaching and learning were devised. Theory and practice became integrated, laboratory and field experiences were found to be educational, vocation and culture were perceived as being interrelated, technical equipment to facilitate learning was invented, and individualized learning was encouraged.

Plurality of sponsorships and diversity of types of institutions and their programs became accepted policy. The colleges and universities founded voluntary accrediting associations to exert ethical controls and to assure appropriate standards of education. This was in the American spirit and tradition and contrasted with practice elsewhere in the world, where the governments supervised the programs and controlled the institutions.

Universities as organized centers for learning date back a thousand years. Seen in this perspective, these changes in education in the United States during the past century and a half are all the more remarkable. The innovative spirit has permeated American higher education (Henderson, 1970). Tradition has been accepted when it has proved its merit; but changes have been made as the need for change has become evident.

In addition to looking at the past for guidance, it is essential to discover new directions by examining contemporary needs. Such examinations have been made in various surveys of higher education. The findings and recommendations have contributed much to our knowledge. But underlying the surveys are the issues about higher education. They are symptoms of needs.

This book is concerned primarily with fundamental issues, rather than with problems that call for immediate solutions. The more immediate problems of seventeen colleges and universities, together with descriptions of their causes, are discussed in detail in *Academic Transformation* (Riesman and Stadtman, 1973). These institutions serve well as case studies. In this volume, we analyze the basic issues of higher education in the context of criticisms being voiced by students, by faculty, by administrators, and by those spokesmen for the public who help determine public policy and provide the necessary resources for the institutions of higher education. However, the emphasis is on longer-run trends and on principles that give perspective and that should govern public and educational policy. A few examples of problems will suggest our frame of reference.

Is higher education becoming more and more depersonalized in favor of education in mass groups? Such a trend is alarming, because education really occurs only as each individual changes and grows. Are the courses of study sufficiently relevant to students' needs? Students contend that the university should address itself to the issues of social change and should also prepare graduates to work effectively in reducing such things as racism, pollution, poverty, and the use of force in settling international conflicts.

Should the faculties give more attention to improving the teaching-learning process? If we are in a period of social change —a postindustrial revolution era—do the objectives of general education need reexamination? How can we best develop our human resources as we reorder the nation's priorities in favor of universally available resources for health, better management of our natural resources, reduction of pollutions, and curtailment of centralized power?

Is there a real shortage of funds for higher education? In reordering the nation's priorities, where should higher education be placed when allocating our gross national product? Should the colleges and universities become less competitive through cooperation and through better definition of the functional role of each? How can the state achieve good overall planning and coordination in the authorization of programs and the allocation of resources and, at the same time, free the professional personnel—faculties and administrators—to determine and implement educational policy and program? What role should faculty unions play? How can the knowledge of students as the consumers of education be utilized in decision-making?

How can the educational process be ordered and conducted to avoid triviality, superficiality, and dogmatism in favor of a learning that progresses in both breadth and depth? How can intellectual freedom be maintained?

Purpose of
Higher Education

★★★
★★★

Thoughtful men have posed many models for the well-educated man, and these provide insights into the central purpose of higher education. It is also instructive to observe the changes that have occurred in our thinking about purpose as society has evolved through successive stages of industrialization. Historically the emphasis has been on educating the good man, the intelligent man, for a life of cultural and scientific attainments. As society becomes more industrialized and egalitarian, demands are made for greater attention to vocational education. As society becomes more and more complex, the institutions are pressed to assume social obligations—to train for employment, to solve social problems, to help set ethical directions for society. The purposes of higher education are severalfold. They are concerned with student growth and development, the discovery and refinement of knowledge, and social impacts on the community. But all of the programs should be oriented to a central

purpose. Some of the more significant definitions of that purpose are described below.

Models of the Educated Man

The ideal of the cultured man was impressively described by Cardinal Newman in his classic book, *The Idea of a University* (1941 edition, pp. 196-197):

> But a university training is the great ordinary means to a great but ordinary end; it aims at raising the intellectual tone of society, at cultivating the public mind, at purifying the national taste, at supplying true principles to popular enthusiasm and fixed aims to popular aspiration, at giving enlargement and sobriety to the ideas of the age, at facilitating the exercise of political power and refining the intercourse of private life. It is the education which gives a man a clear conscious view of his own opinions and judgments, a truth in developing them, an eloquence in expressing them, and a force in urging them. It teaches him to see things as they are, to go right to the point, to disentangle a skein of thought, to detect what is sophistical, and to discard what is irrelevant. It prepares him to fill any post with credit and to master any subject with facility. It shows him how to accommodate himself to others, how to throw himself into their state of mind, how to bring before them his own, how to influence them, how to come to an understanding with them, how to bear with them. He is at home in any society, he has common ground with every class; he knows when to speak and when to be silent; he is able to converse; he is able to listen; he can ask a question pertinently, and gain a lesson seasonably, when he has nothing to impart himself; he is ever ready, yet never in the way; he is a pleasant companion, and a comrade you can depend upon; he knows when to be serious and when to trifle, and he has a sure tact which enables him to trifle with gracefulness and to be serious with effect. He has the repose of a mind which lives in itself, while it lives in the world, and which has resources for its happiness at home when it can-

> not go abroad. He has a gift which serves him in public, and supports him in retirement, without which good fortune is but vulgar, and with which failure and disappointment have a charm. The art which tends to make a man all this, is in the object which it pursues as useful as the art of wealth or the art of health, though it is less susceptible of method, and less tangible, less certain, less complete in its result.

Newman's essay was written when the objective was to educate for cultural elitism, and with a curriculum that was compact and well focused. With the blossoming of the industrial age and the welling up of demand from all men and women for education, the objectives and programs became more complex.

Although the Newman model in many ways is obsolete, the goal of developing the intelligent man is not. A later American model has been the scholar or professional man—one who has objectivity, flexibility, and breadth of learning. Man's brain is capable of a high degree of development; it has been called a tool that can be sharpened. It can reason and therefore delve to the heart of a matter. It can evaluate and therefore make critical judgments. It can plan ahead for future action and thus provide direction.

In thinking about the intelligent man, we are reminded of the goals of the ancient trivium and quadrivium of liberal education. It was the trivium that provided the tools of thinking: grammar, the proper use of language; logic, the training in accurate thinking; and rhetoric, the facility in expressing one's thoughts and ideas. The quadrivium added certain skills in the use of symbols, especially from mathematics. This view of education has a timelessness about it. Indeed many of the writers that subscribed to it contended that human nature does not change and hence liberal education should be the same for all men in all times.

A more recent writer, Theodore M. Greene (1943) recaptured the goal of developing the power of the mind by posing the following outcomes for the education of the student: training in the accurate and felicitous use of language as the essential condition of all reflection, self-expression, and communication with others; training in the acquisition of factual knowledge of ourselves, our society and other societies, the physical world and ultimate reality, so far as it is humanly knowable; training in mature and responsible evaluation and decision in the controversial areas of science, social policy, morality, art, and religion; training in synoptic comprehension, that is, in the escape from the multiple provincialisms which bedevil mankind, and in the attainment of larger and more inclusive perspectives.

These ideas are derived from the concept of intellectual discipline. Stated in terms that may be too simple, a college-educated man should have verbal facility, a background of basic facts, a perspective about values, and an ability to transpose and integrate knowledge so that it becomes wisdom. Presumably these qualities, secured best through liberal education, should result in an improvement of culture. Greene (1943, p. 115) thought so, as demonstrated by his words: "Our greatest weakness today is our lack of genuine culture. This deficiency manifests itself in the superficiality in many of our standards, the poverty of many of our individual experiences, and in the inadequacy of our social consciousness. It can be corrected only through liberal education."

Since 1943, when Greene wrote on liberal education, we have made great strides in technology, but we have used it for materialistic ends. America still lacks genuine culture, and our recent behavior in various parts of the world has suggested that our ethical standards need further refinement. Whether liberal education can be a potent influence on the culture of men is debatable, but in the long run it certainly can be an influence. Indeed, if we could achieve for large numbers of men and women the four goals posed by Greene, this surely would have an impact on the character of our society. But the trend has been otherwise, for a consequence of the devotion to technological advance has been the shrinking of general and liberal courses in favor of specialization, much of it skill training.

The emphasis on technology has its roots in the shift in interest from the humanities to science. Newman wrote when concern with the humanities was at a high point. The age of science, stimulated by discoveries—such as those by Priestley in atomic structure and by Darwin in evolution—was just emerging. Once launched, the study of science swept into the universities as a new tide of learning. The vogue became objectivity in analysis—the use of inductive reasoning rather than the older, deductive method. New facts led to new theories and older, pontifical ones were discarded. The laboratory, coupled with empirical field research, helped to free the mind of man from instinctive behavior, from ignorance and fear. Both in strengthening the quality of men's thinking, and in raising the standards of living of most people, the age of science has been of tremendous benefit.

John Dewey (1916) was a strong advocate of the scientific method as a mode of thinking. He was concerned about developing comprehensive and accurate ways to think through the use of critical inquiry. Thus the scientific method has usefulness far beyond the confines of science. Dewey said that the training received in college should carry over into one's adult life. Discipline is not really effective when a tool is sharpened in college, unless the tool is useful after college. Too often the transfer to postcollege activity does not occur. The student should be trained in problem-solving so that he is able to use analysis and synthesis in novel situations.

Scientists often have defined objectivity as lack of responsibility for the uses of knowledge. They discover increments of knowledge but leave it to others to determine the consequences. This is a failure in social responsibility. Critical inquiry is more than an examination of facts; it is also a route to the discovery of the best answer to a problem. A discovery and the uses to which it is put are equally important to the welfare of society.

As a consequence of the trauma of the Great Depression of the 1930s and of the tragedies of the war of the 1940s, Robert Hutchins and others attempted to reorient the curriculum toward the humanities. We needed to gain a better sense of values. Something was terribly wrong with our economic system, and war as a method of settling disputes between civilized nations was unthinkable. The contention of the humanists was that, if a man knew what was good and what was bad, he would choose the good. Hutchins (1953) found a solution in the great books—they contain the best thinking of which men have been capable, and they reveal how the men who wrote them arrived at refined ideas.

Other educators, in contrast, felt that the too-exclusive devotion of the student's time to great books was seriously confining. Such a curriculum devotes much time to facts (in anthropology, economics, or physics, for example) that have been disproved and to theories that have been sloughed off as men have achieved new insights. It is essential to build upon existing knowledge, but much time and labor are saved when we begin our thinking with observations that have been screened through many minds. To produce an increment to knowledge, the scholar must know what has been known before. The accumulated wisdom gained from past human experience, and stored in the literature that has survived, is an important element in education. But often the best knowledge is the product of current investigation that adds increments to what was previously known.

The objective of reading great literature was to acquire the best knowledge. A coordinate objective was to produce the best possible man. As Mark Van Doren (1944) said: "The aim of liberal education is one's own excellence, the perfection of one's intellectual character—not merely to know or do, but also, and indeed chiefly, to be."

This is reminiscent of Newman's view but also adds a dimension. In Britain, liberal education had been closely associated with the gentility of society. Van Doren clearly meant something more than a cultural veneer. His call for a perfection of intellectual character refers to the ability to make value judgments and to use them in living the good life. This aim is similar to one advanced by Everett Dean Martin (1926, p. 28): "To my mind, an educated person is not merely one who can do something, whether it is giving a lecture on the poetry of Horace, running a train, trying a lawsuit, or repairing the plumbing. He is also one who knows the significance of what he does, and he is one who cannot and will not do certain things. He has acquired a set of values."

This question of a common orientation to values is very much in the minds of educators who contend that in our universities the specialists are losing the ability to communicate with one another. Good communication, a common heritage, and a reasonably common set of values are necessary; otherwise society falls apart. Men are interdependent, hence a college needs to do something more than just graduate individuals who are individually and culturally perfect. There is no assurance that merely knowing differences between right and wrong, justice and injustice, and honesty and dishonesty produces men who will live in a perfect relationship with their fellow citizens and neighbors around the world. It is difficult, if not impossible, to dissociate being from the activities of living.

Walter Moberly (1949), writing just after World War II, contended that the best course of direction is not through the study of classical culture, nor through the medium of scientific humanism, nor even through the imposition of religious dogma, but rather in the Christian concept of living. Although he would readily include all of these facets within the framework of higher education, Moberly felt strongly that the state of the world demanded a turning to Christian values; hence, it is the responsibility of the university to instruct in these values.

Numerous liberal arts colleges in the United States, affiliated with churches, subscribe to this view, although they sometimes express religious views that are narrower than Moberly advocated. The objective of some is to inculcate selected religious beliefs. One is reminded of the religious-oriented institutions in other parts of the world where intelligent men, who are equally devoted to their cause, teach a non-Christian religious view. A Buddhist university in Japan, for example, has sincerity and tenacity of purposes in adhering to Buddhism. In India, the Benares University, which teaches Hindu culture, and the Aligarh Moslem University, sincerely devoted to the Moslem culture, are both substantial institutions.

Because higher education is a rational process of investigation and of learning, it is logical to analyze what the great religions of the world have to tell us about values. Many of the Christian values seem superior as a way of life, but some of the biblical commands have motivated us to attempt to impose our religion upon other people of the world—and it becomes increasingly clear that we cannot do this. Nor can we impose our beliefs about democracy by the use of armed force or the intrigues of the Central Intelligence Agency. In America, indeed in western culture, we do not possess a monopoly of wisdom about values.

Social Ethics and Social Action

Critics of the colleges and universities charge that the impact of education and research is directed not toward change but toward perpetuating the status quo. Thus, the colleges educate students to fill niches in business, government, and the professions, and these persons accept without question the mores of their environment; the institutions do both applied and pure research, a portion of which is devoted to producing more devastating war materials, more dangerous and pollutive chemicals, and more efficient ways to organize for power and privilege. Research professors permit their findings to be kept secret for private gains or to be classified by the government, instead of following the scholarly tradition of publishing all findings. Some critics contend that the University now undergirds capitalist society in the same way the church earlier supported medievalism.

Another facet of this criticism is that, although students find lots of opportunity for vocational training, they have access to little direct help in preparing themselves for social action. They desire skills with which to make the communities in which they will live more integrated and effective social units. But the institutions do not create programs in which such knowledge and skills can be learned.

Colleges and universities hesitate to engage in social action, or in training for it, because of the risk that they will become politicized. We see, for example, nations abroad that have created centralized governments that in turn have molded the universities in the service of the state. These institutions commonly indoctrinate students with a political ideology and train them to meet the state's needs for manpower.

At first glance, this plan seems to produce a uniformity of goals and to provide an efficient use of educated personnel. The value in this course of action can be seen best in newly developing nations. A sense of mission gives a dynamic character to a nation. To carry out the mission and the ongoing work of the society, educated persons are needed to fill leadership roles and to supply knowledge and skills in the technologies, the professions, and government. This marshaling of human resources establishes goals of immediate interest to the state. In the long run, however, the policy may injure the state and vitiate human aspirations. When an institution is the servant of government, it cannot be a true critic of its society or a proponent of change that is controversial. If the university becomes a partisan on controversial issues, its objectivity will become restricted. The traditional role of the university to inquire, and not merely to teach, will be undermined.

John S. Brubacher (1972) has described the university as the primary source of expertise on social and scientific problems. It consists of libraries that are a storehouse of expertise, laboratories and seminars that are fountains of new expertise, and classrooms that are avenues for the communication of this knowledge. He concludes that the "role of the university is to operate as a central handler of sophisticated and esoteric expertise." He says that the university provides the expertise; then it becomes the citizen's role to determine how society shall use the knowledge.

Nevertheless, universities in the United States *have* influenced social change. As noted earlier, the establishment of the colleges of agriculture and engineering set off a century of great advance in agriculture and industry. Moreover, they were established for this purpose. The teaching of evolution profoundly changed religious thinking and, indeed, the power of the church. The recent discovery of the power of the atom and how to harness it has been having tremendous effect on the uses of power in the world. In all of these cases, the universities have taken leadership roles in education and also in society. The discoveries were made by individuals, but the institutions became advocates and users of the new ideas.

Recognizing that our society has been built on a system of individual morals, we have become conscious of the need for a better understanding of social ethics. Social ethics are concerned with the good of man as he functions in groups or within the fabric of a state. Society is not necessarily destined always to improve. It may also retrogress. Societies do decline and fall. Some critics say that contemporary society has begun a decline. They cite, among other evidence, the overwhelming destructiveness of modern warfare, the devastating exploitation of natural resources, and the threat of starvation caused by the uninhibited growth in the population of the world.

Both students and faculty should lift their sights in considering the mission of the university. The older view, that the role of the university is to educate individuals so that they will lead more satisfying lives, should not be discarded. But there is more to the mission than that. The greater social worth of the institution lies in its abilities to enlarge the social vision of the students, to prepare students to work creatively for social advance, to subject existing knowledge and institutions to critical evaluation, and to search for better ways in which people—all people—may satisfy their highest aspirations in forming the good society.

Culture and Vocation

The early editions of *The Dictionary of Modern English Usage* tacitly assumed that there is a dichotomy between cultural education and vocational education. The definition of cultural education read: "It is the education designed for a gentleman (Latin *liber*—a free man), and is opposed on the one hand to technical or professional or any special training, and on the other to education that stops short before manhood is reached."

H. W. Fowler, the editor, was describing what had existed as liberal education in some institutions. Indeed, even today we find in some places the assumption that some individuals are qualified to do intellectual work and others to work with their hands; then the jump is made to the conclusion that intellectual training and vocational training are different and should be separated.

In Great Britain, the dichotomy between culture and vocation resulted from the structuring of society as an elite educated class and a working class. This had been a characteristic of Grecian society—one of the reasons why Blacks feel frustrated when their study in college begins with the culture of Greece. Since World War II, the institutions in Britain have greatly expanded their technical training programs—so much so that Eric Ashby (1968) has warned that the university may be pressed to put too much of its resources into utilitarian and vocational training. He has said (1968, p. 13) "this is a short-sighted policy for, in a time of rapid technological change, this sort of training is less relevant to tomorrow's world than is a rigorous education in the humanities or social sciences or pure science." In the United States, because as a democracy we aim for the full development of each individual—his competence for work and his ability to create a good life for himself—the intertwining of the cultural and vocational elements in the education of each individual is important. We are beginning to appreciate that this principle applies to all persons, women and men, non-Whites and Whites.

Some of the newer democratic countries have been having a struggle with this problem because their universities, founded during the colonial period, had been based on the dichotomy concept. For many of these people, this had been a congenial notion of education. In India, for example, the Brahmans, who constituted a high proportion of the university students, felt that it was not appropriate to their position in society to engage in practical work. The need in India, however, is not for more civil servants or persons with high verbal facility. It is for educated persons who can lead the people in achieving better lives, and who can demonstrate how this can be done.

The American ideal was well expressed by Horace Kallen (1949, p. 307) in his pithy phrase: "The root of culture is vocation; the fruit of vocation is culture, alike in the institutions of society and the personal life." From the social point of view there can be no separation of these two elements. Nor should there be in education.

General education, a movement that was aimed at educating both for culture and for vocation, received much implementation during the 1940s and 1950s. It was given special impetus by the Harvard report, *General Education in a Free Society* (1945). General education was a restructuring of the values in cultural education as ascertained from the way people live and the functions they perform. The problems of living and earning a living were to be analyzed in the light of relevant knowledge. Milton B. Singer (1950, p. 125) defined general education as "the education in those things which are of general significance to the student, that is not merely of significance as doctor, lawyer, business man, engineer, economist, or labor leader, but of significance to him as a citizen and as a human being." General education was an element that should be common to all learning in a democratic society. It was also a new way to assist the student to secure an integration of knowledge.

General education placed emphasis on experience as an important factor in learning. The individual assimilates an idea best when he experiences some applications of it. He will comprehend the meaning of a generalization if he applies it in some novel situations. Such experience is the essence of learning. And so we find the sciences and also the social sciences drawing heavily on laboratory and field projects. Colleges deliberately organize experiences as a means of making the learning process more effective.

Under the whole man concept, then, education is something quite different from the sharpening of the mind. It advocates the cultivation of the whole person. Growth in intellectual capacity and power is a primary, but not the sole, aim.

The general education idea had much value, but interest in it has declined because our technologically oriented society has been demanding specialized training rather than general knowledge. The universities reward specialization and thus induce faculty to specialize. Students demand relevancy and do not always understand how breadth of knowledge—at least as portrayed in the usual courses—prepares them to deal effectively with the problems that confront them. Most educators believe in "broad learning experiences," an expression advocated by the Carnegie Commission on Higher Education (1972b). But the dilemma of devising courses that convey general knowledge continues to plague the colleges.

Liberating Education

Much has been written on what constitutes the free man and, more especially, on what education is the most liberating in that it produces the free man. Men have striven constantly to gain true intellectual freedom, and during the past century and a half women have engaged in their own struggle for equal intellectual freedom.

To answer the question, "What constitutes a liberating education?" one must first ask what being liberated means. We assume people are free when they have become masters of themselves, of the forces of nature, and of their own destinies as communities and nations. They have become masters of themselves when they have learned to utilize harmoniously and creatively their own individual abilities—intellectual, physical, and emotional. They have become masters of nature when they have freed themselves from superstitions, and to the extent that they understand nature and can harness its forces. They have become masters of their destinies as communities of people when they have learned how to plan and organize cooperatively for the future to achieve the greatest possible human happiness.

A few illustrations will make these generalizations more specific. People are free insofar as they possess the tools of learning and techniques of action: to verbalize, to calculate, to analyze and synthesize, to create, to organize, and to administer. People are free who possess, or know how to acquire, the available knowledge pertinent to the courses of action that they are undertaking. Persons are not wholly free who are handicapped with unnecessary psychological inhibitions, who are the victims of preventable diseases, who harbor irrational prejudices against men of differing views or other cultures or other races, or who practice religious bigotry. People become free as they learn how to organize into social groups to secure, on a basis of equality of opportunity for all men, such advantages as economic sustenance, physical comfort, health services, educational opportunity, economic justice, and leisure time for cultural creativity. Achievements such as these bring about liberation. People have become free in proportion to their attainment of goals such as these. That education is liberating which aids in this process.

At first glance, it might seem that all of education is liberating. But the fomenting of racial antagonisms is not liberating; neither is the teaching that men are inhibited by original sin; nor are the nationalistic distortions of history; nor is the teaching of economics as a dogma instead of as a science. These teachings are not liberating because they are not consistent with the best available knowledge, and they close the door to the discovery of new knowledge. Hence they tend to limit man's understanding of himself and his environment, and they lead to courses of action that do not in the long run have social justification.

A liberating education has a dynamic quality. Students are prepared to comprehend great issues and to mobilize the knowledge and skills needed in solving them. When Copernicus described his new system of astronomy, when Locke propounded his views on the natural rights of men, when Darwin formulated his theory of evolution, each was dealing with a crisis in men's beliefs or with a practical problem in human relations that had validity for the society of the day. The fruits of investigations such as these form much of the basic knowledge that can be made available to students, and also the basis for learning about the process of problem-solving.

Students of today are sensitive to human relations problems, but they are not always able to cope with them. One way to help prepare students for this effort is to give them experience in the world about them. Educative experience will give them a larger understanding of human needs and aspirations, will increase their factual knowledge and their ability to observe facts, will demonstrate to them the importance of checking assumptions through practical observations and trial and error, and will motivate them for constructive work in society.

Another element in a liberating education for today is our willingness to draw on the experience of other contemporary national and racial groups. Society throughout the world is closely interdependent. Discoveries in science occur irrespective of cultural boundary lines, and there is good communication about them. Developments in the social, economic, and political fields should be studied with similar tolerance and objectivity. As a nation, we shall find ourselves lagging in cultural achievement if we fail to take full advantage of the knowledge gained through the technological and social experimentation of other nations. The too-strict worship of our little body of western knowledge can lead to intellectual inbreeding and sterility.

A liberating education, then, is an exploring education. The student seeks wisdom wherever wisdom can be found—in the record of the past, in the accounts of contemporary experience, and in his own participation in the world about him. He seeks wisdom from all of the cultures of the world, whether western, eastern, African, or other. The student searches for knowledge because he realizes that the whole truth, even in matters spiritual, has not yet been discovered. He uses the scientific method. Knowledge becomes dynamic, like the world we live in.

In this approach to learning, how does the student discover the values by which he will live and work? He must make choices in determining his future courses of action, and these choices must be based on what he believes are fundamental values. These values are most reliably found through analyzing human experience. The analyses made in the past can, of course, aid the student. Experience also aids in showing when action is good or bad, social or antisocial.

Does this view leave the human race adrift without any moorings? It does not necessarily deny the existence of a fundamental purpose in life. But as far as the human race is concerned, that purpose is not static, and our concept of that purpose can be continually enlarged. A liberating education prepares the individual to make his own analysis of human experience and determine by his own reason what he considers, for the present, a socially justifiable course of action.

In summary, a liberating education liberates people from ignorance, superstition, fear, prejudice, unnecessary physical handicaps, and the need to use force in trying to solve recurring crises. More positively it is the education that helps produce people who, because of their perspective of human experience, their sensitivity to the limiting forces of the time, and their knowledge of social dynamics, can aid in the further evolution of man and society. Some concept of purpose, such as this, should permeate the programs of higher education.

Roles of Institutions

★★
★★

The purposes of higher education are achieved by defining and implementing the objectives of the colleges and universities. Objectives pertaining to the education of students are best achieved if the desired outcomes for students are specified for each educational experience as well as for each course. Objectives for the expansion of knowledge need to be related to the research function of the institution. Objectives for community services should be determined by surveys of community needs and by linking the projects undertaken to the resources of the institution.

Differentiating Roles

Irrespective of differing views about the nature of higher education, we relate it to the level of education beyond the high school. We see no particular value in limiting the term *higher education* to some phase of this level of education, because to do so would inhibit the evolution of programs of innovative institutions. The term *higher education* parallels the designations used for elementary and secondary education.

Within higher education there should be differentiation in the purposes and functions of institutions for many reasons. We are now educating a heterogeneous group of students who vary in their interests, aptitudes, and previous achievements. Their interests include the whole range of human activities, and they need education for widely differing roles. Their needs are not uniform or standardized. Higher education includes many sub-categories of institutions beyond the high school, but a discussion of three broad groups—colleges of liberal arts, universities and complex institutions, and community colleges—will reveal and illustrate the basic concepts about roles.

Our resources in higher education should be allocated to help maintain quality. Unnecessary duplications of programs and dissipation of resources should be avoided. The social needs should be met by varying the objectives of the institutions and by assuring quality in each program. Differentiation of college roles and provision for mobility by the student should be arranged by state planning and coordinating commissions in higher education. Each state should make it possible for a student to study in the college that best meets his needs.

Although institutions should differ, there is one respect in which their objectives should be the same. In a democratic society, one aim is to assure to each person the best possible opportunity to live the good life. A college can best contribute to the realization of this aim by engaging each student in education that is cultural. Thus, a common core element, varying in its scope and intensity should be present in all educational programs.

The Liberal Arts College

The objectives of liberal arts colleges should rest on the cultural purpose described in Chapter Two. The programs comprehend the four broad divisions of liberal subject matter—the humanities, the social sciences, and the natural and physical sciences. In this respect, liberal arts colleges differ from vocational or professional schools which have as their primary objective the competence of the individual in a specialization.

The liberal arts colleges, however, vary considerably (Schmidt, 1957; Keeton, 1971). The several hundred independent liberal arts colleges can be roughly divided into three categories by the objectives revealed in their programs and activities. One group is composed of institutions that follow tradition, maintaining a substantial program of interrelated arts and sciences and restricting the scope of the program to secure concentration of effort. Illustrations are Haverford and Oberlin Colleges. A second group includes colleges that use a basic curriculum of arts and sciences but make an effort to be innovative and distinctive. Illustrations are found in the members of the Union for Experimenting Colleges and Universities. The third group—and it appears to be the largest one—comprises institutions that serve functional roles related to a special clientele, a church, or a particular community. There are, for example, several hundred church-related, liberal arts colleges. The fourth group includes liberal arts colleges within universities, or in institutions that have two or more college units. These colleges are usually the core unit of their universities. The program at such a college is much the same as that of the independent liberal arts college although, because of the size of the college, it may have more departments of major studies. A few universities have developed colleges that have broad cultural curricula, but with a focus of interest and instruction in one major area. These colleges are innovative. An example is the University of Wisconsin at Green Bay, with four distinctive colleges of liberal arts.

An examination of the course enrollments of the hundreds of liberal arts colleges indicates that they emphasize teacher education, preparation for business administration, and training for positions in the church. In many colleges, the real emphasis may be on departmental training—that is, specialized programs—rather than on integrated education. To the extent such variations from the traditional curriculum appear, the cultural aspect is subordinated to vocational and specialized objectives.

These variations in programs provoke a number of questions. Should a liberal arts college confine itself to traditional academic content which has been the special province of the liberal arts? Or can it devise a program irrespective of precedent? Should it have a compact limited program or one with many majors? Should the college emphasize departmental disciplines or an integrated education? Should it emphasize vocational objectives?

The liberal arts colleges contend somewhat fiercely that theirs are genuinely cultural programs, often with the added purpose of developing Christian character. The latter aim is harmonious because it is based on the Judeo-Christian contribution to western culture, which is the corpus of existing liberal arts curricula. These colleges, however, have become the victims of pressures that have distorted their traditional purpose. Their faculty members are specialists who were trained in the graduate departments of the universities. Many of them lack integration and breadth of knowledge, and some of them have little interest in educational objectives beyond the reproduction of specialists in their particular areas. It is for this reason that the colleges that have attempted to launch general education courses, integrated in subject matter, have found the task difficult.

The colleges also have been under pressure to specialize because of the increasing multiplicity of occupational outlets. Furthermore, as the student bodies have become more representative of the general population, the motivation of students toward preparation to upgrade their socioeconomic status has caused the colleges to give more emphasis to vocations. And accrediting societies in the professional fields, intent on competence in the graduates, impel specialization. The chemistry profession, with its specialized criteria, is a good example.

Similar in effect is the tendency of the smaller colleges to emulate the universities in their programs. In part, this is due to the origin of the teacher, who emulates his teachers in graduate school and continues to crave their respect for his work. His professional reputation may be at stake; it will be determined by the record made by the graduates of the college who have majored in his department. When they enter graduate school, they must demonstrate that they have a solid foundation in the subject that they will study as a specialization. Thus, the graduate school is often a strong influence in determining the education of undergraduate students. This influence is especially strong in the liberal arts programs within universities. The persons who compose the specialists in the graduate faculty are, for the most part, the same persons who design courses and teach them or supervise the teaching assistants at the undergraduate level.

Although vocational and specialized objectives should be included among those of a liberal arts college, an institution that places primary emphasis on comprehensive and integrated knowledge should not let itself become too much the victim of the specialized pressures. To do so defeats the primary function of the college.

Students today say that the college lacks relevance. They express concern about the nature of the liberal studies. They want knowledge that will help them to understand social issues, and they want skills that will enable them to work toward solutions of these kinds of problems. The nearly exclusive attention by the faculty to western civilization, and to the past, leaves students unsatisfied. The student complaint suggests that the curriculum should focus on the issues of society, digging into man's past experiences for knowledge that is relevant to their solution, and that the content of liberal studies should be reordered to include all cultures, seeking knowledge and wisdom wherever they may be found.

The objective of relevance, however, has another twist. It may mean the study of the here and now and the wholly practical knowledge. The curricula provided by the Free Universities, student sponsored and organized, have been overloaded with such courses. This can lead to superficiality. Attention to immediate relevance may leave out the theoretical groundwork needed for more intensive study. It also overlooks the content of liberal education that is of the greatest value—the body of learning that has been stored in the minds of men, in libraries and museums. That learning, when mastered by an individual, enables him to begin using knowledge where other men have left off.

The key to the resolution of the pressures to emulate the

university in its spread of curriculum, or to address social problems, or to prepare for specialization and vocations, does not lie in adding courses that adjust to each pressure. Instead, the objectives must be clearly defined, so that the varying needs are met. A basic curriculum can be compact in size but comprehensive in character. The teaching can produce diversified outcomes for the students. Likewise the content and the methods need not be uniform in all of the colleges. If a liberal education is defined by identifying objectives that are cultural and liberalizing, the content and the methods may vary and also be innovative. The focus should be the education of the student, not the transmission of a given body of knowledge. However, it is the function of the college of liberal arts to draw on cultural knowledge in educating the student. Other functions can be left to other types of colleges.

The University

Universities differ in size and complexity (Perkins, 1973). We have, on the one hand, the universities of established reputation, such as Harvard University and the University of California, Berkeley. At the other extreme we have a loose use of the term *university*. A small college may have acquired the right to use the name *university* before the laws restricted its use. But there are also universities whose programs are essentially undergraduate, but that have one or more professional schools, such as law or engineering. Some of the states have witnessed interinstitutional fighting over the designation *university*. State colleges have grown into complex institutions consisting of several colleges and schools with enrollments running into the thousands, and many have been winning this battle to be renamed *universities* (Harcleroad, Molen, and Rayman, 1973). We now have two types of universities—the complex institution with several college and professional school units, and the university that has these subdivisions plus substantial research and doctoral programs.

A number of writers have attempted to define the university. One of the more traditional statements was by Ortega y

Gasset (1944), who identified the mission of the university as the core within a strong liberal education. On the American scene, Abraham Flexner (1930) attempted such a definition by pleading for a restriction of the work of the university to areas of knowledge that were intellectual in nature and in which substantial knowledge had been accumulated, and to theoretical research. Flexner felt that the university should not be concerned with the current events and problems of the world about it, because such events and problems do not conform to the purpose of the university. And further, Flexner believed that indulging in such activities would negate the fundamental purpose of the university. University activities, he thought, should be concerned with the discovery, refinement, and dissemination of truth, irrespective of whether the results were acceptable or unacceptable outside the university.

Flexner attacked Harvard University for having initiated the Harvard Graduate School of Business Administration. He contended that this type of school did not belong in the university. This appears now to have been a misreading of the nature of a professional school and of its potential contributions to the organization and functioning of modern society. The evolution of a school of business administration, or of other new professional schools, is not unlike that of the older professional schools that Flexner readily accepted. The formal study of medicine began centuries ago, as at Salerno, but the real history of the medical school as a part of the university began with the nineteenth century. A typical example is the medical school of the University of Michigan. Students were first admitted in 1850. At that time the school consisted of a single professor of anatomy who kept a cadaver hidden in a back room because the state law did not as yet authorize the dissection of bodies. Presently two additional men were added to teach other subjects. But it was not until some decades later that a medical curriculum of the type we know today, requiring also a premedical foundation in the liberal arts, was generated. The study of medicine started as apprenticeship training, as did the study of law. In recent years these schools have achieved high status as educational institutions engaged in fine intellectual instruction and substantial scientific research.

The newer professional schools that Flexner condemned have been going through a similar growth. The more stable of them today provide intellectual instruction based on growing bodies of knowledge in their particular fields. These schools should also raise the level of men's conduct in human affairs and should serve human wants and needs.

However, as a society, we will make a mistake if we fail to sufficiently differentiate the complex, teaching university from the research-oriented university. The latter should be characterized by the superior strength and quality of its library, its laboratories, its plant, and its faculty. A characteristic of advanced instruction is the amount of resources that must be devoted to each student. In university research, large funds are spent in examining hypotheses, often with negative findings. The cost of such programs naturally rises geometrically in proportion to those at lower levels. Because appropriations for such purposes must be limited, there is danger that a state may dilute the character and quality of advanced graduate programs by scattering resources too widely among institutions. Also the multiplication of programs creates an oversupply of graduates, saps teaching strength, and scatters laboratories.

Engineering education provides an illustration. In 1973, about one hundred universities were conferring doctor's degrees in engineering. The American Society of Engineering Education (1968) estimated that by 1978, one hundred fifty institutions will be offering the degree. Doctorates in engineering include a substantial grounding in science. Yet graduates in the science of engineering go principally into research and academic positions, and so the number needed is not large. To staff and finance too many doctoral programs would dilute the quality of each of the very programs where quality is of utmost importance. The preponderate need for engineers is at the level where the application of theory to practical problems is needed. We also need planners and supervisors who have training equal to the one or two year professional master's degree. Most of the programs in engineering should be of these types (Henderson, 1968).

These problems are created by the uncontrolled growth of the new regional universities. Their objectives should relate to the needs of their regions, and a large proportion of these needs can be satisfied by programs that are undergraduate, or are professional at the master's level.

Objectives of the university should also be concerned with services to the state and the community. In the days when the University of Wisconsin had its most dynamic growth, it claimed the entire state as its campus. Thus the scope of the work of the institution was expanded enormously. It may not be clear whether the addition of these functions added strength to the university as a university, but it is clear in retrospect that universities of this type have made excellent contributions to their respective communities. These activities seem not to have detracted from the main job. They have resulted, as in Wisconsin, in major economic benefits. Research and field work have provided students and faculty with additional stimulating opportunities to learn and make their learning more genuine. To some degree the modern university may be said to be a center for research and learning related to all fields and keeping pace with and anticipating change and growth in its society. As such it is not merely educating future leaders for society; it is also taking an active leadership role.

Although professional schools for the most part are within the structure of a university, they commonly behave as autonomous units. They have achieved considerable autonomy because they attract much separately appropriated financial support. Their academic policies are more subject to influences from the respective professional societies, and to controls by the state, than to influences from the university. Yet their social orientation would be improved if they were more subject to influence and control from within the university.

The focus in objectives is to train for competence in some profession. The test of competence is predetermined by the requirements for licensing and by the codes of professional recognition and conduct. Such requirements must be met. Obviously, it would be grossly unfair to graduate students who are unable to practice their professions.

The state prescribes only the minimum requirements needed for licensing. This does not induce high quality. Besides, the codes of the professional associations result in the disciplining of very few practitioners—those who engage in conduct that is highly unprofessional. Hence, the regulations and codes have not been effective in stimulating practitioners toward the highest goals in meeting genuine human needs. The university must do this.

The professional schools are defining their technological objectives very well, but they are remiss in meeting human needs. Lawyers tend to serve corporate clients; medical doctors cater to affluent patients; engineers collaborate with interests that exploit the natural resources. Several professional schools have been favoring students from elite families, and men rather than men and women. They have been emphasizing research rather than teaching and research.

A fresh approach is needed and is occurring at a few innovative schools. The orientation should be to people and their needs, society and its problems. The role of the university is to provide this orientation and to evaluate the programs in this broad frame of reference. The university, including its professional schools, should not lose sight of the central purpose of higher education to produce good men who will help build the good society.

The Community College

The public community college is an innovation of the twentieth century. The first community college was established in 1901. Now such an institution is available in almost every community in the United States (Monroe, 1972).

At first, it was called a junior college and offered the first two years of an arts and sciences program. It emulated the private junior college, which had been launched in the latter part of the nineteenth century. A junior college prepared students for further education at a more advanced level in a college or university.

The technical institute, which was devoted to vocational training developed parallel to the community college. In most foreign countries, vocational and cultural schools have been developed separately. After puberty, youth had to attend one or the other. The choice was usually based on grades on qualifying examinations. In the United States, however, the focus has been on the individual and his development. In a democracy the individual needs both cultural and vocational education. In addition, he should have the freedom to shift his goals as he matures—hence, he needs some breadth in his education. This is especially important to youth from the lower socioeconomic strata. Initially, they may want to prepare for a specific job, but the college experience may stimulate them toward larger intellectual interests. Here again, the college needs to orient its various objectives to the overall purpose of higher education.

In the course of time, the programs of the two types of institutions became more similar. The junior colleges began to offer vocational courses, and the technical institutes moved toward balancing their curriculum by including some general education. The public colleges, located near the people, began to offer programs for adults also, and this work expanded greatly. The narrowly focused junior college became a comprehensive institution, and it adopted a new name—community college.

The community colleges serve three types of students: those who desire to take college-parallel work in the expectation of going beyond the two-year curriculum; those who desire terminal courses, usually with emphasis on the vocations; and the older students, who attend part-time and have special interests related to their occupational advancement or their leisure time activities. The colleges also serve as cultural centers for their communities.

Because it is a young institution, the community college has yet to define its full identity and resolve some of its problems. The program that prepares students for transfer to a senior college continues to be the most prestigious one, and this is certainly legitimate for a portion of the students. The roles of the college in counseling students and identifying those who should strive for a more advanced education are appropriate at this level. Doubtless the two-year college will register more and more students who will transfer. But senior institutions have exerted too much influence on the junior programs. Concerned with the adequacy of preparation in particular courses, or with sequential courses within each department, university faculties exact requirements of the community colleges that throttle the efforts of the colleges to define their own objectives. Recently, this tendency has been lessened somewhat, but the two-year institutions need to take more initiative in declaring their own educational objectives. The community colleges are able to sense the needs of students, they have a firsthand view of the needs of their communities, and their faculties are devoted to teaching. The criterion for transfer should not merely be the credits the student has in history or mathematics, but rather his motivations and how is he progressing as a genuine learner.

The public community college is the most urban of any of the colleges. Typically its students commute from their homes and many work part-time. Students come out of the ghettos as well as from the suburbs. Students from the poorest of families manage to attend college. The student body is heterogeneous in personal characteristics and in interests and talents. Many are from minority groups. The cultural growth of these students does not necessarily require the study of European history. They seek knowledge about their own backgrounds and pride in the cultural achievements of members of their own races. These students want skills with which to attack the grave problems that confront their own communities. They want social as well as vocational skills.

Some of these colleges have made substantial headway in vocational education. They have made more use than other institutions of community surveys to identify future job opportunities for students. They have devised programs of varying lengths to meet various skill training needs. A few colleges have not hesitated to initiate programs that lack endorsement by the educational establishment. However, the need for colleges to become more effective in preparing students for employment is great. The community colleges should tackle this problem more imaginatively and vigorously, and they should be given larger financial support for this purpose.

The increase in interest in lifelong learning gives the community college an opportunity to extend its already large service to persons beyond the usual college age. The community colleges are not inhibited by traditions relating to admissions, curricula, or degree requirements. They are close to the homes of people who work, have families, and must commute to college.

Institutional Objectives

If objectives are to permeate the life and work of the institution, they must be thought through and accepted as a basis for action by those who compose the institution. In formulating objectives, it is useful to go through a series of stages in thinking:

(1) Because the institution should orient its work to the achievement of the good society, a statement of a broad goal of human development is appropriate and serves as a frame of reference.

(2) It is essential that the faculty prepare criteria for determining the clientele to be served and the specific functions to be engaged in—even if an outside agency, such as the state or a church, has already defined these criteria in a broad sense.

(3) In every institution there are pervasive objectives. Examples include: advancing the students' intellectual competence; training in communication, in memory, and in critical thinking; learning how to use source materials, how to work constructively as members of a group, and how to choose ethical aims. Faculty must make a conscious effort to identify these objectives and to design courses in accordance with them.

(4) Specific objectives need to be identified. If education for breadth is to be included, appropriate recognition of this function should be obtained by thorough faculty discussion. Breadth will not be achieved unless the faculty accept responsibility to get beyond their specialized interests. Education in depth requires specialized or vocational programs. Because of the enormous array of possible vocations, it is essential to reduce the scope of possible service to manageable proportions. It may be desirable to teach for clusters of vocations rather than for discrete occupations.

(5) It is important to determine the methods to be used, the learning materials that can be provided, and the activities to be undertaken.

(6) An analysis of the educational outcomes to be achieved by the students in each course is essential. This step is usually neglected by the faculty, who are content to prepare a stub outline of subject matter and thus fail to interrelate input and output. The course-by-course analysis of objectives and outcomes is based on all of the preceding analyses but is essential as a follow-through if the objectives worked out in the preceding steps are to be implemented. The analysis should include the choice of methods and materials of instruction, because the means that are used determine the outcomes.

The procedure outlined above takes account of most of the factors involved in any analysis of objectives. The first objective, to provide a frame of reference that relates to human development, may serve as a basis of inspiration and guidance. The institution thus sets its overall course of direction. The intangible objective of intellectual competence is included, and an attempt is made to add to its achievement in every course and educational experience. Social objectives may be achieved through attention to the development of attitudes and social skills. The problem of outlining a program that is relevant to the interests and aptitudes of the clientele of the institution is also solved, because the clientele has been identified.

This leaves the way open for one college or university to serve students with one set of characteristics and another institution to serve students with other interests and talents. Assuming that it is desirable to have some general education included in the program of every student, the faculty of each college may determine the relative emphasis to be given to this phase of the work. The planning also may result in defining clearly the scope of the specialized vocational and professional courses.

This planning procedure, applicable primarily to the education of students, is suggestive also of the types of analysis that need to be made of other primary aspects of the institution's total program, including research and community services. If the state, through a planning-coordinating agency, has defined the roles of the respective public institutions, each of the latter will have a frame of reference for its own planning.

In order to plan well, the institution should have good information. This can be obtained from a self-study. In the United States, each college or university has a unique character. This freedom of each college or university to develop in accordance with its own formulated objectives permits diversification among institutions—public and private, universities and colleges, liberal arts and technical programs, four-year institutions and two-year colleges.

In a self-study, the institution compiles information about its students, about its research and service programs, about the needs of the community or clientele that it serves, about the resources in plant, funds, and faculty at its disposal, and about the social role that the institution should attempt to perform. Data will be available about the registered students and about potential students, about curriculum, library, plant, records system, financial management, personnel policies, and so forth. Such a self-study needs to involve all the personnel of the institution, because the results that will flow from the study will depend upon the manner in which the findings and recommendations are implemented.

Empirical studies of the needs within the surrounding community can assist in identifying programs that should be offered. These surveys can be facilitated by appointing advisory committees, each composed of citizens who represent a special vocational or cultural interest. The committee and the faculty collaborate in surveying a particular area of interest, and they make recommendations for the scope and content of the program.

Regional associations of colleges and secondary schools have long based their accrediting on the degree of fulfillment by a college of its own objectives. They do this for two reasons. First, this is a convenient way for the institution to interpret its achievements, and it provides the committee with much information that otherwise would be difficult to collect. Second, the associations have desired to stimulate the institutions to advance in quality, instead of allowing them to be content to meet the minimum standards required for accreditation.

The multitude of problems facing higher education causes the parties that bear the responsibility for solutions—faculties, administrations, boards of control, legislators—to seek data beyond anything required heretofore. Judgments can be made about the institutional objectives and their implementation only when this information has been obtained.

★★★★★★★★★★★★★★★★ **4** ★★★★★★★★★★★★★★★
★★★★★★★★★★★★★★★★   ★★★★★★★★★★★★★★★

Barriers to
Higher Education
and the Good Life

★★
★★

During the period from the early colonial days to the present, there has been an evolution in the American philosophy of what higher education should be and the clientele it should serve. From a strictly aristocratic philosophy, the country gradually shifted to a philosophy of meritocracy. A philosophy of egalitarianism in higher education has been emerging more recently. The aristocratic philosophy posits that education is primarily for the elite, and this view was maintained until about 1940. The meritocratic philosophy—that all of the able segment of the masses should be educated—drew strong support until the 1960s, when it was joined by the egalitarian philosophy advocating universal access to higher education. Each of these three philosophies has its advocates today. Hence, although it is apparent that egalitarianism will be the prevailing philosophy from the seventies onward, some colleges and universities will continue to attract and accept only the intellectually elite. It is mandatory that the great universities and distinguished colleges maintain their high standards of scholarship—and this implies giving preference to applicants of high intellectual achievement or ability—for these institutions are essential to the advancement and quality of our society. Institutions reflecting all three philosophies have their places in serving the people in a democracy. Egalitarianism and equality of opportunity do not require that any individual should have access to any institution he chooses, nor to any program, regardless of the prerequisites for entry, but rather, that an individual should have the chance to pursue his education consistent with his interests and abilities.

The early colonial colleges were founded to train leaders who would become ministers, lawyers, and doctors. In the early days of the republic, higher education was not considered necessary except for a small segment of the population. It is doubtful that there were many college students except the sons of the socially prominent and wealthy. The ordinary man had no need of an education beyond the three R's and perhaps a knowledge of the workings of government in a democracy. Indeed, as late as 1900 it was an achievement to have been graduated from high school; only 11 percent of the school-age population had more than a primary school education. Not quite 4 percent of the eighteen-to-twenty-one year old age group went on to college (see Table 1). About three hundred years passed before this aristocratic philosophy was jarred into giving ground to a philosophy of meritocracy.

From 1900 to 1940, the number of years of education completed rose steadily. High school attendance rose sharply, accompanied by an equally constant, but more gradual increase in the numbers going on to college. By 1940 the college population numbered 1.4 million, 15 percent of the college-age group, while 73 percent of the school-age population were in high school—over seven million boys and girls.

Certain periods of American life have produced upsurges in the college-going population. One of these followed the Civil War. Graduate instruction was introduced into American educa-

Table 1

Undergraduate Degree-Credit Enrollment in the United States

Year	Number (in thousands)	Percentage change	Percent of population aged 18 to 21
1870	52		1.7
1880	116	122	2.7
1890	154	33	3.0
1900	232	50	3.9
1910	346	49	5.0
1920	582	68	7.9
1930	1,053	81	11.9
1940	1,388	32	14.5
1950	2,422	74	26.9
1960	3,227	33	33.8
1970	6,840	112	47.6
1980 (est.)	10,080	48	59.2
1990 (est.)	9,660	−4	67.4
2000 (est.)	12,700	31	72.6

Source: The Carnegie Commission on Higher Education, *New Students and New Places* (New York: McGraw Hill, 1971). Table adapted from Appendix B, Table 1, p. 127.

tion, and some colleges were transformed into universities. An additional influence at that time was the effect of the Morrill Act, which established the land-grant colleges. Another growth period occurred after World War II when the meritocratic philosophy, espousing the attendance at college of all youth who had shown good progress in high school, received wide acceptance. An influential advocate of this policy was the President's Commission on Higher Education (1947), which declared that 49 percent of youth had the ability to take two years beyond high school and 32 percent should be encouraged to take four years. Not to develop the nation's resources was considered a loss to the country and to the individual. Previously, although some scholarships were available for some students, most young people who wanted to attend college were expected to provide their own financial support, either by working or from family resources. After 1940 this expectation was transferred, in part, to the states and the federal government. Such support has been supplied by the public institutions, federal and state loans and scholarships, work-study programs, and grants-in-aid.

There were, of course, other influences: the country's complex and rapidly expanding economy, the technological revolution that required a better educated working class, the increasing mobility of people and the increased communication among them, and the growing needs in the professions. Concomitantly, the general population developed rising aspirations for improving their status, and higher education had become an assured method for achieving upward mobility. The trend received momentum from the World War II soldiers, who, as veterans, were eligible for educational benefits under Public Law 346, the "GI Bill of Rights." Young men who would not otherwise have attended college grasped this opportunity to procure further education. During the Depression preceding the war, these same men had held jobs as delivery boys, grocery clerks, filling station attendants and the like. After the war they entered colleges by the hundreds of thousands, and many proved to be excellent students.

Notwithstanding this impetus, in 1950 only 27 percent of the college-age population (including the older veterans) were attending college. There were still many able high school graduates who did not go on for further education but instead went directly to work. To a large extent, they lacked the motivation or the finances to attend college. But this group also included many women whose socialization did not include the expectation of higher education.

College Attendance

Why do some bright and capable high school seniors want to go to college and others do not? That question has intrigued many investigators. High academic ability, high school grades, sex, race, and socioeconomic status are the familiar determining factors. Using the data file of twelfth grade students (approximately one hundred thousand) in the national sample of students in Project TALENT,* the Commission on Human Resources and Higher Education analyzed the pertinent responses to determine what factors influence young people to want to pursue a college education. Because of the number of factors that have some influence on college entry, the commission used a multivariate approach, studying each variable while holding the others constant. Their results were consistent with other studies, but the size of their population added credence to the information. They found that the most definitive pressure for college entry (not necessarily for successful completion) was "college commitment" in the senior year of high school. College commitment encompasses several variables: plans for going to college, parental encouragement, and encouragement by friends (Folger, Astin and Bayer, 1970, pp. 153-155). Trent and Medsker (1967, p. 27), in their study of ten thousand high school graduates, found that similar expectations exerted a strong force for college attendance.

> From the outset of the study, differences in parental encouragement and academic motivation distinguished those in the sample who did enter college from those who did not. While still seniors in high school, over 57 percent of those in the sample who later entered college reported that a college education was extremely important to them, compared with 12 percent of those who did not enter; only 29 percent of those who reported a great deal of interest in college failed to attend. A question about parental encouragement yielded a dramatic difference. More than twice as many college attenders as nonattenders reported having been encouraged to enroll.

"Ability variables," the Commission on Human Resources found, comprised another positive force for college at-

---

*Project TALENT was a nationwide study of American youth in 1960. The study was made under the direction of the American Institutes for Research and the University of Pittsburgh and supported by the U.S. Office of Education. (See Folger, Astin and Bayer, 1970, page 407 and those following, for more details.)

tendance. These included vocabulary, general information, creativity, abstract reasoning, and math aptitude. These ability variables were the best single indicator for the educational progress of male students after admission. For women, marital and family status were as good predictors for academic progress as the ability variables (Folger, Astin and Bayer, 1970, pp. 153-155).

The socioeconomic background variables of college entrants bears an influence, one-half to three-quarters as strong as academic aptitude, on college attendance and college progress. These variables include family income, father's occupation and education, mother's education, and the number of books in the home (Folger, Astin and Bayer, 1970, p. 155). The adverse effect of the family's socioeconomic status (SES) on college attendance has been demonstrated in numerous studies over the years. Illustrative of the effect of SES is a report of a comparison of two cohorts of one hundred male high school graduates in Project TALENT. These young men were from the lowest and the highest quintiles of SES backgrounds, and all of them were in the highest quintile of academic ability. Less than half of the low SES young men got the opportunity to complete four years of college. Table 2 presents a tabulation of their higher education.

Table 2

Influence of Socioeconomic Status on College Attendance
of Men

High Ability H.S. Graduates	High SES		Low SES	
Did not attend college		9		31
Attended junior college		9		17
Graduated from senior college	3		5	
Attended senior college		82		52
Graduated from senior college	63		32	
Total four-year graduates	(66)		(37)	
Total		100		100

Source: J. K. Folger, H. S. Astin, and A. E. Bayer, *Human Resources and Higher Education* (New York: Russell Sage Foundation, 1970, p. 322).

Despite the strength of the meritocratic philosophy demonstrated by the number of high school students in the top fifth of their graduating class who do continue their education, the influence of low socioeconomic status has not been entirely eliminated. In 1954, an estimated 47 percent did not go on. By 1960, 15 percent of the boys and 24 percent of the girls failed to enter college immediately. Of those also in the top fifth socioeconomically, 91 percent of the boys entered college immediately. But in the bottom fifth socioeconomically, only 69 percent of the boys did. For the girls, the comparable figures were 90 percent and 52 percent (Folger, Astin and Bayer, 1970, p. xxiv). When ability and economic status were held constant, social status had more influence on college attendance than academic ability. Only one out of every four students from homes of semi- and unskilled workers went on to college compared, to three out of four from professional homes (Trent and Medsker, 1967, p. 26).

A young person is more apt to go to college if he lives in the outer ring of a large metropolitan area. Presumably families living in the suburbs have a higher socioeconomic status, and there are better elementary and secondary schools in the suburbs. There are also sharp differences in the enrollment rates of poverty and nonpoverty sections of metropolitan areas. Only 19 percent of the eighteen- and nineteen-year-olds in poverty areas attend college, compared with 44 percent in nonpoverty areas (Carnegie Commission. 1971b, pp. 34-35).

The location of institutions of higher learning is another factor that determines who will go on for further education. When Trent and Medsker (1967, p. 26) analyzed the rates of college attendance as related to the presence or absence of a college in the community, they found that the rates ranged between 25 and 65 percent. The highest rates occurred in communities that had junior colleges, the lowest rates where there was no college. A divergent view of the proximity thesis is taken by Spaeth and Greeley (1970, pp. xvii, xx-xxi). They maintain that postsecondary school attendance is determined more by ability and family status than by the nearness of a college. Their conclusions, however, were based on data that related to college-age youth and did not include information about metropolitan centers or education of adults.

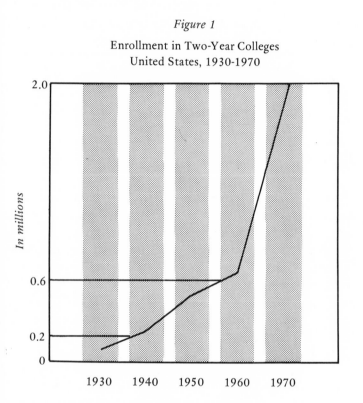

Figure 1

Enrollment in Two-Year Colleges
United States, 1930-1970

Source: Medsker, L. L. and Tillery, C., *Breaking the Access Barriers.*
New York: McGraw-Hill, 1971, p. 17.

Certainly the growth of the open-door community colleges has been an influence in the shift in educational philosophy to egalitarianism. In 1970, the public two-year institutions accounted for 38 percent of the postsecondary institutions and 28 percent of the postsecondary students in the United States. This was nearly double the number of institutions and more than three times as many students as reported in 1960 (Figure 1). Community college students come from all levels and all groups—inside and outside of the regular college-age population

—in sex, race, age, and socioeconomic status. Because of their nonselective admissions policy, community colleges have students with all levels of ability. At the low end they have those who could not find entry into another college, and at the high side they enroll more students who are academically able than do the selective baccalaureate and master's degree institutions (Folger, Astin, and Bayer, 1970, p. 163). They have older students in quest of a second chance, women undertaking an education after raising a family, and both men and women seeking to learn new occupational skills.

Women and Minorities

Female sex, ethnic minority status, low tested aptitude, and low socioeconomic status are the major causes of nonattendance in higher education, according to recent studies. It is well documented that women's educational attainments have never equaled those of men. Even at the highest socioeconomic level, women do not attend college in quite the same proportion as men. The difference is not as marked, however, as it is at the lower socioeconomic levels, where the greatest effect on women's entry into college exists.

In a study of Wisconsin high school graduates, only one-fourth of the girls, but one-half of the boys, in the highest ability quartile, but the lowest SES group, attended college. Seventy-five percent of the girls and 90 percent of the boys in the highest SES group and the highest ability quartile did (Sewell and Shah, 1967, p. 13). Low SES interferes with college entry at all achievement levels; but in the blue-collar, White families the girls get short shrift and boys get encouragement and finances if any are given. The opposite is true in Black families. At least in the past, the women have been given first consideration for a college education because they had more opportunities to get positions in professions such as teaching (Carnegie Commission, 1971b, p. 29).

The Task Force in Higher Education states unequivocally that women are discriminated against in higher education. The report cites three major barriers blocking women's equal participation: overt discrimination by college and university officials, practical barriers such as rigid admission and attendance policies and lack of services and facilities, and deeply ingrained beliefs among both men and women regarding women's abilities and desires. These barriers compound discrimination by increasing the likelihood that women cannot receive equal opportunities from other social institutions during their lives (Newman, 1971, p. 51).

Low SES is not the only factor that mitigates against women in higher education; to a large extent the institutions themselves are responsible for blocking or bypassing women. Although women earn better grades in high school and in college than men do (Bayer, Royer, and Webb, 1973, p. 13), a lower percentage go on to college and to graduate school. Women do not receive as much encouragement to pursue college studies, and some graduate departments actually discourage women from going on for graduate work. The Task Force cites the myths that society holds against educating women: they are a poor investment because they do not persevere and graduate, and if they do graduate, they do not make use of their education in the working world. Statistics, however, refute these allegations. Of the students of both sexes entering college, women have a fifteen percent higher graduation rate four years later than men and, moreover, do as well as men in completing graduate studies (Newman, 1971, p. 53). The myth that education is wasted on women is not borne out by the U.S. Department of Labor statistics presented in Table 3. The more education a woman has, the more likely she is to be found in the labor force.

Fortunately, recent shifts in society's views about women's role and place are having a salutary effect on college attendance. In a survey of college enrollment in the fall of 1971, the Carnegie Commission reported that, although the growth in the number of new college freshmen was leveling off, women were beginning to make gains in attendance at all levels of college and university education. In 1971, women made up 41 percent of the total enrollment, 44 percent of the undergraduate enrollment, 46 percent of the first-time freshmen, 35 percent of the

Table 3

Women Workers

Education	Percent of total in labor force
Elementary school (less than 8 yrs.)	23
Elementary school (8 yrs.)	31
High school (4 yrs.)	50
College (4 yrs.)	56
College (5 yrs. or more)	71

Source: U.S. Department of Labor, Employment Standards Administration, Women's Bureau, *Women Workers Today*, 1971, rev.

graduate enrollment, and 36 percent of the first-time graduate enrollment (Peterson, 1972, p. 5). Ten years earlier, women made up 37.7 percent of the total enrollment, 38.5 percent of the undergraduate enrollment and 29.3 percent of the graduate enrollment (Folger, Astin, and Bayer, 1970, p. 380). Most promising were the gains made in graduate education. Unfortunately, there are still strong pockets of resistance to women in parts of many universities. With respect to women on faculties, even with greater participation in graduate education and large increases in the hiring rates, the Carnegie Commission does not see women and minorities represented in rates equal to those in the total labor force before the year 2000 (Carnegie Commission, 1973d, pp. 122-123).

Women, of course, are not the only class that have been discriminated against in higher education. Many racial and ethnic minorities are also underrepresented—Black Americans, Chicanos, American Indians, and Puerto Ricans. Oriental-Americans, both Chinese and Japanese, are well represented in higher education (Carnegie Commission, 1971b, p. 25). Demands from these minorities have increased since 1960, and the institutions have been responding. For example, the number of Black students enrolled in college doubled over the period 1964 to 1970 (Janssen, 1972, pp. 1-2). Peterson compared enrollment figures of 1970 with 1971 and reported that total Black undergraduate enrollment increased by 17.2 percent, graduate enrollment by 38 percent. For students with Spanish surnames, total enrollment increased by 19 percent, graduate enrollment by 36 percent. More recently, the enrollment of Blacks declined for the first time since 1960. The American Council on Education's yearly survey reports only 7.8 percent of the entering fall enrollment were Blacks in 1973 compared with 8.7 percent in 1972. Tuition increases and competition for financial aid are believed to be the cause (American Council on Education, 1973). College attendance by minorities falls well below that of white students. Ethnic minorities made up 24 percent of the national college-age population, but they comprised only 5 to 6 percent of the total college enrollment in 1971 (Peterson, 1972, p. 15). As has been pointed out, the greatest detriment to be overcome is the early deprivation in poverty-ridden and disadvantaged families, and the accompanying lack of intellectual motivation and family expectations for higher education.

Qualifications for Admission

It is often assumed that all of higher education requires a particular kind of conceptual and abstract reasoning ability. No doubt some subject matter—such as philosophy—does, but universities have not limited themselves to such areas. From the beginning of the first university in Europe at Salerno, medicine, for example, has been in the curriculum, and the teaching of medicine is heavily weighted with practical knowledge and skills. The methods of teaching that have been used in college also reveal the true nature of the learning that has been required—explication of the text, note-taking, fact-recalling on examinations, and similar methods not seriously concerned with the development of abstract thinking. Programs in higher education have become highly diversified—some demand abstract thinking, most do not. Whether a person is educable depends on the correlation of his particular aptitudes with those needed for the program he tries. In a system of diversified programs, the aptitudes required are varied, and success or failure is relative rather than absolute.

As has been shown, finances and family expectations may preclude attendance in college for low SES students, but low ability rarely does for high SES students. High SES students are often sought after, and students in the lowest quartile of the high school graduating class can always find a college ready to accept them. The admissions practices of individual colleges and universities vary widely. Some maintain limited enrollments and select students carefully for success in their programs. Others admit all who apply. Many public institutions are required by law to accept all applicants with a high school diploma. Public community colleges, some by policy and some by law, admit virtually any high school graduate who applies, as well as some students without diplomas who seem sufficiently ready for college.

It is a common misconception that private colleges and universities are more selective in their admission of students than public ones. This is true of a number of the older, better-financed, more prestigious institutions. They number about one hundred and accommodate only a small percentage of the entering college freshmen. Most of their students are in the top 20 percent in academic ability. But because many of the colleges in this limited group are small, they can enroll less than 15 percent of all top ability college students. As a matter of fact, the community colleges enroll more students from the top 20 percent than do these prestigious institutions (Folger, Astin, and Bayer, 1970, p. 163). The general run of many private and public colleges and universities, however, admit almost all who apply, their published criteria notwithstanding. Many of these institutions require a certain standard of accomplishment once the student is enrolled. According to estimates made by the Commission on Human Resources, of the public and private institutions in the United States, about 4 percent are very highly selective, 28 percent are highly selective, 33 percent are of average selectivity, 28 percent of low selectivity, and 7 percent are of very low selectivity (Folger, Astin, and Bayer, 1970, p. 163). The Commission estimated selectivity from the average IQ scores of Project TALENT sample students entering each college. The most selective colleges enrolled students who had an average IQ of about 130 or better, but they enroll only about 4 percent of all entering freshmen (Folger, Astin, and Bayer, 1970, p. 162).

It is not the admission practices with these varying standards that are faulted, but rather, the follow-up or lack of it after the students are admitted. Many colleges appear to function on the basis of expediency, accepting students to solve a budget problem or to outstrip a rival in size. Once admitted, the students are left on their own, and they are often ill prepared, both academically and psychologically, for the experience. Lacking any integrity of purpose, these institutions make no effort to assist the students to grow in relation to their interests and abilities. Aggravating the situation is the fact that the policy filters down, so that any integrity of purpose that faculty and students once held regarding higher education and its values is dissipated.

Studies of attrition in institutions indicate that those with high holding power are generally highly selective and private rather than public. Other factors that contribute to the withdrawal of students are ineffective teaching, impersonal faculty-student contacts, lack of counseling, and the poor attention in both kind and amount that the faculty give to curricular improvements and to the institution itself (Folger, Astin, and Bayer, 1970, pp. 53 and 95). Spaeth and Greeley (1970, p. 67) found college quality and intellectual and cultural experiences extremely important to the attitude of alumni. Even in colleges where the alumni criticized quality, they were loyal if the formation of values had been stressed (p. 58).

Academic Caliber of Students

There are, of course, some educators who cling to the belief that higher education is primarily for the intellectually elite. When enrollments increase, they issue dire warnings that expansion will depress standards in the colleges and universities. This has not been substantiated so far. Increased enrollments have come mainly from the higher ability groups in the secondary schools. John Darley (1962, p. 34), using a representative national sample of colleges, demonstrated that the average ability level of the entering students did not change very much from

1952 to 1959. Substantiating this is a report prepared for the Carnegie Commission which studied college enrollment since 1900. It concluded that the quality of college students had actually increased. The increase was accounted for by the expanding number of the most able high school graduates entering college from 1900 to 1960 (Taubman and Wales, 1972, p. 19). Whether this will continue to be the case with universal access remains to be seen. The highest level of prestigious colleges and universities will undoubtedly continue to hold their superior place; the community colleges may well have valuable but different goals.

The issue raises an important point about maintaining quality education through standards and instruction—in photography or cosmetology, as well as in history or chemistry—in the community colleges. From the social viewpoint it is essential that some institutions be given the function of offering courses that require superior intelligence and intensive searches for knowledge.

Dropouts and Stopouts

Once students have entered postsecondary education, factors similar to those that mitigate against entry affect completion. Nationally, not quite half (47 percent) of the students who enter four-year institutions complete the baccalaureate degree within four years (Astin, 1972, p. 49). (Actually, of course, a higher percentage graduates. Some students enroll in programs that take more than four years, and others transfer to other institutions.) There is a consistent relationship between academic ability (based on high school grades and aptitude tests) and persistence in college. Virtually all students with very high secondary school grades and scholastic aptitude scores complete their education, but over 80 percent of the low ability students drop out (Astin, 1972, p. 29).

Dropouts from college historically have been considered anathemas, both to the institutions and to the students. The institution believes its selection process has been faulty when a student decides to leave of his own volition; educators believe the effect on the student is injurious to his morale. Other critics bear down on the waste of money and time by both the institution and the student. A study reported in 1968 disclosed only 15.5 percent of the men and 5.8 percent of the women withdrew for academic failure, a fact which only compounds the egregiousness of the dropout situation. Reasons for withdrawal are presented in Table 4. Obviously, college was a disappointment to most of the withdrawing students and influenced them to reconsider their career objectives.

Table 4

Reasons Given for Leaving College

	Men	*Women*
Dissatisfied with college environment	26.7	27.0
Time to reconsider goals and interests	26.4	17.7
Changed career plans	22.1	20.7
Could not afford cost	23.6	17.8
Tired of being a student	11.3	6.0

Source: R. I. Panos and A. W. Astin, "Attrition Among College Students," *American Education Research Journal*, 1968, 5 (1), 62.

Perhaps because of their different clientele, the two-year colleges have a higher dropout rate than the four-year institutions. About one-third of those entering the two-year colleges do not return for the second year; only 25 percent of the four-year group do not return. Of those who do return to the two-year college, fewer than two in three eventually earned the associate's degree (Astin, 1972, p. 12). However, the four-year colleges with selective admissions accept students most like those they graduate. The open-door junior college does not. This fact alone would presage a lower degree rate. On the other hand, these students may not be getting the kind of education they are seeking.

Economic factors exert a strong influence on college completion. Students supported by parents, scholarships, or personal savings tend to remain in college. Students employed during the school year tend to drop out, whether they are registered in two-year or four-year institutions. Public junior college students, as a group, come from families in income groups that are lower than those of university students (Medsker and Tillery, 1971, p. 44). The junior college, with low or no tuition, is often a commuting college and hence finances may well be an important factor. The student who works at a job while attending college has a reduced amount of time for studies. Thus, a job may interfere with satisfactory progress. Moreover, the job offers the student an alternative to remaining in college (Astin, 1972, p. 37).

We submit that withdrawal from college is neither as pernicious nor as wasteful as most educators have been believing. Certainly some education is better than none. Also, the time spent in college helps students to crystallize their thinking and their choices of ultimate or immediate objectives. The monetary loss is not as wasteful as the cost overruns and expenditures that are commonplace for military equipment and affairs. Although success in college is usually equated with graduation, dropouts benefit by their tenure, however short. Trent and Medsker (1967, p. 318) concluded that the student who needs to seek self-understanding and developmental experiences may do so better by traveling, working, or studying on his own for a time.

Recently, many have advocated that traditional formal college attendance during the college-age years be made flexible and that opportunities for higher education be made available to persons throughout their lifetimes (Carnegie Commission, 1971a, p. 1; *Time*, 1973). High school graduates, they posit, should be allowed to defer college attendance or to stop out during the college years for work, travel, service experience, and so forth. Hopefully, the censure which has accompanied dropouts and the pressure to enter college immediately after high school graduation may be alleviated. Eventually, we may reach a point where all students attending college are there because of intrinsic motivation. Estimates are that at least ten percent are in college unwillingly, and another twenty percent are attending without commitment (Carnegie Commission, 1973e, p. 18). Furthermore, the commission is critical of professions that do not afford opportunity for advancement without formal degrees. Nurses, for example, should be able, after demonstrating the required knowledge and skills, to take on larger responsibilities in the health services—as the new role of nurse practitioner enables them to do (1971a, p. 14).

There is a trend toward more participation in nontraditional postsecondary education by the nontraditional student.* For example, the percentage of the population between the ages of twenty-five and thirty-five who are enrolled in higher education tripled between 1950 and 1960 (Carnegie Commission, 1971b, p. 3). This tendency is further demonstrated by U.S. Office of Education statistics, which indicated that during the academic year 1968-1969, 11 percent of eligible adults—nontraditional students—had participated in education and training activities. By the summer of 1972, the Commission on Nontraditional Study was reporting that 31 percent of persons between the ages of 18 and 60 had received postsecondary instruction in the preceding year in subjects other than those taken as full-time students (Carnegie Commission, 1973e, p. 27). Scholars of higher education are advocating lifelong learning in the United States whereby all persons can partake of postsecondary education at any time throughout their lifetime for vocational, avocational, or cultural purposes. Together with the enrollment of college-age students in regular college programs, these statistics presage the "learning society" which is becoming a necessity in this time of rapid change and accretions of knowledge.

Overeducation

Other experts believe that we are now faced with the prospect of an overeducated population. The development of the United States has reached a turning point, they postulate, and the demand for educated workers is decreasing. They believe that today there is an oversupply of college-educated per-

---

*Nontraditional students are defined as "young and older part-time, degree-credit and nondegree-credit students attending, often in the evening, and in off-campus as well as on-campus locations" (Carnegie Commission, 1973e, p. 10). Traditional students are full-time day students, of college age, in degree programs.

sons seeking jobs and that there has been since 1968. Job seekers in many parts of the country concur, and there are official
reports which substantiate this view.

The U.S. Bureau of the Census has stated that if the same
education required for jobs in 1960 is still required in 1975,
there will be more high school and college graduates than are
needed (Carnegie Commission, 1973a, pp. 1-2). The Manpower
Report of the President, 1972, calculated that during the seventies two and one-half million college-educated people will be
working in jobs that were not held by college-educated people
in the past. Moreover, the shortage of college graduates that
occurred in the sixties is not likely to reoccur in the foreseeable
future (Carnegie Commission, 1973a, p. 3). The U.S. Bureau of
Labor Statistics estimates that during the 1970s, only 20 percent
of the jobs will require postsecondary school education. But according to the Carnegie Commission, two-thirds of the persons
graduating from high school will take some form of higher education at some time, and over one-third of the college-age population (eighteen to twenty-one) is in college at any given time
(Carnegie Commission, 1973a, pp. 2-3).

An oversupply of educated workers in the labor market
causes various occupations to be educationally upgraded. That
is, the educational requirements are raised, but the job requirements remain the same; or the job can be redesigned to attract
and require a more highly educated person; or a proportion of
college-educated persons will be working at jobs they would
have had anyway if they had not gone to college (Carnegie
Commission, 1973a, p. 2).

Since 1950, educational upgrading has occurred in many
occupations. Not all these changes have been warranted. The
stratagem of raising the educational requirements alone, without redesigning the job, was tested in court in 1971 (Griggs *et al*
v. Duke Power Co., 1971) and was found wanting. The decision called for "the elimination of artificial, arbitrary, and unnecessary barriers to employment that . . . cannot be shown to
be related to job performance" and of "devices and mecha-
nisms . . . unless they are demonstrably a reasonable measure of
job performance"; and that requires, instead, that "any tests

used must measure the person for the job and not the person in the abstract" (Carnegie Commission, 1973a, p. 9). Although the raising of educational requirements necessary for the job was considered irrelevant in this case, some occupations become more complex with advancing technology or new discoveries and do require more education.

Nevertheless, there will be a certain number of college-educated persons who will be doing work that does not tax their potential, as there always are. The thesis has been put forward that to educate people beyond their station in life is frustrating to them and dangerous to society. When this occurs people lend themselves to political causes—either of the extreme right or the extreme left—causing ideological upheavals that otherwise would not occur, such as the situation in Germany prior to the Nazi takeover. Perhaps this could happen in countries where college graduates hold rigid attitudes regarding the kind of work that is fitting for them to perform or in underdeveloped countries where there may be a temporary imbalance between trained manpower and jobs to absorb them. Certainly for years American women have been overeducated for their jobs as typists, but they have not instigated political uprisings. Furthermore, in the United States a person does not have a fixed and unchanging status; Americans are flexible about work and often work in fields unrelated to their education. According to the Commission on Human Resources, many college graduates go into occupations that do not require a degree in the field in which they received their baccalaureate degree. In one study, less than 60 percent of the business majors were working in business or commerce, and only one-fourth of the natural science majors were at work in their field (Folger, Astin, and Bayer, 1970, pp. 232-233). And not all law school graduates practice law. Professions are no longer limited to a few prestige occupations. New professions continue to evolve out of the needs of a given time and change as the requirements of society change.

Certainly there are people who prefer jobs that require less rather than more intellectual involvement. Not all college graduates enjoy the intellectual life, as any faculty member will verify; many go to college for vocational reasons and prefer work of a more concrete kind. Recently many of these students have been demanding more practical courses, and many colleges are responding with major curricular changes (Watkins, 1973, p. 2). But the benefits of a college education, quite apart from the vocational training are important. Assessing the impact of a college education is difficult; nevertheless, there is general broad agreement that every year of higher education offers additional benefits. College graduates have more knowledge, skills, and interests than persons with less education, and they make greater use of printed material to add to their store of knowledge, skills, and interests. Additionally, there is a general salutary impact on most students of most colleges, and there may be the added impact of a particular college on its students. College-educated people are usually considered to be more open-minded and tolerant, less materialistic and moralistic. They are more satisfied with their work, receive higher salaries, and suffer less unemployment than persons without a similar amount of education. They tend to be more thoughtful, deliberate, and informed (Withey, 1971, pp. xii, 128-129). Certainly there are people who do not complete college who are well informed, and others with master's and doctor's degrees who can be provincial and narrow. These are broad generalities and from incomplete data; nevertheless, the consensus is that higher education, like clean air, cannot be bad, but could always be better.

As a matter of fact, there are forces working to counteract the oversupply of workers vis-à-vis the number of jobs available: the shorter working day, the four-day week, longer vacations, and earlier retirement. In addition, there is the ever-increasing demand for services. There is a need for personnel in social welfare, insurance, repairs and construction, recreation, technical and managerial positions in business, industry, and the administrative agencies of government. There are shortages in some professions, mainly in the health fields. Professional workers are needed in the care of the aged, in child care centers, and in preventive mental health services. It seems unlikely that there will not be enough work to go around.

When people had to work sixty or even eighty-four hours

a week to earn a subsistence living, a twenty-or-thirty hour week would have been considered the apotheosis of the good life. Now that we are on the threshold of such a possibility, the short week is viewed with consternation rather than with appreciation. It is an opportunity for all persons to work less and enjoy a fulfilling life with a variety of activities. It is mainly the people working at the highest ability levels who enjoy their work and spend long hours at it. Persons in routine jobs abhor overtime, as was illustrated by the United Automobile Workers' opposition to compulsory overtime during contract negotiations in 1973. Eventually the workers will be the elite. In the meantime, what is needed is a national leadership dedicated to altering the priorities, so that the benefits of an advanced civilization in a cultured society will be available to everyone.

New Students,
New Problems

★★★
★★★

When students arrive at college, they bring their problems with them—academic, identity, life style, choice of vocation, financial, and health problems. Academic problems in colleges have changed during recent years. Although there have always been students who flunked out, sometimes the causes were not so much academic inability as lack of motivation. Certainly there were some students who needed remedial work and others who had various problems that blocked their progress. Students at one institution might have very different intellectual capabilities than those at another, but all had similar school backgrounds in one respect. That was, they were all high school graduates who had been, to a greater or lesser extent, successful in their academic pursuits. Today, students who did not do well in high school are entering college.

The New Student

The new student (Cross, 1972) in higher education today is one who has never been effectual in the traditional secondary school curriculum. Some have received inferior education in inferior schools. Others have not been successful because of low ability or low motivation or, more often, both. Many of these new college students come from environments where neither their families nor their peers considered academic achievement a laudatory goal. Cross (1972) defines new students as those scoring in the lowest third among the national samples of high school students on traditional tests of academic ability. They are students who in previous generations would not have considered entering college. The open door of the community junior college has given them hope that they can pursue postsecondary education, and through it secure better jobs and a better life. Black youth, from communities where unemployment rates are terribly high, now think of a college education as essential to employment. Although a number of studies indicate that grades in school do not alone necessarily predict success in life, college graduates nevertheless earn more (about 10 to 25 percent more) throughout their lifetimes than those who do not graduate from college. To the extent that more men were attending college during the sixties, those who did not go on were kept out more by low academic ability than by low economic ability. (Women, on the other hand, are kept out for reasons of economics even at high ability levels.) But beginning in the seventies, men in the lower ability category in high school—that is, in the lowest third—showed a high increase in college attendance. The greatest percentage of these men entered the local community college. Furthermore, this group will probably increase as the philosophy of universal access in higher education becomes dominant. Hence, the colleges need to be prepared for students who have never done well in traditional academic studies and who have consistently been assigned the lowest academic rankings. The colleges must meet their new clientele with workable and welcome programs. Such an undertaking requires counseling personnel who are sensitive to the needs of these new students and programs of study different from the traditional programs in traditional colleges.

In addition, new students must be helped to change the image they have of themselves as failure-prone students according to Cross (1972, p. 39). Programs must be provided that enable them to catch up and that give attention to reorienting their approach to learning. The latter is probably the single most important assistance that the colleges can give. New students need to have repeated opportunities to encounter successful classroom experiences that rekindle their desire to learn. Learning is innate within the human animal—the desire of infants and young children to do things for themselves demonstrates this. Children are constantly learning. It is when the child enters school that his eagerness to learn is diminished. Studies indicate that failure-threatened personalities will try jobs they are certain of doing well, but withdraw when there is a potential for failure. Conversely, good students actively try new problems because their past experiences have been successful; poor students are passive because their past experiences have taught them that to try usually means to fail.

Successful remedial teachers build up favorable learning situations for new students by starting them at work below their tested ability and then by gradually moving them into new and difficult material. New students who progress successfully can hopefully assume responsibility for their own learning. Beyond this, it is important that community college educators develop relevant programs around the interests and skill potentials of new students.

In the primary and secondary schools, the curriculum is defined by the three Rs and the general education necessary for adequate adult life. The subject matter is set, and teachers accept the fact that all pupils cannot learn it. So adjustments are made in the quality of accomplishment. Seldom are adjustments made in the curriculum. Not successful in required traditional schoolwork, the new student knows failure as an ever-present concomitant of school attendance. Little wonder that he becomes failure-prone. Cross (1972, p. 152) believes that, for these reasons, part of postsecondary education must be in different kinds of education, so that all students can perform well in some subjects. New students do well working with people and working with things. These are the fields where labor shortages exist—in services and in technology maintenance (Cross,

1972, p. 154). It is up to the educators to devise programs based on subject matter in these areas, so that this third of the college population can prepare successfully for a satisfying vocational and avocational life.

In the face of declining enrollments, many four-year colleges with traditional programs will be accepting new students. These students should be accepted only if there is a chance that success is within reach and if the institution has the facilities and the trained personnel to assist them. Unless the colleges have the resources to cope with the problems of new students, they should resist the temptation to expand their role in education, however appealing the cause.

Counseling Services

Counseling is as much a part of college today as classes are. Originally an informal part of the college president's duties, in universities counseling has become a full-fledged facility engaging professionals trained in psychology and specializing in problems that beset college students. The director may be a top-level administrator and a member of the president's cabinet. At a small college, he may be the psychology instructor, or a faculty member who approves students' registrations.

Faculty who are concerned with academic counseling help students to plan their programs so they can reach their educational goals. These counselors may meet with students continually throughout their college years. A student, seeing the same counselor for four years, may in reality be getting more than academic advising. The counselor's knowledge of the student may enable him to direct the student toward courses that fill in the areas where his knowledge is weak or his outlook is narrow, or toward courses that test his values. In contrast, some counselors succumb to the student's inclination to take easy courses and collude in underwriting a second-class education. To some extent the academic counselor can assist with vocational planning, but he should not preempt this role. A teacher will be knowledgeable and persuasive about his own field of interest. But it is the general or career counselor who can best assist the student to examine a variety of possible choices and can also assist him in analyzing his chances for having a successful career.

In formal programs at large institutions, counseling becomes a part of the overall student personnel services, which include admissions, records, health services, housing, and financial aids. Nevertheless, counseling is a basic service concerned with the personal, psychological, and physical development of the student—with his search for identity and his occupational choice.

Character formation has been one of the purposes for going to college—an added emolument, as it were, to the educational and vocational ones. Through liberal studies and student activities, a college education was expected to round out the person, help him to find himself, hone the rough edges, and make him a gentleman. This has been termed the *initiation function,* helping the adolescent become an adult. The achievement of identity is still one of the anticipated benefits of college attendance. Because the formation of identity is resolved in the later years of adolescence, during the very years when youth are in college, the college can hardly ignore this crucial period of maturation. Identity formation, however, has only recently been the subject of intensive study. Probably the best-known authority in the field is Erik Erikson, psychiatrist and Harvard faculty member (now emeritus). Erikson (1968) describes identity as the way a person sees and thinks of himself in relation to his world and how he thinks others judge him. Identity is not static—it is a continuing process. It forms as the person advances through predetermined stages depending on his readiness and ability to move into new situations and deal with other individuals.

During infancy and childhood, identity formation occurs unconsciously. At adolescence, when the individual has the necessary physiological and psychological growth and is on the verge of adulthood, the identity crisis occurs. The word *crisis* is used to signify not a time of turmoil but a necessary turning point in the development of the individual. The crisis may come on gradually and be resolved tranquilly; or it may bring a period of anxiety and conflict. It is an interim period during which the adolescent will make decisions important to the emerging adult. College students particularly feel pressed toward making many decisions all at once, in handling relationships with the opposite sex, managing their own sexuality, preparing for careers, dealing with intimacy with roommates and peers, and living up to expectations of families and friends.

The intermediate period between adolescence and adulthood Erikson terms a moratorium. It is a time when the individual can delay making permanent decisions that will be critical to the adult, and when the enduring pattern of the identity is being set. It is a time when the promise of finding oneself and losing oneself are closely allied. Eventually, the adolescent becomes an adult, and in the process takes on his abiding identity, his real self. If his identity crisis is resolved positively, the individual will have a feeling of confidence and psychosocial well being about himself.

Black students, in particular, may find the search for self-identity especially difficult in a largely White institution. White institutions, in accepting Blacks, need to have a definite program for helping them to establish a positive identity concept through programs and through the attitudes the institution holds toward the presence of Blacks. Particularly important are the intangibles which emanate from the milieu of the campus. Is the Black race fully recognized and accepted as a worthy part of the pluralistic American society? Is there respect for Black culture and for the differences in Black experiences? Are there courses in Black studies? Do Black students see Black staff members, faculty, and administrators on campus? Is there a counseling and guidance program offering help to Black students in personal, financial, and vocational counseling? Does the institution support the Black Students Union, or tolerate it as a second-class outsider? Needless to say, Black counselors for Black students are needed for identity and personal problems (Vermilye, 1972, pp. 49-66). Counseling programs must be genuine, not mere window dressing, and an integral part of the educational program. The president of Morgan State College explained well what Blacks need to overcome: "Hundreds of years of socioeconomic deprivation have left their mark. Black students with castrated egos, damaged self-images, and poor academic preparation must be given the opportunity to have their personhood restored" (Vermilye, 1972, p. 73).

Some students use drastic ways of finding out about themselves. Desire for self-revelation was often cited as a reason for the increased use of drugs by students in the sixties. Although the use of drugs—or at least of hard drugs—seems to be decreasing during the seventies, alcohol, marijuana, and tobacco have been accepted by the college clientele for experimentation and use. To the extent that these substances are physically or psychologically injurious, experts agree that marijuana is the least dangerous of the three. On the other hand, its illegal status at the present time increases its use and exacerbates the problems of the college counselors. A student's refusal to have a drink is accepted less critically than his refusal to smoke pot. To handle such problems, institutions of higher education generally have regulations in consonance with their objectives and the law. Nevertheless, to the extent that counselors are responsible for dealing with student lawbreakers, or with students who become high on alcohol or drugs, a counseling rather than a disciplinary approach is usually more effective. The student seeking an altered state of consciousness may be in need of counseling because he may be trying to escape from his problems instead of facing them.

According to Erikson (1968, p. 132), a crucial part of one's identity is one's vocation. He believes that the inability to settle on an occupational identity is a problem that most disturbs young people. Previously, a college education, if it did not definitely settle one's vocation, was at least a certificate for entry into a well-paying job. This was true when the economy was expanding so fast that the demand for qualified workers was greater than the supply. But it is no longer true. A U.S. Department of Labor study (1973, pp. 41-42, 45) on the job status of 1970 and 1971 college graduates reported an unemployment rate of 7.4 percent. (This was only about half the rate for high school graduates for the same years.) Fifty-five percent of the working group said their earnings were substantially or somewhat lower than expected. One-third of those who were earning less than expected were in work not at all related to their major field of study. Among those who looked for work from five weeks to more than ten weeks, the main reasons for the length of their search was that no jobs were available. It is believed that this situation will continue into the eighties.

Studies like the above and those of the Carnegie Commission and the Commission on Human Resources and Advanced Education indicate the need for more sophisticated vocational counseling in the colleges. The Carnegie Commission (1971a, pp. 47, 167) called upon federal agencies to develop more adequate data on employment of college students and suggested that postsecondary institutions strengthen their occupational counseling programs.

The demands of different occupations for personnel change with technological advances and with demand and supply, as well as with what is the vogue. During the fifties, the demand for teachers was never fully met; in the seventies they have become a glut on the market. The demand and supply of engineers went through the same cycle. College students want to know what chances they will have for employment in specific professions or occupations. To a large extent, students have been voluntarily responsive to the changes in the job market. This is fortunate, because in the United States the system for making decisions about vocations has been one of free choice. Some countries manipulate the supply and demand of workers by limiting the numbers of persons who enter educational and training programs. The individual-choice system has worked fairly well for us, although we have been experiencing large personnel deficits in the health professions and in some of the trades. Moreover, the system is not equally open to all young people, particularly not those in the lower socioeconomic groups.

The counseling of women will be increasingly important in vocational planning. Women will be working for twenty-five or thirty years of their lives, whether single or married, parents or childless. They are becoming intensely aware of their position in the job market and are resisting being shunted into low-level, dead-end, handmaiden jobs. They are demanding, and getting, admission to several male-oriented occupations and professions. In conjunction with the increased numbers of women attending college (young women and women returning after their children are in school) the institutions are being called on for more flexibility in their regulations. Admissions requirements, full-time course loads, or continuous study requirements need to be—and are being—modified to meet the life styles of dual- or triple-roled students, both women and men. It has become even more important that institutions of higher education give serious, sincere, and active attention to child care centers for the children of students, staff, and faculty. As women have pointed out, money has always been available for large stadiums, gymnasiums, athletic fields, and marching bands for male students. Child care centers do not cost as much.

Chronic health problems of a physical nature are usually diagnosed at the lower levels of education; treatment, however, may extend into the adult years. Additionally, college students can become involved in all kinds of illnesses from mononucleosis or gonorrhea to serious accidents. Moreover, colleges have long closed their eyes to the fact of sexual activities on campus. Health services need to accept the facts of life and offer contraception and sex education to their students as a matter of course. Many institutions now do. For all these reasons, colleges need to enlarge their provisions for medical care or medical counsel.

In Loco Parentis

The early colonists established academies and colleges so that their children might understand the laws of the land and receive training for employment, and so that the children learn the principles of their religions. Hence, the housing, boarding, and disciplining of the students were necessary not only because of pioneer conditions but to keep them under constant supervision in order to assure that they lived up to the strict moral code of the religious sects (Leonard, 1956, pp. 106-107). Child-rearing was authoritarian, and harsh punishment was the rule.

Moreover, students on campus were much younger than they are today. Some were only fourteen and fifteen, and most colleges had preparatory departments because the public secondary school was not yet established (Henderson, 1968, p. 66). In this environment, the concept of *in loco parentis* was established and flourished. Today students are usually eighteen when they enter college, and some are older. More mature in many ways than were previous generations of their age, these students come from homes that permit freedoms during the high school years that were unknown to their grandparents in college. Some students have done military service or held full-time jobs before coming to college. They have become recognized as citizens with the right to vote. These students demand adult status in college. The women, who mature earlier than the men, have been held to the most rigid and closest supervision. With the women's movement, women are now demanding that restrictions placed on them be no different from those on men. Unfortunately, it is well known that although students demand release from parietal rules, their parents, the community, and the college administrators want those rules maintained. Many of these parents have permitted the very freedoms they now hope the college authorities will curtail. Added to this is the fact that the president and his administrative associates are responsible for maintaining and projecting the image of the institution and also for providing for students (and faculty) an environment conducive to scholarship and personal growth. Administrators are caught between students and most faculty on one side, and parents, trustees, and alumni on the other. When a situation erupts, administrators often find themselves making expedient decisions. It is time that everyone concerned recognize and accept the fact that the concept of *in loco parentis* has been challenged and is now moribund; procedural due process is taking its place. But in conjunction with this change, there is the recognition that the educational institution has the right to enforce its own reasonable regulations. Because the institution has this right, the efforts of the administration need to be directed toward marshaling the entire campus to develop a group concern for the right environment. Announcing that a standard exists

does not make it so. Beyond this there must be continuous rein-
forcement through indoctrination and example. The day of dog-
matic pronunciamentos is past, but opportunism should not
take their place. The institution that wants a distinctive or
scholarly environment must work to achieve and sustain it. This
requires leadership, group involvement, and common understandings about values.

Broad

Learning Experiences

★★
★★

The programs of contemporary colleges and universities present a startling contrast with the curriculum of a century and a half ago, when a tightly knit package of knowledge was presented to all students. The phenomenal growth has raised many questions and has created many problems (Dressel, 1968). One of these is to identify, from the vast array of possible subject matter and experience, the elements that should provide cultural knowledge and skills.

    Widespread use of the scientific method has influenced the manner in which human knowledge has developed. Earlier in the history of higher education, deductive reasoning was the prevailing method of developing knowledge. When there was a limited body of knowledge, authoritarian in type, it was easy to determine what the content of an education should be. This body of knowledge could be passed on to students as the cultural heritage. Doctrinal values could be inculcated. When the new method of critical inquiry into the nature and origin of natural phenomena was developed, additional knowledge began to be accumulated at a terrific pace. Each investigation developed new facts and brought forth fresh ideas, and also additional questions for study. The search for truth displaced the rote learning of truth.

Although natural phenomena were the bases for the earlier investigations, when scholars began to turn from the study of the classics to empirical studies of their own society, the social sciences emerged and began to flower. The tendency of the social sciences to divide and subdivide, due to the additional increments of knowledge, is a familiar phenomenon on nearly every campus. The humanities, which in earlier times constituted so large a portion of the curriculum—indeed almost the whole of it—acquired new partners in the sciences and the social sciences. Relatively, the humanities have lagged in change. Nevertheless the flowering has occurred there, too, as evidenced by the accumulation of literary and historical materials and the rigorous analysis that has been applied to the meanings of changes and events that have occurred in recent times.

Underlying much of this change has been the evolution of our economic life. As educators began to see that knowledge was useful and that education should not be limited to "things of the mind and spirit," a vigorous assist was given to the beginnings of industrialization. Knowledge helped enable industrialization to proceed. Industry, commerce, agriculture, and the advancing professions exhibited new needs and opportunities for educated personnel. As our economic society became more complex, the varieties of knowledge and skills that were useful increased tremendously. Education, in turn, has helped produce persons trained in diverse types of knowledge and in varied skills.

The fragmentation of knowledge in American institutions was begun when the German model for graduate study and research was adopted by the American universities. The growth of the graduate level of instruction and research in the United States would have occurred in any event, although there is little doubt that the German example was a stimulating one. Fortunately we did not wholly accept the German pattern. An important factor was our commitment to the concept of liberal education; under the leadership of the liberal arts faculties, the new universities balanced specialized study with continuing emphasis on the humanities and other liberalizing subject matter. Nevertheless, the graduate schools in our universities became departmentalized and, in turn, the whole of the institution became segmented. The tendency of individual departments to emphasize their specializations was one of the actions that helped to disrupt the unity that had prevailed when the classics were the heart of the curriculum. The various disciplines into which the curriculum has been fragmented make invaluable contributions to knowledge and to the education of students. But much of knowledge is interdisciplinary, and hence there is need also for an integration of knowledge. Furthermore, the student, if he is to acquire both breadth and depth of learning, must be helped to assimilate both types of knowledge and to integrate them in his own life.

Departmentalization has resulted in changes in the college curriculum. The content of the breadth component in education, as distinguished from specialized education, has grown proportionately smaller. There have been periods when the urge to specialize has very nearly swamped our institutions. There have been advocates of the segregation of cultural and vocational education following the European example. Finally, the pressures from the increase in knowledge and rigidities in the curriculum have made it difficult for faculties to devise curricula that provide the student with both breadth and specialized competencies. Fortunately, the belief that the well-educated man is a man possessing breadth of knowledge as well as depth of understanding has persisted in American thinking.

It was perhaps natural that there would be a strong skewing of the various college curricula in the direction of specialization and applied subject matter. As new professional schools were developed, the mood of those who initiated a school was in the direction of fully cultivating the subject matter encompassed by the particular professional interest. Thus, in the fields of engineering, agriculture, business administration, and in the training of teachers, the newly organized schools went overboard in emphasizing applied materials and specific skills. This earlier period was followed by a strong movement to provide a better balance between the general and the special elements in the curriculum of the professional school. However, specialization is again attracting financial and other support. Students from the lower socioeconomic segments are motivated to improve their economic status, and legislators want youth to be prepared for occupations so that unemployment is reduced. And so the issue is still alive: What should the content and role of instruction be if cultural knowledge and skills are to be provided?

Distribution Plan

Heretofore there have been two principal ways in which faculties have attempted to provide for breadth in the curriculum. One of these is the distribution plan. Under the distribution plan, it has been taken for granted that the college curriculum divides naturally into departments or, at least, divisions, of subject matter. In a liberal arts college, these areas comprehend the common fields of human knowledge. The objectives of the distribution are twofold: to prevent the student from concentrating all of his attention on the courses in a particular department or field by requiring him to make selections from each of at least several of these fields; and to give the student an opportunity, through sampling these several fields, to make a wise selection of a specialization in which to major. Ordinarily the spread will encompass some course work in the broad areas of the humanities, the social sciences, and the sciences, and also in English composition. The plan frequently involves making the course selections from among the courses that already exist in the departments, usually the introductory courses. If one of these courses introduces the field in which the student decides to major, it will have launched him in a study in depth.

The distribution plan has been the one most widely used and is still being used by a majority of the colleges and universities. It developed as a means of correcting the specialized tendency of the elective system that was in vogue during the latter part of the nineteenth century. Sometimes a faculty will stipulate the particular courses that every student must take. In other instances, the college requires a distribution, but gives to the student considerable option in making his selections from among fields, and sometimes of courses within each field.

Some colleges provide special sections of introductory courses for students who do not intend to major in those departments. For example, a liberal arts college with a large number of students who plan to teach in public school may feel that each of its students should have some knowledge of physical science, although the difficulty of mathematics deters many students from taking a course in science. A special section of, perhaps, physics or chemistry, may be taught with less emphasis on the mathematics of science than in the standard course. The justification for this variation is that, although a full grasp of mathematics is essential in understanding science as a special field of study, it may not be essential for a person who is going to teach science at an elementary level or who may want to take some science as a part of his liberal education. Occasional variations of this type are made in the nonscience fields.

Because of the emphasis on English, languages, and mathematics so often found under the distribution plan, the method has resembled the trivium and quadrivium, usually with the addition of a bit of history and of science. Very probably the theory is similar; that is, the student should be required to become proficient in communication tools, symbols, and self-expression as a foundation for the remainder of his college work. Other institutions require that students take a given minimum of hours of credit from among a minimum number of specified fields. In this plan, the basic aims of the trivium and quadrivium have been so adulterated as to have become innocuous and unrecognizable.

Critics of the distribution plan point to several deficiencies. The courses generally are introductory to a sequence of specialized courses, hence the introductory course is itself specialized. This type of course does not provide a workable understanding of a broad area of knowledge—a beginning course in botany, for example, gives only a meager view of modern science. Students fail to see the relevance of the course to their own program. If the student is not motivated to take a particular course and has some options, he may select the courses that are reputed to be easy. Often the elementary courses are taught by the least experienced of the faculty.

Finally, the system of choosing the general required courses from among the departmental courses has frequently resulted in considerable logrolling within the faculty. A department will consider that its work is being undervalued or neglected if it is not represented in the required distribution. Many faculty feel that all students should take a course in each department early in their college careers because this enables the departments to attempt to influence the students toward majoring in the department. Higher enrollment in departmental courses also provides a source of leverage in securing larger budgetary appropriations for a department, and this is thought by some chairmen to be an index of prestige. It is significant that the Harvard faculty, in making its 1945 report on general education, recommended strongly that those courses that were to serve the purposes of general education, as defined in the Harvard report, should not be under the control of individual departments but should be a matter for overall faculty concern and control. This faculty procedure is essential when planning any program to achieve breadth objectives.

The distribution plan has the merit of causing a student to sample areas of knowledge other than the one he considers his special interest. Some of these courses will also introduce the student to the vocabulary, the basic concepts, and the methodology of other disciplines. The plan need not suffer from all of the weaknesses mentioned above, because the faculty can design a better program. The focus should be the education of the student, not on the self-interests of departmental faculty.

General Education Movement

The second plan for achieving breadth of education emphasizes synthesizing knowledge for the benefit of the student. The term *general education,* used in its narrower sense, repre-

sents an attempt to design a new curriculum, rather than using existing departmental courses to achieve breadth of education.

Advocates of this term feel that the concept is appropriate to the American scene, because general education has not
been bound by the tradition that surrounds liberal education
and has not been associated, as liberal education has, with class
privilege. They also argue that a fresh approach is essential to
achieve the objectives being sought. The distribution plan starts
with courses that already exist and includes materials that the
professors choose as means of passing the cultural heritage to
the students. General education, in its initial stages, ignores precedent and attempts to analyze the functions of man in life
today and the aspects of knowledge that should facilitate the
performance of those functions. Obviously even a well-educated
man cannot know everything. Nor are dabs of information
about many fields of great value; they may be unrelated among
themselves and unrelated to the student's life. Hence, careful
selection is necessary. The advocates of general education have
defined specific objectives:

(1) To retrieve a unity of knowledge for the student,
something that was lost for a time when the single-package curriculum of a century ago was abandoned; to assist the student
to relate the part to the whole.

(2) To enable the student to acquire intellectual competencies, such as skill in critical thinking and in communication.

(3) To select the most significant knowledge that has accumulated through men's past experience and thus assist the
student in finding his way in the morass of available materials.
In part, the objective is also to break away from the use of se-
quentially oriented introductory courses in specific knowledge
areas as the units for a curriculum in general education.

(4) To provide a historical perspective of our civilization
and of world cultures; to get away from the past tendency of
liberal education to confine itself to western culture.

(5) To acquaint a student with and to stimulate his interest in the environment, physical and social, in which he lives; to
prepare him for effective living in a complex world, the events

of which are increasingly influenced by the advances being made in science and technology.

(6) To help the student relate his education to living today, to his occupation, his family life, his community activities, and his endeavors to lead a richer life; to make culture functional in relation to his living rather than leisure-time sophistication.

(7) To provide the student with a framework of knowledge into which he can fit his special intellectual and occupational interests; to assist him in achieving a social conscience and a mature philosophy of life.

(8) To make general education an essential part of the education of everyone in a democratic society rather than of the privilege of a few, so that there may be some common understandings about historical directions and ethical bases for the conduct of individuals and the ordering of society.

The method defines the educational objectives, including the intangible and pervasive ones, then uses originality in selecting historical threads and events, major intellectual concepts, essential problems of society, and techniques from among the several fields of knowledge that have most strongly influenced the course of civilization and that have the greatest relevance to its present and future development. The aim further is to relate this knowledge to the lives of the students. In this type of objective, general education has been influenced by the philosophy of pragmatism, and by its application in the progressive education movement.

The implementation of the objectives has taken many forms, not all of them successful, although some of the experimentation has been extremely interesting. Many institutions have sought to break away from the departmental limitations and barriers and to integrate subject matter by providing divisional courses. These courses are planned with the nonmajor in mind. The divisions used are ordinarily the humanities, social sciences, and sciences. Almost always a fourth course in communications is added. The subject of communications is often more comprehensive than the usual introductory English course and includes writing, reading, speaking, and listening. The divisional pattern may vary from these four courses—there may, for example, be five or more divisions—but the theory behind the plan remains the same. The objective in each course is to give the student a survey of knowledge from a broad area and to attempt to secure an integration of that knowledge through the medium of a single course.

Probably the oldest example of this type of course is the one in contemporary civilization at Columbia University, begun after World War I and successful over the years. This course was an effort to broaden the horizons of knowledge of American students at a time when the United States was emerging on the world scene. Many colleges and universities pride themselves on having established divisional courses, although some of them have departed from the survey concept in the planning. Ordinarily the divisional courses are required to be taken during the first two years of college, on the theory that they constitute a broad foundation for the additional or specialized studies that the student will undertake. Usually these courses constitute about half of the courses to be undertaken by the student during these two years. This design of curriculum—the completion of the general education element during the first two years— provides a considerable degree of articulation between the programs of two-year colleges and those of the four-year institutions. This design has practical importance in curriculum administration but is not a good application of the theory of general education.

A better plan is one based on the assumption that students need a longer period of time to develop an adequate grasp of the broad fields of knowledge and to assure the achievement of particular educational objectives. Each of the divisional courses may, therefore, be arranged as a set of sequences continuing through two or more years. Because more time is devoted to the study, the achievement of knowledge goes beyond the superficial and elementary. Such extended study also provides the time needed to enlarge intellectual skills and to develop mature insights. In one example of this plan for the social sciences, the first year would be devoted to these sequences, giving the student a foundation of facts and ideas. During the second year, the student would acquire knowledge about the major problems of contemporary society by making a thorough analysis of selected problems. The final year would be devoted to a synthesis of the intellectual process. The primary aim of the final year would be the maturation of the individual's personal and social philosophy. It is interesting that when Columbia University recently revised its plan of general education, it adopted the concept of continuity of objectives throughout the four undergraduate years and also the years in professional and graduate school.

Another plan is to vary the method of selecting the areas and materials of study in the hope of avoiding superficiality and of achieving thoroughness appropriate to college-level work. Possibly the assumption is that the high school has already given the students some general education and hence a broad picture of human knowledge; or possibly it is assumed that it is not essential at this stage of one's lifetime growth for the student to attempt to secure a comprehension of all human knowledge. Thus gaps are left in the knowledge available from the field, and topics selected from a wide range of possibilities are given intensive study. Here the most significant historical trends are noted. Problems of major import to society are discussed. Only those ideas or concepts which seem to have had strong impacts upon the development of civilization are studied. For example, the study of a historical trend in the social sciences might focus on the development of our concept of civil liberties. In literature it might be better for the student to get a thorough understanding of a limited number of plays than to read hastily a whole series of them. The theory of evolution is of great importance. In the physical sciences, the development of the atomic table is today a matter of universal interest and an essential part of our common knowledge. The subject of human relations is so important that a course that applied knowledge from the social sciences to some of the significant problems of human behavior would be highly relevant to the contemporary scene.

Other Plans

There are still other variations in the designs of curricula to meet the objective of breadth in education. A distinctive one exists at St. John's College, where the great books program is used. It is assumed that these books, having stood the test of time, constitute the best that is available in human knowledge, and that it is important for the students, as a part of their general education, to be exposed to the best thinking that men have been able to develop.

A variant exists at Monteith College of Wayne State University—a college of limited enrollment within a large university —where the curriculum endeavors to identify and impart the essential knowledge, the large and important ideas in Western culture, ideas which free the mind and spirit of the individual.

Some colleges, originally under stimulation from a plan at the University of Minnesota, have developed a program of general education especially designed to meet the needs of students of lesser academic achievement. The courses are geared to meet the abilities and pace of study of this group of students. The students who then demonstrate sufficient competence or larger promise of achievement have the opportunity to transfer into other programs.

A few institutions offer the degree of Bachelor of General Studies. This degree is less stringent in its requirements for a major study, and thus emphasizes breadth of achievement. This appears to have been induced by the rigidities in the regular degree programs required by departmentalized faculties.

Daniel Bell (1966), after studying the experiences at Columbia, Harvard, and Chicago, contended that it is not so much the information gained as the intellectual development of the student that counts. He said that the ability to acquire information, to conceptualize, and to clothe specialized knowledge with breadth of significance were the important sequences in learning. Hence, "first comes the acquisition of general background, second the training in a discipline, third the application of this discipline to a number of relevant subjects, and fourth the effort to link disciplines in dealing with common problems." In this view, general and specialized education are not separable but evolve together out of the process of intellectual inquiry.

Movements that recognize that much of knowledge is really interdisciplinary contribute to a solution to the problem of breadth of learning. Many problems cannot be researched well within the confines of departmental walls and need the involvement of the concepts and procedures from two or more disciplines. Often researchers become part-time teachers and develop courses that use knowledge from more than one discipline. Some colleges create introductory courses by providing a synthesis of concepts. For example, a course on matter and energy at one college studies the principles that underlie the famous Einstein formula that led to unlocking the power in the atom. All of these situations are making it more possible for scholars who have received narrow graduate training to broaden their own interests and perceptions. When a faculty member has achieved for himself an interdisciplinary orientation, he is better motivated and prepared to assist students to experience breadth of learning.

Faculty-Student Criticisms

The distribution plan for assuring breadth of education for the student has been regaining acceptance by the colleges, partly because faculty in the departmental specializations generally favor it. Some general education programs in prestigious institutions, notably Harvard and Chicago—programs that were based on carefully defined principles of curriculum planning, and that for a time were hailed as promising solutions for general education—gradually became adulterated and less effective due to the revisions forced by the specialists within the faculties.

In the meantime, in most institutions there was a steady attrition of students from the survey courses in general education; and the students made vociferous demands for greater relevance in the curriculum. Relevance means, in part, concern with future vocation. Liberal education historically had been the privilege of the elite, who enjoyed a high degree of social and economic security. The new students want to discover their prospective vocation and plunge into preparation for it. Those who are most insecure economically may not be able to remain in college for the traditional four years.

Relevance also means concern for the environment,

peace, the elimination of social ills, and so forth. Blacks, for example, are motivated not only to gain blue or white collar employment, but also to lift their own people from the mire of cultural lag and disadvantage. Surveys of existing knowledge have seemed to them to be irrelevant and superficial. Surveys of Western culture have largely ignored the contributions of other civilizations to cultural growth—contributions which for minority students are a source of pride in their origins.

Women, too, have become aware of the biases in the traditional ways women are portrayed, not only in the general education courses, but in all college courses. Like Blacks, women are largely invisible in literature, art, history, and many other subject areas. Relevance to women has come to mean equality and proper recognition.

Youth have rejected many traditional values. The values that appear to motivate leaders in politics, business, and the armed forces—the dominant influences in American life—seem to youth to contradict the idealism that has been expressed in the Judeo-Christian religious heritage and in Western philosophy. And so they conclude that the study of values perpetuates the acquisition of a cultural veneer that leads to a dichotomy between rhetoric about beliefs and actions in vocation and during leisure. This calls for a scrutiny of values—especially of the practice of excluding the wisdom found in other human experiences—and for a reexamination of the ways in which we provide educative experiences.

The answer to these criticisms does not lie in a return to the distribution plan or to more specialized study. On the contrary, the basic objectives of general education are sound, but need fresh approaches in implementation.

Developmental Theory

During the past several years, many studies have been made of the characteristics of college students. The studies shed light on the problems of education, and from them have emerged some principles of education that have a bearing on the problems of general education and of achieving a synthesis in learning.

Joseph Katz (1972, pp. 142-143) calls this the developmental theory of student learning. He has provided a good statement of the principles involved:

(1) Students learn if their studies connect both with motivation and with aspirations among them, achievement of personal identity, occupational identity, a satisfactory life style, a sense of competence.

(2) There must be self-direction in the student's process of learning, and he must have autonomous participation in the planning and execution of what he learns.

(3) The student's learning must issue in a product that has its own self-contained integrity and must be more than make-believe or a testing hurdle.

(4) The student's work must be useful to himself and, wherever possible, useful to others. This contrasts with situations in which the primary product for the student is a grade which may or may not be an ornament on his record and a career token but which has few other consequences.

(5) Learning is facilitated when students learn in groups which are oriented to a common task and in which what is found out is mutually complementary.

(6) The professor or other adults must be interested in the student's work and convey this through task-minded encouragement and evaluation.

(7) The professor himself must treat the subject matter in an inquiring mood, and he must be interested in the subject matter he is teaching. (Hence students will always rate the "enthusiasm" of the teacher as an important incentive to their own learning.)

(8) There must be no neglect of other developmental tasks that students face during their passage through college—such tasks as the achievement of self-esteem, of competence, of acceptance by and integration with others, and many more. If obstacles are put in the way of the achievements of these tasks, the effect is one of depressing the students' willingness to learn. Hence often not much more than examination complicity, that is, temporary memorizing and forgetting, can be expected. But if cognitive learning is tied to the achievements of other developmental tasks, gains can be achieved for both. For instance, a stu-

dent's sexual anxieties and needs can be the vehicle for a better understanding of the physiology of the body or of the social nexus as well as for psychological maturation.

Katz attributes many of the failures in education to faulty teaching and counseling—a subject discussed in Chapter Nine.

A few institutions have been experimenting with programs based on these kinds of principles. California Polytechnic State University is known for its "upside down" curriculum. The plan permits a student to begin vocational exploration and preparation in the freshman year. As he proceeds with his study, he draws on basic theory and information as he needs it; and he broadens his scope of study to enrich it with cultural knowledge. At any time that he withdraws from college, he will have attained occupational competence relative to the level of his study at the time. In most colleges, the student begins with much breadth and little specialization and in the upper years reverses these increments. California Polytechnic does the opposite. The student achieves breadth when he is ready for it, and the concepts and information are more meaningful to him as he gains maturity.

At Antioch College, a special effort is made to intertwine the general and vocational elements of an education. A basic aim is to enrich the student's personal experience in preparing him to live a better life. One of the objectives of the study-plus-work plan is to assist the student in understanding the wisdom of the past by having him engage in directed personal experiences in the society of the present. In doing this, he may learn how to observe the operation of an industrial plant, the processes by which it makes its contribution to our economic order, the composition and problems of the people who make up the personnel that undertake the operation, the physical and social environment of the enterprise, and the cultural, recreational, economic, and political activities that make up the life of the community. Other forms of experiential learning are also being tried—notably having the students assume active roles in trying to resolve community and social problems. The student, thus, is being taught how to become a keen observer and careful analyzer of society today as a basis for extracting greater wisdom from the cultural heritage embedded in the college courses. The experimentation with different types of jobs, too, assists the student in making a clearer choice for his future career and in relating the cultural attainments to that career.

The program at Sarah Lawrence College is an illustration of an attempt to avoid arbitrary requirements and to induce the student in her self-interest to select desirable courses of study. A variety of courses are designed with the general student in mind. The faculty, then, makes a special effort through individual counseling to assist the student in thinking through the criteria for the content of her own education. Thus, she is not required to take any particular course. It is expected, however, that because of the counseling, she will choose to include the breadth element in her education. To the extent that she has learned how to do this for herself, she has gained an advantage for her continuing study and further intellectual growth after she has left formal education behind. Assuming that higher education, even though it is higher, is nearer the beginning than the end of the lifetime education of an individual, the effort made at Sarah Lawrence to induce the student to choose wisely in educating herself would seem to be theoretically correct and highly commendable.

A few institutions encourage student initiative and responsibility, but also a close working relationship with faculty through a contract plan. The student designs a plan of study and projects the achievements toward which he will work. These, when approved by faculty, become his program. The evaluation is then based on his achievement relative to his own objectives. Students do not have to leave college merely because they have covered specified substantive matter. This plan has merit for all students, but would be especially helpful to those who enter college with deficient backgrounds. When placed in full academic competition with other students, the low achievers usually fall still further behind their peers, a frustrating experience. Students of higher abilities are released from the need to keep pace with the group. They have freedom to move ahead.

The University of Wisconsin at Green Bay has devised a curriculum that focuses on man and his environment. It achieves a comprehensive curriculum through the cluster college plan; each college unit, of which initially there were four, has a central focus. The colleges are environmental sciences, human biology, community sciences, and creative communication. The faculty have identified twelve areas of study; a student chooses one of those areas for an intensive experience but includes relevant materials from other areas. A central objective is to acquire the skills with which to obtain knowledge and use it effectively.

The recent inclusion of women's studies in the college curriculum has been a highly successful innovation. In 1970 the first anthology of women's studies listed seventeen courses. In 1971 the list had grown to seven hundred courses in 178 institutions, and by 1972 there were well over eight hundred. The content of women's studies courses differs significantly from that of traditional courses on or for women. They examine the image of women, and they explore the nature of women through psychological, biological, historical, and literary means. By design or chance, they encompass the principles of education that Katz provides in his developmental theory of learning. Some classes are interdisciplinary; some are taught by teams and groups; others are seminars. The teachers endeavor to break down the traditional classroom barriers and create an egalitarian and cooperative spirit in the class. Many dispense with titles and last names as students and teachers learn together as equal participants. Grades and examinations may be minimized. In some classes, emotion is used (along with formal teaching materials) as a learning technique through the use of personal journals and consciousness-raising periods. Students are responding vigorously to these classes, with many planning different life patterns and careers as a result.

In the traditional curricular offerings women are covered only peripherally, if at all. Hence it is not difficult to understand that women's courses, linked with the liberation movement and giving women the primary focus, are welcomed with such fervor. From them women have been able to derive self-esteem, worth, and a sense of identity. They are relevant to the political, social, personal, and academic endeavors of women. The strong and positive response to these new courses augurs well for the growth and continuance of women's studies (Robinson, n.d., pp. 3-6).

In the demands of Blacks and Chicanos for ethnic studies, they express a desire for relevance and for academic content of types that have been ignored. Black studies are concerned with identity and with the history, art, literature, and civic affairs of Black civilization. These courses are intended to build self-esteem and promote cultural growth, and so they may properly be identified as components of cultural education. And it is also important for Whites to have cultural appreciation of histories different from those of the White European.

The developmental theories of higher education are still germinating, but they show promise of contributing to the achievement of cultural change and growth by students. Flexner (1972) points out similarities in the objectives of the older advocates of general education and of the newer proponents of a student-centered approach.

> Both place a high priority on the individual and on his total development; both are concerned with the present social context and with the student's ability to function successfully in that context; both recognize the value of interdisciplinary studies as a means of dealing with contemporary issues and problems; both would provide extra institutional experiences; both emphasize the need for restructuring the curriculum to provide greater student inputs and alternatives; both stress the desirability of informal student-faculty rapport; both urge greater faculty commitment to teaching and the development of the whole student; and consequently both recognize the necessity of reforming the graduate education and training of college teachers.

Specialized Education

★★
★★

The largest portion of instructional time in postsecondary institutions is devoted to vocational and specialized education. Most research funds are expended on specialized inquiries and technical and scientific projects. Thus, specialized education looms large in the programs of higher education.

In many foreign countries, almost all of higher education is specialized. It is assumed that general education has been sufficiently provided by the secondary school—which, some foreign observers contend, advances the student further in learning than does our high school curriculum. A student enrolling in a university selects a special field of study to pursue. By concentrating his energies in one field of knowledge or one segment of a field, he is presumed to be able to penetrate the knowledge in greater depth.

In the United States, the issue of whether the high school should be preparatory and the college specialized has frequently been raised. Advocates of such a change argue that a clarification of roles would result in greater efficiency in operations and in more effective specialized education; and because the majority of students now go beyond the high school, they can prepare for a vocation in the community colleges and elsewhere. The accepted plan, however, has been to offer some vocational education in the high schools, and to continue some general education in college. The reasoning in support of the existing program is impressive. Our high schools have had a long and successful history of providing programs that are comprehensive; we believe that the identification of the vocation or profession for which a student should prepare is a gradual process that begins at an early age and extends at least into the earlier years of college; and we recognize that culture and vocation are interrelated and that the two kinds of knowledge should be integrated. If the goal of breadth of education is valid, this content should continue to shape the student's learning throughout his years in college.

In spite of the weight of these arguments in favor of intertwining the cultural and specialized elements, there are many forces that press for greater emphasis on specialized training. Concern about the high rate of unemployment among disadvantaged youth causes many persons, and especially legislators, to advocate early vocational training as a solution. Business and industry, which are so dominant in American life, want employees with specialized competence for the jobs that require manual and technical skills. The colleges and universities respond to these needs. They also have their own internal pressures; the faculty members themselves have been educated as specialists and achieve recognition by excelling in a narrow segment of knowledge. It is, therefore, in the interests of faculty to give their attention and time to a specialization. Students, too, press for relevance, and to many of them, relevance means preparation for useful activities in life.

The work ethic in America continues to be strong. It is not consistent with American ideology to support a privileged class who do not work. We do, of course, because wealth can be accumulated and inherited. Nevertheless, the image of the American is of one who earns his living through work. As society becomes more complex and as our technology advances, it becomes increasingly necessary for success in work for a person to get special training. One of the most obvious ways to do this is through specialized study in college. Preparation for a vocation or a career is a strong motivation among youth who decide to enter college. Training for competence in a job, or a profession, or in research, is an essential aspect of higher education. However, confinement of the student's attention—and that of the institution—to a narrow segment of knowledge would stifle the central purpose of higher education. We need both breadth and depth in learning.

Technician Training

Technician training programs are generally characterized by their short duration and by their emphasis on the practical applications rather than on theory. A common length is two years— to harmonize with the two-year calendars of community colleges. However, some are a few weeks in duration and others more than two years. For example, short courses in agriculture may be devoted to a single skill; but community college training for registered nurses combines two years or more of study with at least a few months of apprenticeship. Theoretically, different occupations require varying lengths of time for adequate training. If an auto mechanic or a secretary can be well trained in a few months, why take longer? However, by making the length of programs uniform, the community college can provide general education, include basic courses that ensure greater versatility, and require sequential courses when these are needed to assure competence in training. Most of the curricular problems are resolved by organizing the instruction on a two-year basis. A practical consideration is the pressure to coordinate the work of the two-year college with the first two years of a senior college. This assists many students to transfer to the latter for advanced work.

Technicians fill middle-range jobs, the employment level between skilled labor and the professions. The number and importance of workers in this category are increasing rapidly (Harris, 1969). The mechanization of industry and the growing sophistication among the service occupations create demands for workers who possess knowledge that is relevant and skills that assure competence in the employment roles assigned to them.

This level of workers also includes many paraprofessionals. A professional man or woman can extend his services considerably if he uses technicians as assistants. The demand for such assistants has been rising because of the greater tendency in the professions for personnel to practice in groups. When, for example, several physicians collaborate in their practice, they can make efficient use of laboratory, x-ray, accounting, and other assistants, and they need a greater variety of nurses. The utilization of clinics and hospitals for diagnosis and therapy has greatly accelerated the employment of paraprofessionals. Similar changes have occurred in other professions, such as engineering, law, architecture, and accounting. Technical training may also lead to opportunities for self-employment, for example in electronic maintenance, upholstery, cosmetology, or catering.

The principal educational requirement for this type of job is practical knowledge. This requirement is a determining factor in the design of curriculum and in the employment of teachers. The training progresses steadily from the elementary to the more advanced skills. This requirement also differentiates the level of training, for at the higher levels of instruction the component of basic theory is paramount and skills are usually taught after a groundwork of theory has been laid.

This difference in program is one reason why it is difficult to transfer from junior to senior college. In many fields of study the student, upon transfer, finds himself in freshman courses in order to catch up on the prerequisites. A few colleges have overcome this difficulty by arranging what they have called the upside down curriculum. In this program the student begins with the practical and is introduced to theory as he needs it. The student is then qualified as a technician, specialist, or professional, depending on how far he has carried his study. This type of program deserves more consideration for adoption than it has received.

In addition to junior and community colleges, many other post-high school institutions train technicians—industry and military related organizations for example. Some of them are profit motivated, others are nonprofit. A business enterprise or a branch of the military has a special interest in assuring high achievement in technical competence. Many profit-motivated schools provide good training—they need a reputation for good results if they are to attract students and to find jobs for their graduates. But when profit is the primary goal, it may lead to inferior training. The school may also slight general education by limiting the offerings to communication, the teaching of which may be confined to applied skills. Any survey of the opportunities for vocational training should assess these programs because many schools offer superior training.

The public community colleges now offer the most diversified and extensive array of programs to train men and women as technicians. Their programs ordinarily are geared to meet the needs of their own communities. These colleges include general education, are low in cost to the student, and articulate their programs with senior colleges for the benefit of students who may want to transfer. Some of the students terminate their vocational training in the two-year college; others transfer to prepare for higher-level occupations. One of the greatest challenges facing post-high school institutions is the need to bring these vocational and technical training programs to a genuinely high level of quality. Part of the problem lies in inadequate resources—the colleges should have competent teachers and adequate, up-to-date equipment. The communities have taxed themselves generously in order to establish community colleges, but the funds have had to be used for growth in size. The next step is improvement in the quality of instruction.

The training of technicians is also a function of technical institutes, both public and private. Some of these programs are independent and others have been established in professional schools, notably schools of engineering.

Educating Specialists

Senior colleges almost always require a student to major in some field of knowledge. He may be preparing for a vocation or laying the foundation for graduate study or entry into a professional school. The major may be broad or narrow in scope, but it is a form of specialized education. In the graduate and professional schools, the specialization is continued and is more intense.

When the American university began to devote large inputs of energy to research and the available knowledge expanded, a number of problems developed related to organization and policy for the education of students (Dressel and others, 1970). A few of these problems, of various types, are discussed here.

The concept of an intensive study is sound. Intellectual training should include learning how to concentrate on a problem and a field of knowledge. It should include development of the skills of observation, the collection of information and the testing of validity and reliability, and the carrying through of thought processes to conclusions that are based on skillfully analyzed facts. One way to assure a good concentration is to apply some principles of design that are useful in all curriculum construction. A study should have continuity, in a line of inquiry and with other related knowledge; it should be sequential, proceeding from the basic to the particular or the reverse, and from the elementary to the more complex and difficult; and it should provide for integration, in that the part should fit in with the whole (Tyler, 1950).

One of the issues today is departmental organization. The justification for departments is that each represents a discipline. The department enables persons with common interests and knowledge to band together as colleagues and students. Here the concepts, special knowledge, and particular skills relating to a discipline can be learned and understandings can be enlarged. The department is also convenient as a housekeeping tool and for the administration of personnel and financial policies.

However, at the undergraduate level, too much departmentalization can impede the synthesis that should be maintained between breadth and depth. A department becomes a confining organization that erects walls around particular subject areas. Competition for funds motivates self-protective activities by each department. The student often becomes a captive —he is needed as a major to justify budget requests and to satisfy the professors' interests. From the point of view of the student, departmental offerings in individual fields of study become needlessly rigid.

Although continuity of broad learning experiences is highly desirable at the graduate and professional levels, the study in depth, or for a professional career, must necessarily be emphasized. Genuine competence is essential. However, even at the graduate level, there is a movement toward the fusing of knowledge. This is because much knowledge today is interdisciplinary. The creation of such departments as biochemistry, social psychology, and industrial relations confirms this. Furthermore, many problems are so complex as to require teams of experts. In the graduate school, these teams obtain grants for research that require the creation of special centers or institutes, because the departments are too narrowly confined.

In his undergraduate study, the student is often prevented, by departmental dictates, from realizing his goals. His motivation would be enhanced if he were counseled by an informed, disinterested counselor, who could assist him to discover his talents, identify his interests, and select a field to study that the student considered relevant. Removal of the power of the departmental chairman to dictate to the student should not leave him without professional guidance; he should still choose an appropriate instructor as his counselor in designing his course of study. In this design, the criteria of continuity, sequence, and integration should be followed. As a result, the student's major might or might not conform to the standard departmental requirements. The requirement should be for a field of concentration, not for a departmental major. This concept of study in depth would permit the student to be innovative, crossing departmental boundaries to the extent necessary to arrive at an integrated field of his own choosing and design.

The spectacular growth of knowledge also raises the question of whether each institution can include all fields of study in its program. Ordinarily it is not possible to do so, but if the student had appropriate guidance, plus expert help with problem-solving, and freedom to study on his own, an institution could assist the student to unlock any door to knowledge. The University Without Walls idea may point the way to this solution. If no one college or university can teach all of knowledge —because of inadequate space and finances—ways must be found for several institutions to share in the responsibility. Each college would have an identified role; each student could have interinstitutional privileges. Together the units would become a system of higher education.

The line between the specialist who has been trained in a graduate school and one who has graduated from a professional school is thin. The resemblances in education between a chemist or an economist, both educated in departments of liberal arts, and a dentist or an accountant, educated in different professional schools, are greater than the differences. They are all specialists, trained to be competent in a particular field of work. Many graduates in the arts and sciences disciplines will teach or do research, whereas the graduates of a professional school may be more apt to engage in private practice; but lawyers, psychologists, architects, and creative writers may either practice their arts independently or seek employment in business, government, school districts, universities, or elsewhere. Because the objectives are similar, the principles that determine the education of all specialists are much the same.

Professional Schools

We are in a period of rapid social change, with pressures on the professional schools to change (ASEE, 1968; Kellogg and Knapp, 1966; McGrath and Johnson, 1968; Packer and Ehrlich, 1972). The schools are faced with many issues: How can they revise their objectives and change their methods to take account of social change? (The need for professional men and women with different motivations and understandings than those that have been graduated was discussed in Chapter Three.) How can these schools help revise the preprofessional programs to make them more genuinely liberalizing? How can the preprofessional and professional curricula be coordinated and articulated to achieve an adequate foundation for advanced study, and to avoid repetitions that have prolonged unnecessarily the total time for study? In some cases, illustrated by the need of today's medical students to have a foundation in the behavioral sciences, the preprofessional requirements need fresh examination. The needed changes should be identified by the faculty in the advanced program so as to facilitate their implementation at the preprofessional level.

The admission policies in some professional schools have been biased to favor a selected segment of the population. Some professions have been male-oriented; others have favored White, western-descended youth. These biases are unfair to those who have been excluded, but more than that, they skew the practice in favor of privileged groups. In medicine, for example, white doctors are not as readily available to black patients as are black doctors because 85 percent of the black doctors practice in black communities. But the number of black doctors is much too small. A more subtle effect of restrictive admissions criteria is the emphasis placed on high academic achievement. Of course, intellectual competence is essential in the professions. But the selection of applicants with highest grades in the sciences, to use an example, can lead to the training of research personnel rather than general practitioners. As a consequence, society is burdened with an excess of researchers, some of them frustrated and unemployed, and is inadequately staffed with persons willing to take care of the more mundane needs of people.

The knowledge explosion has created a further problem in curriculum design in the professional school. It has been customary to train a student to be a finished practitioner. That is, he has had all knowledge relevant to his future practice poured into him. The divisions of the school have been occupation-oriented, with the aim of graduating persons able to enter the occupation. It is no longer possible for a student to absorb all of this knowledge. Where the length of study has been increased, it has added greatly to costs and has delayed the experiences that make the theory meaningful. Where solutions have taken the form of narrow specialization, the student is deprived of interdisciplinary learning.

The answer to the problem lies in a different direction. The student should be graduated not as a finished product but as a continuing student. He should be trained as a problem-solver. He should have learned how to learn, so that he will know how to accumulate knowledge, discard obsolete ideas and information, and apply theory to novel situations.

An implication is that the professional school should aim more for achievement in intellectual skills and should put less emphasis on the memorization of facts. In business administration, for example, the aim should be to stimulate imagination, induce comprehension, and teach the skills of information-processing and of analysis and synthesis; to acquire communication skills, quantitative techniques, conceptual and behavioral skills; to learn how to make operational analyses and design systems. The student should be concerned with networks, linkages, interactions, feedback, system adjustments, survival and growth, and the weaving of the elements and the activities into the whole. He should grow in his sensitivity to social responsibilities. Can these outcomes for the student be achieved through the usual pattern of courses—marketing, finance, accounting, and so forth—and the standard methods of teaching, or must the curriculum and the instruction-learning processes be drastically changed (Henderson, 1970)?

The computer has become a factor in making changes possible, and also in solving comprehensive and complex problems that require interdisciplinary approaches. It can relate many variables, compress time, and store information. Its speedy processing of data eliminates an enormous amount of chore labor by the student. Thus, problems of great complexity and length can be studied, and games can be devised that require role-playing by the students. Case problems that necessitate decisions can be used, helping the student to achieve good decision-making facility. Students from several specializations or disciplines can work together on complex problems, each contributing from his special knowledge. This type of training is highly significant in preparing specialists to collaborate in the solution of our complex and difficult social problems.

Changing Professions

The principal earmark of a profession—in a narrow sense —is the requirement of a certificate (for example, to teach or to be a certified public accountant) or a license (for example, to practice nursing or law). The requirement is intended to protect the public. The "buyer beware" tradition of the market place has not applied to the professions. It is in the public interest for professionals to be examined to determine their competence to practice; the certificate or license, and also a professionally determined code of ethics, are assurances to the patient, client, or student, that he will receive skillful attention.

The traditional professions were medicine, law, and the ministry. These three formerly dominated the scene, but now they include only a minor portion of the personnel in licensed professions. The growth of newer fields has been phenomenal.

To determine when a program to train professionals should be initiated the criteria that are often used are the presence of a substantial body of knowledge, the existence of continuing research, and recognition of the field. When this subject was being discussed by a group of Fulbright scholars, one of them—a teacher from India—pointed out that these criteria would apply to the field of astrology. These criteria are unrealistic.

The Commission on the Financing of Higher Education (1952) discussed the seventeen occupations for which the state of New York then granted professional licenses. They accepted ten of these as being legitimately professions, including the more familiar ones such as law, medicine, and engineering. But whereas optometry was included, podiatry was excluded, although in both cases the requirement of medical education was much the same. Nursing was included but not physiotherapy. At that time, in New York a person could become a registered nurse after three years of hospital training, a portion of which consisted of drudgery and repetitive routine. Physiotherapy, a profession that grew largely out of World War II, required four years of college study, including a rigorous major in the subject area, for a license.

In the dynamic situation in which America finds itself, a new field can blossom overnight and grow quickly in knowledge. This has happened repeatedly in easily identifiable areas during the present century. It is partly due to the fact that we rely so heavily on research when we encounter problems. We immediately begin to study them. It is insufficiently recognized by scholars in older fields that the newer fields are, in effect, the product of research and experience.

The licensing laws of the various states have gradually been extended to include more and more fields. One new profession is the licensed psychologist. He gives and interprets aptitude and achievement tests and personality inventories of various kinds and counsels through personal interview. Because he engages in a type of diagnosis and therapy, he is required to be licensed in many states.

It seems reasonable to expect that if a state decides it is important to certify or license within a given occupational area, some educational institution should respond with an adequate training program. Many of these would be on the college and university level. However, there are various professional areas, which become the focus of educational programs, for which licensing or certification is not necessary. New York, for example, has a state school of industrial and labor relations. The program recognizes the growing need for trained personnel in the field of personnel relations in industry, labor, and governmental service. A large body of specialized knowledge has become available in personnel relations, and much additional research is being undertaken. If persons of more adequate education find occupations in this area, progress may be made in solving some of the acute problems in human relations that exist today.

There are many other examples of new professional fields. Child development, a field that includes such special occupations as child psychologist and nursery school teacher, is relatively new. In the medical field, there are now physicians' assistants and nurse practitioners. The physician assistant idea, launched by Duke University in 1965, was accepted as a result of the experience in the war in Vietnam. There, practically trained assistants proved themselves capable of relieving the army and navy doctors of many tasks. The first category of nurse practitioners was in pediatrics—a program initiated at the University of Colorado in 1966. It has been estimated that a nurse, with some added training in pediatrics, can assume about 80 percent of the health responsibilities with well babies. These ideas are new in the United States, but Soviet Russia has had Feldshers, a similar practitioner, for many decades.

Under the impact of the subdivision of labor in modern society, licensing in the professions is becoming fragmented. This is because the professions are being subdivided. For example, for the correction of deficiencies in eyesight, there are medically licensed opthalmologists, optometrists, ophthalmic dispensers, and optical technicians.

In the field of nursing, some states license vocational nurses as well as registered nurses. The nursing profession is being further subdivided—at least five levels can be identified. The person with advanced college or university training is most apt to become an administrator or teacher. The nurse practitioner engages in medical practice in that she diagnoses problems and undertakes therapy, under the general guidance of a physician. The registered nurse is the familiar person who works closely with the doctor in the care of patients, and who in many hospitals takes on considerable supervisory functions. Next comes the vocational nurse (formerly called a practical nurse); she is required to have some organized formal training, and can undertake many duties relating to the care of patients. Finally, there has developed a category of nursing aides who ordinarily lack training except on the job; they assist with routine duties and chores that supplement the work of the nurses.

The impact on the college curriculum is considerable. No longer can the professional areas be thought of as closed compartments, nor can they be described as limited in number. In some instances, as in agriculture or some phases of engineering technology, courses of study that had been thought of as appropriate at the trade or vocational level have had to be upgraded, in recent years, to the college level.

The changes that have been occurring can be clarified by an analysis of a more familiar field, the training of teachers for elementary schools. Here is another instance of a vocation that became a profession. Teacher training for the elementary schools started on the trade-skill level. Persons were trained in short courses in institutes and in one-year normal schools. For the most part they were high school graduates who were taught a few tricks about teaching and given some ideas about how to start on the job. The tremendous growth in the demand for teachers made the adequate training of teachers a continuous problem because of the ever-present necessity of recruiting large numbers of new persons and the resulting acceptance of relatively low standards of preparation.

During the period of the rapid growth of the public school system, the supply of teachers was provided by public and private normal schools segregated from other educational institutions. In time and as the high schools developed, liberal arts colleges saw an opportunity to help supply the demand. This move was consistent with the belief in liberal arts colleges that a liberal education is a foundation for teaching, regardless of the age level of the students to be taught. There has, of course, been the need to meet the minimum state requirements for certification. These commonly have ranged from fifteen to thirty hours of credit out of a total graduation requirement of one hundred twenty, so this minimum has not been large.

Inasmuch as most of the schools of education that exist today originally began as institutes or normal schools, it has been necessary to substantially upgrade their programs. Because they started with the professional subject matter, much of the upgrading has had to come through an infusion of basic work in academic subjects.

Techniques for Designing Programs

Curricula in specialized and professional fields have been evolving steadily during the past century and are still doing so. The rapidity with which new developments are occurring is possibly greater now than at any previous time. The rapid and continuous change necessitates good techniques for designing the programs. The commonly used methods have been to follow precedent or to yield to heavy pressures. When conditions are in a state of flux, these methods do not result in the best curricula. The main difficulty is that the institution follows rather than anticipates the developing social needs. If an institution is to be of the greatest possible service, it should anticipate needs and begin the education of personnel, so that they will be ready for occupations at the time of need.

In an effort to discover new needs within a particular industry or within a community, colleges can use survey techniques. Members of the faculty, working with employers and the public, make a field survey that attempts to evaluate the educational needs. New curricula can be developed that present fresh opportunities to the youth of the community and that provide the educated personnel needed within the community. This is a sound means of making innovations that are based on data that substantiate and justify them. Although surveys are used most by public community colleges, the applicability of the techniques to other colleges is apparent.

The question of whether a particular course of instruction belongs on the college level is an exceedingly difficult one. Some persons contend that any course desired by persons who are beyond high school age may appropriately be given by a college. Others believe that a college should provide instruction only in courses that are justified definitely as college level in quality and character. Possibly the more important issue is not who shall give a particular course of instruction but rather what type of credit shall be given to those who complete it. Colleges and universities do not adhere strictly to criteria in the granting of academic credit. For example, they teach typewriting and elementary languages and usually give credit for achievement, even though these skills are also taught in elementary and secondary schools. Universities commonly give courses for adults for which no college credit is offered. As long as college credit is given for courses that meet standards as determined by carefully worked out criteria, the credit may be justified. The basis of giving or not giving a particular course of study, credit or noncredit, should be made by the institution on the basis of its ability to do so within the role that it serves and the resources at its command.

A rational and systematic procedure is needed. This should consist of the use of objective criteria, together with an evaluation scale that will produce a profile from which a judgment about the curriculum innovation can be made. Such a procedure was used in a New York study for the planning of curricula for technical institutes. The study was used to make judgments about the level of the education needed for various occu-

Table 5

Check List of Criterions for Identifying Technical Jobs

Classification

Technical ＿＿＿＿＿＿＿

Subtechnical ＿＿＿＿＿＿

Job Title ＿＿＿＿＿＿＿＿＿＿＿＿＿＿＿＿ Trade ＿＿＿＿＿＿＿＿＿

Professional ＿＿＿＿＿＿

A technical job:	Low				High
1 Emphasizes technical knowledge	1	2	3	4	5
2 Emphasizes technical skill (the ability to use technical knowledge)	1	2	3	4	5
3 Deals with rational processes as contrasted with empirical rules	1	2	3	4	5
4 Has concern with cause and effect	1	2	3	4	5
5 Emphasizes analysis and diagnosis	1	2	3	4	5
6 Requires frequent exercise of ability to use involved judgment	1	2	3	4	5
7 Deals with many factors and a large number of variables	1	2	3	4	5
8 Contends with a large variety of situations	1	2	3	4	5
9 Requires a knowledge of skilled work but not necessarily skill in doing it	1	2	3	4	5
10 Requires a broad background of fundamental science and mathematics	1	2	3	4	5
11 Involves use of a variety of instruments	1	2	3	4	5
12 Requires effective use of language to interpret orders and make reports	1	2	3	4	5
13 Involves the element of leadership in supervisory occupations	1	2	3	4	5
14 Requires understanding of industrial equipment and processes	1	2	3	4	5
15 Frequently involves visualization of plans and drawings, and a degree of creative design	1	2	3	4	5

For each criterion circle the number you judge to represent the degree the job requires: 1-low; 5-high. Omit those criterions which are not applicable. An average score above 3 would indicate a technical job; below 3, a trade or subtechnical job. Technical jobs which usually require four years or more of formal education should be classified as professional.

Source: A Guide to the Development of Programs for the Institutes of Applied Arts and Sciences. Albany: The University of the State of New York, 1946, p. 43.

pations. The procedures included: getting a description of jobs, following definitions such as those in the *Dictionary of Occupational Titles* (U.S. Office of Employment Security); development by educators of criteria; ratings on the scale by employers and employees as to the level of each job in relation to the criteria; drawing a profile of these ratings; selecting the level at which the training should take place; grouping of similar jobs into clusters for the development of curriculums; and determining subject matter to be required in the course of instruction for each cluster. The instrument used in the New York study was that in Table 5.

Although these criteria would not apply to every situation, they illustrate the technique, which frees the mind of preconception as to what the curriculum should be. It enables the investigator to avoid hunches and emulation. The procedure is a systematic analysis and is defensible. Its chief value is that it provides a means under which the development of new curricula can keep pace with the needs of a dynamic society.

Research and Services

★★
★★

Institutions that engage in education beyond the high school have been assuming several roles in addition to the on-campus instruction of college age students. Among these activities are pure and applied research, extension services and continuing education, community services, consulting services, reference bureaus, and cultural events. These roles have been increasing in number and in types and may continue to do so simply because the services are of value to our society.

These activities have encountered opposition. Many students and faculty have challenged the wisdom of engaging in applied research, especially when it is secretive or when the results contribute to our efficiency in killing people or in napalming food crops. They question the ethics of using scientific knowledge for antisocial purposes. Some faculty express concern about external degrees, believing that academic standards will not be maintained. Businessmen object to the off-campus activities of faculty and students when those activities seem to be arousing discontent among community employees. Politicians and persons of wealth do not like protest groups, and this diminishes the ability of the institutions to get funds. Lack of funds handicaps an institution that desires to launch a new program, such as one to grant external degrees. The issue of enlarging the functions of colleges and universities is controversial because the demands to do so are persistent, but there are various opposing forces, each of which is potent.

The change in the functions of higher education during the past century can be seen in perspective by observing the British scene. According to Armytage (1955), by the middle of the nineteenth century the universities of Oxford and Cambridge were pursuing a wholly conservative course based on the theory that the business of the university was with abstract and cultural matters and not with matters that were useful in society. This conservative approach helped to bring about the rise of scientific societies outside the universities. Those societies sought ways to promote research and additional ways to disseminate learning. The early twentieth century brought the founding of many "red-brick" universities, which were devoted to more practical situations. Following the study by the Committee on Higher Education during the 1960s (Robbins, 1963), the technical institutes were expanded into institutions with complex activities. Recently, Great Britain has taken the lead in developing the open university idea. This program is intended for adults and uses the mail and television as media for instruction.

In the United States, during the nineteenth century the universities took on new functions. Impressed by the scholarship of the German universities, American universities initiated intensive programs of research and advanced study. The federal land grant subsidies that followed the passage by Congress of the Morrill Act of 1862 encouraged research and extension activities in agriculture and engineering. Schools of business administration, public administration, education, public health, and so forth, were added. These schools, especially following 1900, engaged in pure and applied research, in extension activities, and in rendering professional services.

These events brought higher education out from the ivy-covered seclusion of the era preceding the industrial revolution. The university continued to educate students, but it also became a creative, energizing, leavening agency in society. This profound change is best illustrated by the medical school. Earlier deemed by Oxford and Cambridge to be unsuited to the university level, the medical school has gone through an interesting transformation. Prior to the twentieth century, this school was largely an appendage of the medical profession, staffed with practitioners who taught the neophytes to practice medicine. Most medical schools were not associated with a university. Abraham Flexner, in his famous report (1910), rendered a notable service by pointing out the deficiencies in this system and suggesting reforms that led to the beginning of a new concept of medical education.

Today medical education is almost invariably a university function. The medical school has shifted from the apprenticeship plan of training to a program founded on the basic sciences and including both theoretical and applied research. Continuing education programs were added for keeping the members of the profession abreast of developments in medicine. Many schools operate their own teaching hospitals. In these ways, the medical school has become a center for research and learning, both for the education of prospective physicians and for the improvement of the practice of medicine. Thus, its role has been completely reversed. No longer an appendage to the profession, it has instead become a center of leadership for the profession. This concept of the role of the professional school today prevails in each of several professional areas.

These changes, as noted in Chapters Three and Seven, have not been wholly beneficial. Medical faculties, for example, have been entrenching themselves in their research laboratories and, in effect, retreating behind the ivy-covered wall. Some schools have recognized the social significance of their actions and have begun to reemphasize the practice of medicine in their training. Agencies that had been generous with grants of funds for research have begun to make more funds available for the development of delivery systems.

Research

One of the functions of higher education is research. This role has come to the fore with the creation and growth of graduate and professional schools within the past several decades. Research is a means of extending the boundaries of knowledge. Education is primarily concerned with knowledge—both with increasing it and with disseminating it. The discovery of knowledge includes the recreation of it, as with the rediscovery of the Greek classics, and in the unfolding of it by probing beyond what men have known before, as Galileo did by converting the magnifying glass into a telescope and further penetrating the mysteries of the skies.

We emulated the German universities in initiating research, but in a larger sense we are even more indebted to the British. It has been a characteristic of the British people for some centuries that they have explored the wide world, searching for wisdom wherever they could find it. Thus the British libraries, museums, and universities became storehouses of examples of human achievement and wisdom gathered from all corners of the earth. This gleaning and screening of wisdom from men's experiences, from past and contemporary scenes, gave the British nation strength in its industry, its culture, and its political structure. America, too, has had this characteristic.

Today, there is no doubt that research is a well-recognized function of higher institutions (Wolfle, 1972). Research is a procedure for continuously examining ideas to test their validity, facts to prove their accuracy, hypotheses to determine their merit, and generalizations to verify their applicability to novel situations and their reliability for repeated use. Research is the means of enlarging our store of knowledge by accumulating increments at the periphery of knowledge. Research is an avenue for education, for teaching the skills of deductive and inductive thinking. This training in precise thinking is the best available means, as John Dewey said, of developing the intellectual powers of students.

Research is also a source of vitality in teaching. The instructor who keeps abreast of developments in his field, who critically examines the data and the concepts that he uses, who makes contributions from his own discoveries, is apt to be a more stimulating teacher than one who is complacent about his knowledge. This does not mean that all teachers should engage in research, or that researchers who have little interest in teaching will be good teachers. It does imply that the teacher who himself continues to be a critically-minded student generally imparts great enthusiasm and superior training to his students.

Research, furthermore, has implications for the welfare of society. Discoveries of raw materials, of disease preventives, of the power in combustion, of new equations, of population control techniques, of ways to reform language, of fresh knowledge about the Bible—to mention but a few examples—provide new insights that enable men to work for the further improvement of man and his society. Whether for eventual good or evil —we think for good—there can be little doubt that the researches in nuclear energy and in space are profoundly changing the nature of our life on earth.

No academically minded person questions now whether pure research is a function of institutions of higher learning. The questions instead relate to such matters as the type of research that is appropriate, the role of research in undergraduate institutions, the neglect of teaching by research-oriented professors, the ethics that should govern policies for research, and the wise allocation of funds.

Research is sometimes classified as either pure or applied. Pure research is the exploration of hypotheses to prove or disprove them. Applied research applies existing knowledge to the solution of practical problems. There is little doubt that research scholars should be concerned with pure research. Most of the controversy arises because of the nature and scope of applied research. This type of work is usually subsidized by parties that want to profit from the findings or to increase their power, and who may use the knowledge in ways that educators think are not in the social interest. It consumes enormous amounts of faculty time and utilizes valuable space. Often the university provides valuable ideas but derives little compensation for them. It can also be argued that those who are in control of the situations that need solution are in the best position to make the applications.

Certainly applied research should not crowd out pure research. Today our universities must absorb the tremendously increased programs of research that are made available through government and industry. Often these projects pay better salaries and take the time and efforts of the better men in the departments concerned. It is possible that these men might have made much more creative contributions to society had their energies not been diverted to research. Moreover, the addition of large numbers of technicians dilutes the academic quality of a university faculty.

In spite of these considerations that suggest that the universities should not do applied research, there are potent reasons why they should participate. First, research contracts are advantageous in increasing facilities and equipment, in bringing prestige, in supplying opportunities for advanced students to gain experience and increased knowledge, and in keeping the professors in some areas in more active touch with the actual problems being encountered. The universities also feel that they are thus able to maintain the confidence of industry and an important sector of the public.

Second, it is usually big industry that can afford to have its own research staff. Many smaller concerns need access to research staff and facilities. There is value in pooling energies so that both small and large companies can participate; this can often be done through a university. At any university, too, professional men of many and diverse competencies are found who can bring their specialized knowledge and skills to solve a particular problem.

Related to the above is the desire of the government for research on problems of national defense. A portion of that research is farmed out to the universities. Thus, for some purposes the government can mobilize knowledge and personnel far beyond what could be obtained by organizing its own programs of research. Here again, the research might be done by private agencies organized for the purpose. But this introduces the profit element, and self-interest could distort the results or limit the scope of the program. In some areas, too, the government needs to be assured of integrity in relation to the research being done —integrity of the type that is traditional among university professors.

In some areas, such as agriculture, it is not possible for

the individual practitioner to do much research. Nations that do not have organized programs of research in agriculture have experienced depletions of soil, inbreeding of livestock and grain, and a diminution in the nutritive values of foods. They lag in the industrial utilization of agricultural products and in the upgrading of rural environments. To some extent, agricultural research becomes a governmental function. In the past, it has worked well in the United States to have the universities collaborate with the government in agricultural research and extension services. A new issue has arisen, however, due to the shift in American farming from the small landowner to the large agricultural corporation. Should the government and universities serve, and in effect subsidize, these profit-oriented organizations in the same ways they served the crop-and-produce oriented farmers? Many students and faculty object to this policy.

A final reason why universities get involved in applied research is that there are other areas, noneconomic in nature, that require research, only a portion of which gets done outside of the university. This includes many types of social and public services—school surveys, studies of migrations of populations, of water supplies, of wild life, of juvenile delinquency, and so forth. Then, of course, there is the health and medical field, in which the vast majority of the research is done through nonprofit agencies.

The government has become a major source of funds for research, notably through sponsored research and special grants. These cover many fields besides national defense and agriculture. The social sciences and education, for example, are beneficiaries. The funds are welcomed by faculty because of the inadequacy of other provision. It is apparent, too, that even nonsponsored research that is undertaken by a professor who is on the payroll of a public institution is in effect being subsidized by government—although the professor will generally have freedom to define his problem and to publish his findings.

Government research is generally in the public interest. A difficult problem arises, however, in its administration. Government agencies tend to become officious in that they want to supervise closely the questionnaires and procedures that are used and to check the content of the publications. To some extent it is inherent in the political process for this to happen, because the departments of government must secure the appropriations and defend their use; and the appropriating bodies are sensitive to publicity about findings that vary widely from the status quo. The dilemma faced by the universities is not easily resolved. It would be less difficult if the colleges and universities could unite on policies that expressed a firm ethical position in the best interests of society.

The advantages that the institution derives from research should be weighed. On the other hand, a line must be drawn that protects the intellectual and ethical integrity of the faculty and students. A number of criteria can be posed for consideration in defining policy. It is not consistent with the purposes of a college or university to hire itself out to special interests whose aim is largely to enrich themselves or to enlarge and consolidate their power. The university should remain free to scrutinize the establishment and not permit itself to be paid to support it. It should remain free of governmental supervision of the type that controls the nature and content of publications. New increments of knowledge should belong to the human race, not to particular segments of it. Secrecy has no place in higher education.

The pressures on the institutions of higher education to engage in research, both pure and applied, and the counter pressures from educators, students, and concerned public to limit these activities, need resolution. The answer lies in the determination of a clear policy that will guide the decisions.

Should research faculty be concerned with the eventual uses to which the research findings will be put? An older view is that scientists are responsible for objectivity in relation to knowledge, and must leave to others the determination of ethical ways in which to apply it. This policy, however, exonerates the scientist from responsibility for anti-social actions. Under a broader view of social responsibility, a university should refuse to be a party to research that is counterproductive to human welfare, although it is not easy to define what this means. Because the subject is controversial, some universities have been analyzing their policies and setting new guidelines for the faculty.

Concerning the rendering of some of the nonteaching services, a useful distinction may be drawn between two-year and undergraduate institutions on the one hand and graduate schools and advanced professional schools on the other. The assumption that the faculty members in undergraduate institutions generally engage in research as well as in teaching is largely a myth. The vast majority of them do not. This is not wholly a matter of personal inclination, although it is partly that. It is in substantial part due to the fact that undergraduate institutions simply do not make allowance in time and facilities to encourage such work. Whatever the teacher does must usually be done on top of a full teaching load plus committee and other responsibilities. He is in no mood to pick up a thread in research after he has graded several dozen papers or laboratory notebooks. To assume that he is going to engage in research and do a lot of publishing is to put a pressure upon him that is frustrating, especially if this criterion is associated with his advancement in position and salary. The pressure also results, often, in publications of doubtful value.

At the graduate level, on the other hand, faculty members are required who can direct and oversee the intensified studies of the graduate-level students, if the students are to be challenged. Furthermore, research—the increase of knowledge—is a natural function for this type and level of institution.

In resolving the problem of scholarly work by faculty, it is useful to distinguish between research and scholarship. True research is original investigation. Scholarship may signify the collation and synthesizing of materials which need not be original. The research man starts with a problem that needs solution or a hypothesis for which proof has not yet been obtained. The scholar may start with a topic or an idea for fresh analysis, organization, and presentation. Scholarship, then, is a desirable qualification for all teachers, because it is central to the education of the students and to communication with professional colleagues.

Other Activities

What services other than research should an institution of higher education render? The number and variety are large and generally well known. We shall not analyze them in detail, but we will discuss a few of them in relation to the implications for the educational program.

Even the smallest colleges and universities promote programs of music, dramatics, lectures, and courses for adults. The institutions appear to have various motives for these activities, including desire for a better cultural atmosphere and life that benefits the college and townspeople alike, for publicity that helps to secure students or financial support, and for a broader student activities program. Cultural activities give an institution a good image and a congenial environment.

These activities have meaning for education beyond formal classes. They introduce learning experiences. Music and dramatics, for example, are active arts. Without the opportunity to perform, the student would have a passive role; while performing he is developing artistic skills and extending his knowledge. Personal participation is necessary for full learning. Through participation, such extracurricular and community activities become part of the laboratory for the humanities in the same manner that science uses laboratories. Community activities and services in the social science area, developed within reasonable limits of time and structured to advance the learning of the individual, are also based on this principle.

A college or university, in addition to making contributions to the cultural life of a community, often can make some contribution toward its economic development. Undoubtedly many of the larger professional schools in engineering, business, and agriculture do this, as do some departments, such as physics, in liberal arts colleges. The fruits of research are applied when adopted in economic enterprise, and some faculty are in demand as consultants.

After its period of pioneering had passed, America reached a point where the conservation of natural resources became a special need. The problem was so large that it required the interest and effort of the federal government as well as of the several states. But the schools of forestry and of agriculture and the departments in the science areas in the universities took an important lead. They also furnished personnel for the work. Beyond the technical problem was the need to develop civic sensitivity to the dissipation and waste that are occurring and to direct the growth of the social motivation of members of the public to join in the effort to conserve our resources. As time went on, various other media of communication and instruction were used, including the public schools, recreation camps, civic organizations, and public meetings. But the catalyst came from the universities. This illustration shows again the interrelationship of theory and practice, and of the institution and the community.

Although there is now general understanding of the need to conserve our natural resources, we are currently faced with more difficult problems. They focus on the contamination of resources, especially the air and water, and on the wastage of used materials. There is also the pressing need to find new sources of energy. The self-interest of business companies, and of the military, causes them to maximize present profits and accumulations of power. Other agencies, including universities, must therefore supply leadership and knowledge that will protect the public interest in the longer run.

In considering the off-campus services of the educational institution, the civic activities and professional services of faculty members as individuals should not be overlooked. These are many and varied. The faculty member is, of course, not only a professional man but also a citizen of his community. His education provides him with some special competence as a citizen. It would be a loss to the community if he did not participate actively in civic affairs or if the institution took steps to discourage him from doing so.

In the typical American university, the faculty members get frequent calls for their services as professional consultants. These can be seen as distractions from their jobs, and can become so if faculty members do not use restraint or if the institution does not have a clear-cut policy about the division of faculty time between institutional and off-campus services. A university is justified in requiring that its full-time faculty limit their professional services to matters that enhance their competence as teachers in their fields and to an amount of time that does not seriously interfere with the main teaching and research functions. On the other hand, an institution may properly encourage its faculty to engage in some such services. A college or university develops contacts with important enterprises, governmental agencies, and institutions; it acquaints the faculty, and through them the students, with up-to-date developments, at least of the practical sort, within their fields; it brings into the classroom and the laboratory questions and problems from the field that need further study; it assists the faculty members to enjoy greater prestige and recognition as professional men and women. And, by permitting outside professional work and the opportunity to earn additional income, the university often retains faculty members who otherwise might be attracted elsewhere.

Continuing Education

The largest area of opportunity for off-campus services lies in continuing education (Houle, 1972). In thinking about it, we must get back to certain goals of a democratic society: the full development of each individual; the development of all human resources; and the development of the human community as a whole—its scale and quality, its integrity as a community of human beings, its survival. These objectives are important in the further education of persons who have left formal education, as well as of students of college age. Thus the field of continuing education is important. Any college or university is justified in participating; a state institution or community college has a definite responsibility to do so.

Extension education became a vital phase of education when the University of Wisconsin, in 1885 and 1886 began to offer short courses in agriculture to young men on the farms. Over the years, the scope and variety of extension, adult, or continuing education courses and educative experiences have expanded enormously. The concept of continuing education— that is, the education of persons after they have left formal programs—is well established. A basic issue, however, is whether every institution should or can teach everything to everybody. The institutions need to define their individual roles and devise means of collaborating in a manner that will enable them to contribute to the service of all needs and avoid unnecessary duplications and expense. They can collaborate through consortia or by mutual agreements.

Radio and television have presented educators with a promising outlet for educational services. Undoubtedly these media can be developed further for teaching, and especially the teaching of adults. The prospects are inviting. Radio and television, and particularly the latter, are extremely expensive. An effective TV course, however, can reach a tremendous audience, especially when kinescopes of the programs can be distributed to numerous TV studios and even used as movies for other extension classes. Thus, the cost per individual benefited can be low. The need to reach large numbers of persons illustrates, then, the need for organized endeavor, either through the cooperation of numerous colleges and universities working together, or through the provision of a special budget for such a program, with the responsibility placed within a major institution.

Some new experiments in higher education raise further questions. Heretofore, colleges have generally required a minimum period of residence at the institution before the student could qualify for a degree. Now it is being contended that persons, regardless of age, should be permitted to study wherever they are and submit evidence of academic achievement in satisfaction of the requirements for a degree. This practice of offering external degree programs would make the institution more widely useful in satisfying the cravings for higher education. The plan is opposed by many who doubt whether achievement can be sufficiently measured by tests, and also by those who foresee a dissipation of limited resources. The movement, however, is being led by prestigious universities and will continue to be the subject of experimentation.

In Great Britain, the Open University has had much initial success. Its aim is much the same as the external degree program. Its instruction is by correspondence. Each course has a carefully prepared syllabus to be used by the student in becoming self-directive.

Another fresh idea is the University Without Walls. It assumes that many resources through which to study and gain educative experiences exist in every community and that these can be utilized by students. Hence, the university—usually supervised by a campus institution—becomes an organization that identifies those resources, mobilizes them for the benefit of students, counsels the enrollees, tutors them individually or through seminars, and measures their achievements. The institution is controversial, partly because it is so different from traditional institutions, but the experimentation is proceeding.

Some educators advocate that the colleges and universities deemphasize the traditional two-year, four-year, or seven-year packages in education in favor of extending education continuously throughout life. Persons might enter, leave, and re-enter the institutions for formal education at intervals that meet their individual desires and needs. The new experiments described above point in this direction.

Effective

College Teaching

★★★
★★★

College teaching deserves to be improved (Lee, 1967). Few faculty are definitely superior teachers, and indeed a substantial portion of them could improve considerably. The remainder should and can be much better teachers than they are. The solution to the problem requires administrative leadership of the most diplomatic and persuasive sort.

Effective teaching can make a contribution to the problem of financing higher education. To the extent that a student can be motivated to learn, he will require less time and concern from the teacher, and the role of instructor will become more inviting. When the best techniques are used for each situation, the teaching effort can be relatively efficient. Because it seems inevitable that, for the near future, faculties will have to carry a heavier burden of work, it becomes doubly important for instructors to become more versatile in skills and competent in methods.

Issues

Unfortunately, a principal stumbling block is the disinclination of college teachers to examine the subject critically and objectively. They seem content with the timeworn statement that to be a good teacher one needs only to know his subject thoroughly. Indeed, it is not uncommon to find an attitude approaching scorn toward the subject of educational methods.

Half or more of any faculty could increase the effectiveness of their teaching by developing a clear understanding of the teaching-learning process, and by special attention to course planning and teaching methods. Suppose, to use an elementary example, that an instructor was not making the best possible use of his voice when speaking in the classroom. If this person were in public life where his continuance in public favor depended on the effectiveness of his personality and of his presentations, he probably would take steps to improve his speaking. College teaching is probably the only major profession where the voice—a primary instrument for professional work—is given virtually no training. The skillful use of the voice, however, is merely one example of several aspects of teaching in which growth in effectiveness is possible. Other examples include: clarification of objectives relating to knowledge, skills, and appreciations; better integration of these objectives with the specific outcomes expected of the students; improvement of methods for evaluating the student's progress; and better understanding of the learning process.

The college teaching profession has from time to time placed its faith in some particular method. When this happens, the particular method comes to prevail and thereafter the members of the profession, like so many sheep, for a time accept the technique unquestioningly. Such a method, for example, was the "explication of the text." Originating from French sources, this mode of teaching was generally used over a considerable period of time, and then was dropped by the wayside. Recently, at a workshop for college professors, a young instructor from a liberal arts college stated that he had discovered a method of teaching that he had found quite interesting and wanted to examine further. This was "explication of the text." Because he was an instructor in English, members of the department of English in the university were asked if any of them might be willing to give him special assistance in the pursuit of his objective. The answer was that no one in the department used the method or had any faith in it or cared about promoting it. In other words, the method—once almost universally used in teaching—was now dead.

Another method that later became the vogue was the lecture. The lecture was popularized by the Germans, whose teaching has been highly formal. Lecturing as a method is now used almost exclusively in some countries; it has been popular among professors in the United States. The lecture undoubtedly is a useful tool in teaching, and there are some situations in which it is much more effective than in others, but it is only one of several possible approaches. The disadvantages of the lecture system show up clearly in the universities of Japan, India, and Latin America, where the system of instruction consists almost wholly of lecturing and examining. Little direction is given to the student, there is no follow-through with the student by way of discussion and clarification, and at most of the universities the libraries are not arranged to encourage independent study. The lecture in these countries is, therefore, much more limited as a medium of instruction than it is, say, in Great Britain where it is supplemented by the tutorial conferences, or in the United States where it is supplemented by discussion, laboratory experiments, and field projects that require the intellectual participation of the students. When lecturing predominates, the students are passive and postpone serious study until the examination nears.

These illustrations point up the fact that professors do adhere to theories about teaching in spite of prejudice against a method. But in doing so they emulate one another and become defensive about their method, instead of giving careful thought and constructive effort to professional improvement.

Although the lecture method continues to prevail, especially when the classes are large, not all faculty in the United States use it. Science teachers make extensive use of the laboratory. In the social sciences, discussion techniques are more common than lecturing. Field experiences are being used more widely than formerly. In some institutions, the tutorial is favored; in others, an honors system approaches this technique; and in all graduate level institutions, the students who are candidates for advanced degrees receive individual tutoring. Versatility, however, is not a characteristic of the usual college teacher.

Principles of Learning

Professors always take pride in their scholarship in their special fields of study. With unabashed inconsistency, they nevertheless remain ignorant of recent advances made in understanding the learning process. When a teacher assumes that his role is limited to that of unfolding knowledge about his subject, he is ignoring the principles of learning. When one says that learning means individual change and growth, it sounds like pedagoguery, but the statement is nevertheless meaningful. Education does not occur unless the individual changes in his knowledge, beliefs, or skills and becomes better informed, more capable, and better integrated.

Most professors would agree that they seek to develop the memorizing and thinking abilities of the students. As an illustration of faulty perceptions about learning, let us discuss memorization. Studies of the syllabi used by college teachers, and more especially studies of the examination questions submitted by teachers to their students, suggest strongly that most instructors put great emphasis on the memorization of factual knowledge. Factual knowledge is, of course, essential in most subjects, but the gathering of it is only the first stage in the process of thinking. Then, too, the gathering of knowledge independently of its utilization results in tremendous failure to retain it. The forgetting factor in learning has been well demonstrated. It is familiar to professors who observe their students "bugging up" for an examination. This cramming results in minimum retention after the passing grade has been secured.

Furthermore, rote memorization is not good education. To the extent that the design of the courses and the methods of instruction aim merely at the reproduction on examination of factual information, the more basic aim of higher education—that of training the student's power of thinking—is neglected. When professional educators say that less time should be given to the memorization of facts and more to other educational objectives, they do not mean that factual information is unimportant, although some facts become obsolete within a short time. They mean that inefficient methods of teaching factual information are being used and thus unnecessarily consume too much of the student's time.

The conditions under which memorization can take place most effectively have been pretty well determined. The interest of the student must be aroused. In proportion to the extent that the student feels a motivation toward learning, he will succeed. Motivation derives from satisfactions, commendation enhances satisfaction. With satisfaction, the student will tend also to reflect on his material, thus embedding it more surely in his memory. Finally, the material to be learned must be given a variety of applications. The repeated use of the material in various contexts and situations assists materially in learning.

The span of attention of an individual is not as long as has usually been assumed by the professor who lectures. College periods usually run for fifty minutes. It takes a brilliant lecturer—whose motivation is pronounced, who knows the art of animating his discussion, and who keeps the room well supplied with fresh air—to hold the continuous attention of students for this long. Unless this is done, a parade of irrelevant matters keeps floating into the student's mind and diverts his attention from what the lecturer is saying. The fundamental reason is that the student is in a passive position, and for most of the period there is no genuine intercommunication between the speaker and the student.

Radio and television have helped us to become aware that a continuous monologue of ten or fifteen minutes consumes the maximum span of attention. Some teachers require that notes be taken as a means of inducing attention. This helps with some students. On the other hand, there is no assurance that note-taking obtains the intensity and continuity of attention that is required for good retention; but it helps in that the material can be reviewed.

Teaching Methods

The student who has been insufficiently trained in problem solving, and hence in developing his reasoning powers, ends as an insufficiently educated person. There are conditions through which skill in critical thinking is best promoted. It is important at the outset for the instructor to understand the distinctions between deductive and inductive reasoning. Deductive thinking involves abstract reasoning, principally, whereas inductive reasoning involves the use of data in problem-solving. Problem-solvers must be keen observers, skillful selectors, collators and analyzers of data, and competent synthesizers of the results. To serve these purposes, problems need to be designed that will give the students practice in these procedures. The problem method is most commonly used in the sciences, including mathematics. Here, of course, the scientific method has been perfected to its highest degree. The techniques, however, apply to other areas of knowledge; for example, empirical research provides a basis for rigorous analysis in the social sciences.

Intercommunication between the teacher and the student is essential if the teacher is to be effective. It is possible to have intercommunication during a lecture by assuring alertness on the part of the student, stimulating a continuous mental reaction by the student to what is being said, and providing an interchange of ideas following the lecture. A quiz has the same effect in a more rigid and sterile way. Intercommunication during lectures requires critical listening by the student, and this is one reason why courses in communications usually include listening as an important aspect of the subject. It has been contended that a person spends considerably more time in life listening than he does speaking or writing, and so greater attention needs to be given to this skill.

Intercommunication obviously takes place much more fully and intensively when classes are taught by the discussion method, or when the students work in the laboratory or on field projects or term papers, or when they are taught by the tutorial method. These teaching methods involve the student more as an active participant than does lecturing.

Although learning takes place within the individual, his learning can be facilitated by group processes. Learning does not occur only between the teacher and the student; in part it comes from stimulation by the group that results in the accretion of information and ideas. Moreover, learning is augmented by self-expression and by interaction with the other members of the group. There is such a thing as group thinking, where the end product in wisdom can be beyond that with which any single member of the group started. Group participation has special significance for interdisciplinary learning and for teaching specialists how to collaborate with specialists from other fields.

Among the conditions that foster group learning are class arrangement and leadership. The teacher is in control of both of these conditions. In lecturing, for example, it is important for the teacher to be heard by everyone and to be able at intervals to talk directly to an individual. The group environment is important: fresh air, a clean blackboard, and a semblance of order in the room. In addition, an arrangement of the group that enables each person to participate easily is essential—not only between students and teacher, but among the students. This suggests a horseshoe arrangement of chairs or a closed circle such as occurs around a seminar table. The teacher as one within the chain of people may then identify more fully as a member of the group.

Some interesting experiments have been made in the design of rooms to accommodate large numbers of people for discussion. The Harvard Graduate School of Business Administration, for example, uses horseshoe seating, with swivel seats arranged in three tiers at successive heights. The positions of the blackboard and projection screen can be adjusted to best serve each audience. Thus the room can be accommodated to both large and small groups. The instructor functions at the mouth of the horseshoe. Any member of the class can see and converse with any other person.

In addition to facilitating participation, it is important to control any members who disturb the group. They need to be brought in as fully cooperating members and given responsibilities commensurate with this membership. This facilitates their learning and prevents them from interfering with the learning of others.

There are various types of leadership that the instructor may want to use, depending on the teaching situation. He may desire to be highly directive, which means determining the goals himself and keeping the discussion on them. He may desire to be a permissive leader, which means passing to the students a large share of the responsibility for defining their own objectives and carrying through an appropriate study and discussion. Or he may choose a course in between these two, a cooperative type of leadership. Here he would be exercising control of purposes and outcomes but would also be throwing a considerable responsibility on the students for helping to define the problems for discussion and devising ways to solve them. These types of leadership that involve progressive learning should be carefully distinguished from the situation in which the teacher surrenders the leadership by permitting a wholly laissez-faire situation to develop. A bull session may be an enjoyable recreation and sometimes it does yield educational results, but because of its lack of direction and indefinite outcome, it cannot be recommended as a classroom technique. Neither can the technique of the instructor who starts the hour by asking, "Are there any questions?" and wonders why dead silence ensues.

A good way to involve students in their own learning is through the nondirective method of teaching. Nondirective teaching requires more skill in leadership on the part of the teacher than does any other type. The theory of this approach to teaching is that much responsibility is vested in the students to define the goals and to work out the materials and procedures for reaching them. If the student has thought through fully his own educational objectives, and if the group can agree on a common pattern of objectives, a high degree of motivation will have been attained and intensity of application is assured. Each student thus becomes a genuine student of the researcher type. The assumption is that under this circumstance, each individual in the group will make some contribution to the knowledge of the whole. The plan involves self-education and is thus highly attractive as a means of insuring that the students, while in college, will acquire the interests, skills, and habits that will enable them to continue to be creative and productive after they leave formal education. This is one of the answers to the student demands for relevancy and personal involvement.

In such a situation great demands are placed on the teacher, because he must define the area of endeavor and, by indirect means, structure the situation so that effective learning takes place. In one sense, he must become a full member of the group as a participating student himself, but at the same time he must continue to be the leader for purposes of stimulation, coordination, and general direction. He must have a thorough command of his subject, because he should be able to follow the leads of the students in their individual explorations. He needs to gain full knowledge of his students in order to encourage and guide each individual as an individual. He must have a good understanding of the group process and of his role, lest the plan bog down because of lack of leadership.

Many students will not be ready for nondirective teaching and must be trained for their roles. Moreover, some will rebel at the whole concept, because they prefer listening to lectures. Usually a class will get under way slowly because of the manner in which the whole group is involved initially in thinking through the objectives. This requires patience and the belief that, even though the start is slow, in the end the students will be ahead.

Learning how to function as a member of a team is becoming highly important. There are many situations in which the range of services and the efficiency of a professional person can be extended considerably when he employs technical assistants, and when he practices within a group the members of which, taken together, possess a diversity of skills and knowledge. Physicians, for example, do both of these things, although they are still slow in utilizing assistants who are not physicians but who are qualified to do diagnosis and therapy under guidance. The solution of many complex problems, especially broad social problems, also requires team functioning. The problems of poverty, pollutions, environmental design, and so forth, cannot be solved by any one specialist. The combined wisdom that emerges from the group thinking of specialists with varying backgrounds is essential. What can be accomplished by such marshaling of group knowledge is well demonstrated by the progress we have made in exploring space.

To become effective in team collaboration, the individual must accept the advantages of the process, and he must acquire participative skills. Some faculties put much emphasis on this phase of the educational program. In public health, for example, there is no central discipline. Instead, public health involves mobilizing the resources of physicians, dentists, nurses, bacteriologists, and sanitary engineers to address themselves to the health problems. Most colleges and professional schools, however, give little thought to team training. Each specialty is closeted behind its own department walls.

The computer was invented at the right time to be of assistance here. It has tremendous potential in education. It can process data swiftly; it can combine numbers of variables in its analysis, thereby simplifying greatly the statistical calculations; and it has memory that is precise, accurate, and unfailing. The computer facilitates the solution of problems that form the bases of many theses and dissertations. It also facilitates collaboration of specialists representing various disciplines. For example, a school of engineering recently asked a group of students representing several engineering specialties, and also the departments of economics, political science, and education, to design a satellite that could be used for educational intercommunication among four countries. The satellite was designed, but the really significant outcome was the training received in group study.

The computer is an intellectual tool for learning that has been likened in significance to printing. Fortunately, many faculty have acquired some knowledge of computer language, programming, and uses—one school of business administration had its entire faculty involved for a term in a seminar on computers. The computer is one of several intellectual concepts and tools that alert faculty now use in appropriate situations in their particular fields. Among these are information theory, decision theory, games, systems problems, simulations, and models (Henderson, 1970). It is important for in-service training to persuade college teachers to become adept in the use of these new and diversified teaching-learning techniques.

The Student as Learner

The focus of most faculty is on subject matter; that is how they perceive their employment agreement. But the teacher's role is to guide the student in his learning. The developmental theory of education, discussed in Chapter Six, requires that the instructor understand the characteristics and needs of his students. He can then assist them in acquiring knowledge, skills, and appreciations.

It is a fortunate coincidence that students are insisting on greater involvement in their own learning at the same time that research findings are making clear that learning is greatest when involvement is maximized. Educational participation increases the motivation to learn and enhances the assimilation of ideas and information. Students can assist in determining what they will study and how they think they can learn best. The faculty have expert knowledge and professional training, and therefore have an essential role in guiding the thinking and in making decisions. It is especially important that the plan proposed by a student provide continuity of learning, build on sequences that enlarge his comprehensions and competencies, and integrate this learning with his other learning experiences.

A few institutions have adopted a contract plan of study (Keeton, 1972). The student outlines his objectives, a proposed sequence of studies and experiences, and the outcomes on which he wishes to be examined. Following any necessary revision to make the plan harmonize with the policies and standards of the college, the student is authorized to proceed. This is a highly individualized procedure and an effective means of helping each student advance from where he is to the defined goals.

Various plans for independent study have been proposed and are being tried. Independent study can be an honors program designed to enable talented students to get maximum advantage from the time in college and to train them to become independent scholars and researchers. Or independent study can involve an entire group of students who leave the college for a quarter or a semester to study, travel, or work on their own. The institutions that use the work-study plan of education place their students in jobs during one or two periods of the year; the students alternate this work experience with similar periods of study at the college. When the learning experiences of the students who are away from the campus—whether for work, study, or travel—are skillfully directed by adequately prepared professional people, excellent educational results can be secured.

The value of experience as a factor in learning was discussed earlier. An infinite number of variations in experience can be planned, but a few broad categories can be cited as examples: study-and-work programs, internships, study abroad, community projects, field studies, problems to be researched, problem-focused discussions, and role-playing. In several of these, such as work experience or role-playing, each individual is active; what happens, happens to him. The role of the teacher is dual—first he designs a situation that will be educative, and then he assists the student to gain the maximum amount of education from that situation.

John Dewey (1950) made the point that experience may be either educative or miseducative. It may also become noneducative. As in all teaching-learning, it is necessary to define the educational objectives in student involvement, and the outcomes in learning that the student should achieve. Without such design, the work or other experience might result in antisocial attitudes, or in skills and habits that are not constructive. It takes skills derived from experience to rob a bank successfully. The experience becomes noneducative if it is needlessly repetitive and lacks progression from the elementary to the more advanced, or if it is not properly integrated with study. The principles of continuity, sequence, and integration, discussed in Chapter Seven, apply to projects and off-campus work as they do to other curricular designs.

Individual students would be helped to learn if college courses were better designed with that end in view. Too often a course is based on an outline of topics, together with bibliography and instructions for a term report. The instructor has focused on conveying subject matter. He should have focused on student learning. To achieve this result, it is necessary to define clearly the objectives of the course and the outcomes expected of the student (Tyler, 1950). A good device for this purpose is a cross-sectional chart—on one axis are placed objectives that relate to growth in knowledge, skills, and attitudes, and on the other is an outline of content that will contribute to the achievement of these objectives. At the interstices where objective and content meet, the outcomes expected of the student can be defined. The content is used to achieve a particular outcome. These outcomes become the basis for evaluations of the student's progress in learning (Henderson, 1970).

Evaluations as Basis for Improvement

A perpetual issue facing all colleges and their faculties is whether the services of the teacher can and should be evaluated. In general, teachers oppose evaluations made by the administration, or by the students, and seldom are able to agree among themselves to make a self-evaluation. The reasons are understandable—teachers think that their training has given them the required competence to instruct others, they resent intrusions by persons who are not professionals, they think that in order to retain discretion in judging the progress made by students they should avoid any semblance of catering to student opinion, and they fear discipline by the administration. Those who desire evaluations believe that teachers can improve their courses and their methods, that deficiencies in instruction on the part of some faculty tend to discredit the work of all, that persons whose performance is inadequate and who do not show improvement should not be retained as teachers, and that in applying cost-benefit principles to the process of education, if the benefits do not accord with good standards, the costs should not be incurred.

Whether or not systematic evaluations are made, faculty nevertheless are evaluated. Administrators and personnel committees make promotions in rank and give increases in salaries. Preliminary to those decisions, judgments are made about the merit of each individual. Students talk freely about their courses and the instructors, praising some and criticizing others. In some colleges, students publish their perceptions about the instruction. These are informal evaluations. So the issue really is whether students, colleagues, and administrators should have to make decisions on the basis of student chatter, rumor, and the casual observations of peers, or whether their decisions should be based on facts that are objectively obtained and opinions that are representative of the whole group and are subjected to statistical analysis and interpretation. Many studies have been made of the reliability of student answers on opinionaires. When the procedures call for objective answers, the opinions are found to be reliable.

Faculty become more amenable to evaluation when they have been assured that student opinion will be gathered objectively, when the criteria of teaching effectiveness are not limited to student opinion, and when the purpose is to assist the teachers to improve their work. In other words, the procedures should be fair. It helps to gain the cooperation of people by giving them a significant role in making decisions. This can be done by arranging for a committee of the faculty to determine the procedures. The work of such a committee will be more effective if administrators and students are invited to offer suggestions; indeed they may be invited to participate, thus increasing confidence in the findings. The fears of faculty that students will give biased judgments can be ameliorated by demonstrating that students will behave responsibly when they are invited to participate responsibly.

Evaluation should not be limited to information obtained from student opinionaires (Eckert, 1950). The quality of course design, the clarity with which course objectives and student outcomes are stated, the nature of student participation in their own education and the kind of self-help materials that are made available, the character of the experiences in which the students are asked to engage, and the quality and fairness of the evaluation of student performance can be judged if the teachers are required to file copies of their course syllabi and their examination questions. The nature and quality of the teacher's preparation, including the continuing exploration of his field of study should be weighed and can be determined from reports by him of his own studies, his uses of vacation and sabbatical periods, and from his publications where they are relevant. The evaluation should also include a survey of his general contributions to the on-going work of the institution and to the community. The weight given to various factors should vary depending on the understanding between the instructor and the institution concerning his role. But for the vast majority of the faculty the factor to emphasize is his teaching effectiveness.

Because faculty are continuously being evaluated for retention, promotion, and salary increases, it is in the best interests of all parties—the teachers, the students, and the institution—to make occasional evaluations on a professional and systematic basis. The aim should be to improve the quality of instruction and of other services. Threats to the security of individuals should be kept to the minimum; but there is no point in blinding our eyes to the fact that the findings from evaluations, whether informal or formal, are used in passing judgment on the merits of instructors. Positive effort should be made to assist an instructor to improve in his professional work; if he fails to do so, he places his own professional future in jeopardy.

For the most part, the improvement of teaching should take place as the teacher engages in teaching and gains experience. As he gains experience, the teacher can give attention to his problems because he will no longer be pressed with the urgency of his graduate studies and will be confronted with realistic situations. In his graduate study, the prospective teacher should attain better preparation for teaching than he commonly gets. The graduate schools should recognize the importance of this training and should enable the student to devote some time to it. This can most effectively be done in the training of teaching fellows or assistants who, while completing their graduate work, are also beginning to get experience and training in teaching. However, it is when he first accepts a full-time job that the instructor needs to use imagination and resourcefulness in identifying the problems of teaching and in uncovering sources of help. This is the moment when deans of colleges and chairmen of departments could be more helpful than they commonly are. Indeed, the provision of expert, technical assistance to beginning teachers should be a highly important role of the administrator who is also an educational leader.

Faculty do not always accept well the efforts of an administrator whom they perceive as having disciplinary power over them. An ombudsman-type consultant can assist them to analyze their teaching problems and to improve their methods. This plan has been tried at some institutions, including prestigious ones, and with success in that the response was good. A more complete service to the faculty can be created by establishing a service and research center. The University of Michigan, for example, has such a center, the Center for Research on Learning and Teaching. Its functions include consultations with individual faculty about course syllabi, role-playing, closed circuit TV, and the phrasing of objective questions to assure validity and reliability. The center also reports on experiments with teaching methods and conducts studies on its own. It keeps abreast of the new literature relating to college teaching. The center communicates information and ideas to the faculty in "memos to the faculty." It is difficult to assess the value of such a center, but over a period of years it should have a significant impact. In any event, it is a valuable resource to all faculty who desire to make their teaching more effective.

College Teachers:
Preparation, Productivity

★★★
★★

Two additional aspects of college teaching need special consideration. One is the preparation of college teachers; the other is the issue of whether college teachers are low in productivity relative to the costs of their services.

During the 1960s the graduate schools were under great pressure to train more college teachers. The schools stepped up their recruitment of students, and many additional institutions added graduate programs. The resulting surge in graduates, together with a curtailed demand for research scientists and the decrease in college enrollment, has brought about an oversupply of persons with doctors' degrees. Unfortunately, many of these individuals have been unable to secure jobs appropriate to their training. This situation has, however, had other, more fortuitous results, including opportunities to screen out the weaker graduate programs and to be more selective in training prospective college teachers.

During this same period, ethnic groups have been demanding an increased share of available jobs. Ethnic groups believe that they should have teachers who understand them and have knowledge of their cultural and vocational needs. Should the universities, in response, train more Black and Chicano college teachers? There has been a disparity in representation, a bias in favor of Whites; and so an adjustment should be made. The urgency of the need for adjustment is the result of the long history of oppression of minorities. Some universities have increased minority representation on their faculties. The problem has another facet, however. Some ethnic groups have been the victims of weak schooling. Many who aspire to become college teachers enter graduate courses and seminars under serious handicaps. To select only those with superior academic records is not the whole answer. Ways must be found also to admit others who appear to have the necessary abilities and who will need tutorial or other help in reaching the required level of intellectual achievement.

The employment of women as college teachers presents similar problems. The discriminations against women as college teachers have been well documented (Robinson, 1971). Women have been considered good enough to get doctors' degrees but not good enough to become college teachers. Now they are pressing for consideration equal to that given men in such matters as appointments, promotions, salaries, and participation in decision-making. They have found an ally in the federal government. Under recent legislation and executive orders, government funds can now be withheld when there is substantial evidence of discrimination.

To understand the attitudes of male faculty toward women as intellectual equals, it is necessary to appreciate the struggle that women had during the nineteenth century to even get admitted to college (Woody, 1929). Women were deemed to be inferior in interests and abilities. And influential educators contended that the human race would be jeopardized if women shifted their interests from the family to intellectual matters. Furthermore, it was thought that women, with their periods of discomfort and the distractions of childbearing and raising, could not give to scholarship the sustained effort that is required for college teaching and research. Women have proved otherwise. It is high time for the colleges and universities to give equal opportunities to women as college teachers. Many graduate departments that have discriminated against women, must now be opened more widely to women.

Should all college teachers possess earned doctors' degrees? The normal pressures are in this direction. If teachers in graduate schools give direction to doctoral candidates, the usual qualification is the possession of the degree themselves. However, mere possession is not alone a sufficient criterion of the kind of competence that is needed. Indeed, there will always be instances where evidence of other achievements and of unique interests and abilities should supersede the necessity of an advanced degree, and in some cases of any degree. An author with distinction in creative writing, or a technician with varied experiences in his field, are illustrations. In some professional schools, notably medicine and dentistry, the doctor's degree for membership on the faculty has long been a prerequisite. In other schools, such as in engineering and business administration, the doctor's degree as a preferred qualification has recently become popular. This may or may not be valid. In engineering, as noted in Chapter Three, those with doctors' degrees tend to go into science rather than into the work force that solves the nuts and bolts problems. Medical schools shifted their interests strongly toward the scientific aspects of bodily health, and neglected to train a sufficient number of practitioners.

Among the colleges of liberal arts, the tendency has been to employ teachers who have doctorates. These faculty should have breadth of learning and also competence in some field of knowledge, narrow or broad. In a way, the advanced degree is a symbol of that type of erudition. The products of some departments of graduate schools, however, will have had their education skewed badly in favor of a narrow specialization. If a given college absorbs too many persons with this kind of imbalance, the objectives of liberal education will become thwarted. A mathematician, for example, may contend that his discipline is solely concerned with equations. Such a view overlooks the value of mathematics as a means of communication, as the basic component of statistical procedures and interpretations, and as an element in the training of elementary and secondary teachers. It also slights the historic role of mathematics as one of the keys to the integration of knowledge. For purposes of preparing teachers for liberal arts colleges, the doctoral or other advanced program should stress continuing breadth as well as depth of learning.

In community colleges, the work of faculty members is so clearly instructional in nature that teaching skills, as well as knowledge of the subject matter being taught, are essential. A doctor's degree is not necessarily a strong asset, nor is it a disadvantage unless it is primarily a research degree. A research degree may actually disqualify a person for teaching in junior college. A more appropriate degree is a master's, preferably a two-year master's, in which attention has been given to breadth, specialized competence, and teaching competence. Two years of graduate study provide sufficient time in which to get the necessary preparation for teaching at the junior college level. A number of universities have devised programs for two-year degrees that fall between the usual master's and the doctorate, and that take special account of the needs of prospective college teachers or of in-service teachers at the post-secondary level. In this degree the academic content can be pursued to considerable depth, but the research problem and dissertation are not included. Such a degree can also serve as recognition of the work done by a graduate student who has met all requirements for the doctorate excepting the dissertation. This degree goes by various names, but one that expresses the idea is master of philosophy.

Graduate schools are highly departmentalized, each department training its own specialists. Each teacher is an authority on his own subject as a result of his intensive research. This is regarded as an essential qualification for teaching and research at this level of education.

But research is not a function of undergraduate institutions. Why, then, is the prospective teacher trained for research rather than for teaching? The requirements for the doctor of philosophy degree almost always include competence in research methodology, plus a major research project that becomes a book-length dissertation. The answer to the question is based largely on history. In the era of science, training in research was the way to change college teachers from their pre-science allegiance to authoritarian literature to the use of open-minded inquiry. The conversion after 1850 was swift. Teachers gained their reputations by making original discoveries, such as identifying a fossil for the first time and describing the implications of that discovery. When the primary social need was to change the methods of learning and the number of scholars being trained was relatively small the research approach to the training of college teachers was justifiable.

Times have changed. Research is as important as ever but can now be done best in problem-oriented groups and in specialized institutions. The knowledge that has been discovered through research is as important to teaching as ever, but it is readily available to every inquiring person. It is more important that the teacher be well informed and continuously alert to fresh information than that he be an original investigator. These qualities are essential to good teaching, and so a portion of the training should prepare a teacher to continue to be an inquiring student during his teaching career.

But some of his training should be devoted to developing an understanding of students, of how individuals learn, and of how best to assist them in changing their perceptions and perspectives and in developing their competencies (McKeachie, 1969).

The answer to the best way to train college teachers is not as glib as the above may sound. A mere transference of methodology from the secondary and elementary school levels will not be rewarding. And to do so would create emotional resistances. Furthermore, post adolescent problems today differ from those of the earlier years. New content and new methods are needed.

Fortunately, much research has recently been done on the characteristics of college-age youth. Also, there is evidence about the relative effectiveness of various methods of teaching, about the effects of the involvement of students in their own learning, and about ways to design superior courses of instruction. Some materials are available for assisting graduate students to learn how best to function as college teachers.

Moreover, it is the custom of universities to involve their graduate students in undergraduate teaching. This situation could provide a natural laboratory for the training of superior teachers, although a transformation of the program would be required. As it now operates, the principal aims of the program are to help the departments recruit doctoral candidates by giving them assistantships with stipends. Faculty members are relieved of departmental tasks that are considered onerous and that distract them from their research. The student, eager to get his degree as soon as possible, may carry the teaching as an overload. He accepts the dictates of the department about contents and methods, and he pays no attention to the literature on teaching or the counseling help that is available. So the student learns bad methods as readily as he learns good ones. He does not evaluate his progress in becoming a teacher, and he acquires attitudes and habits that later are difficult to break.

How can prospective college teachers be provided with training appropriate to their academic and counseling functions? A doctoral program other than the PhD may be the solution. Of course, such degrees exist—doctor of education, doctor of business administration, doctor of public health, and so forth. Applicants for teaching in community colleges frequently present as a qualification the EdD degree. For some roles in the two-year college, the education degree is superior to the PhD, because preparation for it has emphasized knowledge and skills relating to the educational process, as well as appropriate academic content.

A doctoral degree long talked about, but only recently being implemented, is the doctor of arts. It is intended to provide breadth and depth of scholarship, but without emphasis on original research. It aims at rigorous intellectual development. It is conceived as a program that takes account of the role as college teacher. The Carnegie Commission on Higher Education has recommended the use of this title and training for college teachers (Spurr, 1970).

The problem of oversupply of teachers would be simplified if all teachers beyond the high school were required to possess the doctor's degree. For the reasons indicated, this would be unwise. In many situations other requirements are more important, because they enhance the effectiveness of the teacher more than the usual degree does. The growth in the number who apply for teaching positions was stimulated by an earlier alarm about expected shortages due to huge increases in college enrollments. The imbalance between demand and supply can presently be adjusted if greater care is taken in counseling graduate students about potential careers, and if some of the weaker doctoral programs are curtailed or eliminated.

Productivity

College education is advantageous to the individual and to society. The interest of people in college is demonstrated by the huge number of young people who want to go to college, and by the many parents who hope that their children will go. Moreover, the evidence is strong that educated people are displacing the unskilled in employment. Technological advance has been rapid because educated personnel have been available. Our doctors, lawyers, engineers, scientists, teachers, and other professional men and women are educated in colleges and universities. The social benefit of education, although difficult to estimate, is apparent.

Yet it is difficult to assemble the resources to pay the costs of education. The state, which supplies a large portion of the funds, is under pressures from many competing interests. Education deserves its share, but how can this share be kept under control so that health, welfare, highways, conservation, and other services will not be throttled?

One answer is to demand greater efficiency in the use of money, including efficiency in the colleges and universities. The largest and seemingly most flexible item in the college budget is teaching. The financial problem has caused the state, and also administrators responsible for finances, to press teachers for evidence of their productivity.

At first glance the answer is simple: apply a quantitative measure to the teacher's activities. How many hours does he teach? How many students? What is the total number of credit hours earned by students under his direction? These kinds of measures are used because they are feasible to administer. Furthermore, to the business-minded trustee or legislator this unit-cost formula approximates methods used in business, where the product of the assembly line is standardized and can be counted. The method is not intrinsically bad, because the results can be used in maintaining a degree of administrative control.

In Chapter Thirteen we note the differences between business and education and describe the essential nature of the job of the educator. In brief, the important products of his effort are intangible. The accumulation of credit hours is only presumptive evidence that students are being educated. It is therefore a serious mistake to think that the grinding out of large numbers of student credit hours is an appropriate index of productivity. To a degree it measures efficiency in the use of money, but it does not measure the effectiveness of teaching.

In similar manner, quantitative formulas are misapplied to research, to the counseling roles of the teacher, and to the participation of faculty in educational planning. In research, for example, the unit-cost formula results in pressure on individuals to respond with quantity. In the kind of research that faculty do, what is needed is quality. Fewer publications and more significant ones should be the goal. Quality cannot be counted. The counseling of students is the principal means through which the faculty can assist the student to identify his interests, assess his abilities and special talents, and recognize his limitations and problems. Counseling will not be effective if paced at ten-minute intervals. The most effective education is self-education, but it proceeds best under guidance or with tutorial help. The planning of educational programs, both for individuals and for a department or college, can be done best when there is active, representative participation by those whose learning makes them expert. Faculty may spend much time in committees and conferences, but developing an educational program requires much individual thinking and group consultation. This time is seldom measured by the cost-benefit experts.

The measures of efficiency need to be used with care (Newman, 1971). To proceed otherwise is to reduce the educational process to routines and common denominators. The colleges are already burdened with the problem of dealing with large numbers of students. Teachers should not be pressed to lecture at a sea of faces rather than inspiring individuals to learn.

Better understanding by the public and public officials of the harm that can accrue to teaching from the use of misguided controls could contribute to a solution of this problem. Among those who do understand this but seem to have forgotten it are the officers in university or college systems. These officials become far removed from the scene where the education takes place. They are involved with data rather than with people. They have incentive to work in harmony with state officials—who are even farther removed from the campus, the classroom, and the laboratory.

The college teachers, in spite of division within their ranks about the appropriateness of the actions, are resorting more and more to collective bargaining as a means of protecting and advancing their interests (Carr and VanEyck, 1973). This pits faculty against administration in a manner that clashes with the collegial ideal of unity of faculty and their educational leaders. However, the continued growth of regulatory agencies and policies outside the college inevitably brings about countermeasures—collective bargaining, for example—among faculties as a means of exercising power. Hence, unions such as the National Education Association and the American Federation of Teachers are becoming stronger and larger. The faculty achieves clout through the unions.

The steps being taken by the state and by administrators to hold college faculty accountable for a time-clock type of performance are wrong in principle. In the professions, including college teaching, the greatest benefit for society is obtained when the profession maintains a high standard for its own conduct. The effort to gain accountability, then, should be an ef-

fort to enhance professional standards. An academic administrator should provide incentives and leadership.

Faculties should not rely wholly on defensive actions. To
offset the criticism of inadequate productivity, they should
evaluate their services at regular intervals. They should examine
and control the activities that distract or remove energies from
the teaching; they should revise the outmoded class-hours-per-
week criterion as a means of expressing their work loads; and
they should train themselves—on the job or otherwise—to be
more effective in their teaching. They should also educate themselves about the functional roles of various levels and types of
post-high school institutions, adapt their assignments as faculty
to the appropriate function, and develop a contemporary concept as to what constitutes prestige in the profession. The latter
action is necessary as a means of alleviating the pecking order of
institutions and of persuading faculty that it is not always necessary to emulate the professors in the most prestigious universities. From the viewpoint of the state, this reform would reduce
considerably the unnecessary duplications of curricula and of
research activities.

It would also relieve some criticism if the faculty would
make more efficient use of the money allocated to them. This
would require devising better schedules of work. College plants
are terribly expensive to build and operate and should be fully
used before additional requests are warranted. The same applies
to laboratory space and equipment. Yet the usual class schedule
creates excessive demands at some hours and relatively little at
others. The extent of idle facilities each day, each week, and
each year is scandalous. A partial exception is the public community college, which typically operates a substantial program
from early morning to late afternoon, in the evenings, and on
Saturdays. The community colleges have no problem in doing
this because, being a relatively new institution, they are not
psychologically bound by the traditions that call for a nine-to-
three schedule.

Another facet of the problem of schedule is the controversy over year-round operation. Traditionally, schools and colleges slow down or close during the summer months. This cus-

tom, which was valuable when our society was rural, is outmoded. A schedule that uses facilities fully throughout the year can be flexible for faculty, who can plan their activities so that all terms of the year are covered. But members of the group may alternate in taking periods to refresh their knowledge or for personal reasons. Various forty-eight-week calendars have been tried—four quarters, three semesters, two semesters plus a split term, and of course the familiar winter and summer differentiated programs. The last has been successful but does not make the best use of the facilities. The summer session often is not integrated with the winter terms. Among the others, the four-quarter plan has the best logic and the most flexibility; but this plan and the others have been meeting resistance from students and faculty. Any proposed change from the traditional plan of two semesters, followed by an extended vacation, arouses a variety of objections—course syllabi and texts, laboratory schedules, and personal plans would all need revision. Most of these problems, however, can be solved by offering fewer courses, on a more intensive basis, during a shorter calendar period. In spite of the difficulties, the social interest in using facilities fully is dominant. The main problem lies in the difficulty of transforming the habits of people. People resist change.

We are being pressed by events to expect the college teacher to be a quantitative purveyor of knowledge and skills, and to judge his productivity on a quantitative basis. However, it is inconsistent with the concept of higher education merely to purvey information. The role of the teacher is to stimulate the student to learn—just as happened when professor and student sat on a log. The presence of large numbers of students does not change the essential task of education. Lecturing to a mass of students in an auditorium or by closed-circuit TV where the students can be counted, can serve a purpose, but a limited one. The teacher needs also to have diverse methods at his command, and to maintain the objective of inducing growth and development in each student. His productivity, difficult to measure because it is intangible, lies in achieving this objective.

Mass Education,
or Education
of the Masses?

★★★★★★★★★★★★★★★★★★★★★★★★★★★★★★★★★★★★★★
★★★★★★★★★★★★★★★★★★★★★★★★★★★★★★★★★★★★★

The enrollment of huge numbers of students in institutions with limited resources has created the need for new approaches to the education of the individual. Education takes place only as each individual changes and grows—as he educates himself. The growth of the campus in size inhibits the education of the individual. He registers via a computerized card, enrolls in classes where his fellow students number into the hundreds or thousands, is the recipient of lectures rather than an active participant in the classroom, does routinized experiments in the laboratory, stands in line for books and for meals, and wanders among the milling crowds on the campus. How, then, can he become educated?

This mass phenomenon is a relatively new development.

153

Our heritage is very different. First, there is the Judeo-Christian principle that it is the individual who should be cherished, and there is the British tradition of individual rights and freedoms. Second, our colleges heretofore have placed much emphasis on development of intellectual abilities and on individual achievement. And finally, the colleges have had a well-established tradition of emphasizing the community life on the campus, including good intercommunication between faculty and students.

The college of the past assumed responsibility for the moral, physical, and intellectual life of the student. Housing was arranged to promote the feeling of belonging. "College," "hall," or "quadrangle" came to mean a communal group of students and masters "engaged in the pursuit of preparing liberally educated men for church and state." The communal aspects of Oxford and Cambridge were of great significance to the United States. Our basic college, the liberal arts college, was designed on similar principles, and our universities, for the most part, became campus institutions.

From the British system, we got the concept of a college where the student works at the elbow of his professor. Adoption of honors plans strengthened the tutorial relationship between faculty member and student. We broke the enclosing circle of the classics and permitted the student to elect courses that appealed to him. In our colleges, the student was not merely preparing to pass an examination; he was preparing for life.

The trend toward mass education is a break from this tradition. What is happening at the college level is a projection of the trends at lower levels. Our children go to schools that are graded by age levels, their peer groups encompass narrow age ranges, and they sit for hours each week watching TV programs that are designed for particular age groups. The age layers run only one or two years deep, well into the college period. This concentration of children on the activities of their peer group, coupled with the preoccupation of the parents with nonfamily matters, reduces communication across age groups. Thus the youth have really known only one group, their age peers.

Now these youth are going to college in such large numbers that communication between mature and immature students, and between teachers and the individuals in the classes, is materially reduced. At the same time, peer influences continue to dominate the thinking and the activities of the entering students. This situation raises serious questions about the educational process and about the nature and quality of the college as a community.

There is, of course, evidence from numerous empirical studies that the learning of the student advances irrespective of class size or of teaching method. This is one of the bases for assuming that the student-faculty ratio can be increased and that classes can be large without loss of educational effects. This evidence in support of mass teaching should be weighed properly. However, we think that it is the retention of factual subject matter, rather than change and growth in each student, that has been tested.

There is evidence that neither students nor faculty are now interested in the former style of community life—extracurricular activities, social events, athletics, teas at the professors' houses. The students have larger political and social interests; the faculty are being distracted from involvement with students by their research and their off-campus consulting activities.

On the whole it is unrealistic to assume that we can return to the ivy-covered compound on the hill that encloses an intellectual and social life distinct from that of the surrounding community. Nevertheless, education needs to be effective, rather than merely efficiently managed, and the campus life of the past ten years or so leaves much to be desired.

One way to meet individual demands is to operate an open-ended campus and an open-ended curriculum. The argument in favor is a potent one—the young people of a community have a right to attend an institution that is supported by public funds, and the college has a duty to provide courses that are relevant to student and community needs. Certainly we have moved so far in the direction of egalitarianism in higher education that we can no longer deny the right of high school graduates, and for that matter many post-high school age persons, to attend a public institution. Also, one way to individualize education is to let each student study what he wants to study.

From these arguments emerges the generalization that each institution should do everything for everybody. This is patently impossible. To the extent that a college moves in this direction, it dilutes its program, proliferates the efforts of its faculty, and reduces the depth of learning of each student. When quantity prevails over quality, the long-run effect will be mediocrity.

The way to resolve the problem of quantity versus quality is to develop a system of education composed of several institutions that have differing functions that contribute to the whole. No one would dispute the desirability of maintaining a limited number of law schools, schools of dentistry, or programs in watch repairing. If every college tried to train dentists, there would be a great surplus of dentists, and most of them would be incompetent because of totally inadequate training. Society could not afford the cost of training nor the consequences of superficial training. It is in the social interest to limit the number of schools of dentistry to provide for high quality of instruction. This example clarifies the need to differentiate the roles of institutions, and to mobilize resources behind particular programs to assure quality results in education.

If we conceive of the community colleges, or the public colleges and universities, as systems, we can then plan (1) to provide every high school graduate, and also other qualified persons, with an opportunity to enter a college, and (2) to provide one, or two, or twenty, or a hundred programs in a knowledge area, depending on a balancing of the individual demands and the social needs. This planning assumes that a high-level public agency will identify social needs and identify the function of each institution to which funds are appropriated. It must also determine the answer to a ticklish question—the minimum qualifications, additional to high school diploma, for admission to each program.

Under this plan, each college would have a defined role and freedom to create programs within that role. Thus it could concentrate on teaching what it could do well. At the same time, each student would find a place where he could study what seemed relevant to his career and his personal development.

We should recognize that there are two perceptions about quality of achievement. One is quality that results in an appropriate degree of competence in a subject or discipline. A dentist, to be licensed for public practice, must meet specific standards in his knowledge of dentistry; an electronics technician must possess requisite skills; a teacher of literature must know literature. The other aspect of quality is the kind of achievement that evidences good progress in a student's learning—the development of his intellectual skills, his fund of knowledge, his style of living. The programs within a system can be differentiated to take account of these differing objectives in achieving quality results.

It would be difficult to give any pat answers to such questions as how to motivate the unmotivated student, how to supply, at the college level, deficiencies in foundation that should have been acquired in elementary and secondary programs, how best to help the slow learner catch up, how to meet the instructional needs of the student with talents other than intellectual abilities, and so forth. These questions reveal how complex the problem is (Cross, 1971). They also reveal how deficient the college programs are in meeting needs of students who come from homes that are not intellectually or socially elite. The answers given here do not examine learning theory, but do address themselves to program devices. The aim is to reach the individual whose problems or whose aspirations may be obscured if he is an anonymous member of the mass of students.

Counseling is basic to all modes of attacking the problem. To counsel is to interact with a student. Even in group counseling, the interaction of the counselor is with individuals who have problems in common. An aim is diagnosis. The student is free to reveal his concerns, or his status in college may have revealed them. He should be assisted to identify his interests, aptitudes, and resources, his strengths and goals, and his weaknesses in previous achievements. For this purpose, data can be secured—mostly through systematic inventories that he can take. Much progress has been made in devising tests that can supply subjective and objective data. Data from either source become the basis for self-analysis and for counseling interviews.

New methods for processing data can produce information, with several variables under control, that is superior to information formerly available to counselors. The computer is useful in individualizing education when the data are used to diagnose problems or to plan action programs. Data analysis has produced a large accumulation of knowledge about the characteristics of college students.

Obviously a counseling program does not educate the student in English, mathematics, or history. But it may inform the student about himself. It may suggest to him courses of action that can lead to a better education. It may stimulate him to overcome deficiencies and to select for study subjects in which he stands good chances for success.

Unfortunately, counseling in colleges is limited by insufficient resources. Academic faculty do only limited counseling and often do not support the counseling staff. The agencies that allocate funds discover that it is easy to reject or reduce the requests for counseling staff, because their work is less tangible than the maintenance of a chemistry laboratory. It is difficult to marshall data to show the value of counseling to students. Even students may downgrade the program, partly because it is sometimes the fashion to do so. In spite of all of these negative aspects, a good counseling program can help the individual to find himself and to ferret out opportunities that meet his particular interests and needs; it can help him in his process of self-education.

The admission to college of students who are deficient in background, even though they have a high school diploma, is rapidly becoming noncontroversial. We have become sensitive to the plight of disadvantaged youth whose inferior grounding is not due to any fault of their own. For many, the problem exists because the schools they attended were inferior. They should not be again penalized by being prevented from entering college—not if there is evidence of motivation and potential ability to undertake successfully a type of program that the college offers. These students should be tutored or placed in workshops and courses that will enable them to catch up. For example, a number of law schools have participated in a summer seminar for Black students who failed the law school entrance test. The students have been tested for their abilities and selected because they seemed to have adequate potential to be good lawyers. A large majority of these students were then successfully placed in law schools. Many undergraduate colleges offer noncredit courses that are designed to overcome deficiencies in such subjects as English composition and mathematics. Others have pre-college semesters or summer sessions that give students the grounding needed for college work.

These instructional efforts deserve better support from faculty than they normally get. The teachers of students who are deficient in preparation should possess special skills for diagnosing the problems of each student, and unusual skill in tutoring or teaching. The inadequate preparation of many students—especially Blacks and Chicanos—is a situation for which society bears considerable responsibility. The work of assisting these students to gain a foothold on the ladder to knowledge and a better career provides strong challenge. The colleges should allocate ample resources for this purpose and should reward the teachers for an important service.

An enrollment of twenty, thirty, or forty thousand students in an institution does not mean that all classes must be large or that all faculty must remain remote from students. A complex institution will be composed of many programs, some of which will enroll large numbers of students; other programs will have few students. The extreme example is found in a doctoral program where each student has a chairman of his committee and a supervisor of his studies and his research. In his research, the student has an original problem of his own. His seminars will probably have only a few students and will be conducted with maximal participation by them. At the conclusion, the student will be rigorously examined by his committee. By its very nature, a doctoral program is highly individualized.

Some specialized programs, including some in the professions, will draw a limited number of students; or they may function primarily through laboratory or case study instruction. The Chinese language, geology, and logic are examples of programs in which enrollments are always small. Dentistry, horticulture, and kindergarten teaching involve skill training in which the individual is held to an expected level of competence. Such courses require supervision of the individual and an evaluation of his achievement in skills. The enrollment in each class in law is usually large, but legal cases are used in the instruction; each student is required to analyze the reasoning of the court in the light of some principle or precedent in the law. The training of a physician includes substantial clinical experience, and that experience is individual to each student.

Where the enrollment is not large, the student-faculty ratio is apt to be low. Where supervised training is involved, a professor is always at hand to guide the student. Under these circumstances, the interaction between faculty and students will usually be continuous. Thus a university, although it is huge, may contain programs, departments, and schools that are individualized. It will also have many courses and seminars that are small—sometimes so many small courses that the institution may appear to be supporting uneconomical operations.

The largest enrollment in a university is usually in the college of arts and sciences. Because this is true, a few institutions have organized the programs in the arts and sciences into several college units. The plan emulates the Oxford-Cambridge college pattern. Indeed, the Claremont College group—a decentralized group of colleges that has existed for more than a half century —was modeled after Oxford and Cambridge. Newer clusters of colleges include the University of California at Santa Cruz, the University of the Pacific, and the University of Wisconsin at Green Bay (Gaff and Associates, 1970). Instead of having one college that has grown without limit, each of these institutions has created additional colleges as the enrollment enlarged. A variation has occurred in some universities, where the large college of arts and sciences has been retained but new colleges have been founded for programs with a special focus, or as residential colleges, or as branches. Examples are Monteith College at Wayne State University and the Residential College at the University of Michigan, as mentioned in Chapter Three.

These colleges usually have their own facilities, a nucleus of faculty who are devoted to the program, and a student body that is small by comparison with most. All of these character-istics facilitate the education of the individual. To the extent that these colleges are experimental—and most of them are at least innovative—they attract students who are motivated to participate. Thus, within a large institution it is possible to orga-nize in ways that achieve for the students some of the advan-tages of the small college (Keeton, 1971).

The small, independent college—with a campus of its own and teachers who devote themselves to teaching, including the beginning courses—maintains an educational environment that is congenial for individual development. These colleges are usually limited in resources, especially for in-depth teaching in the sci-ences. On the whole, however, they provide a good education at the undergraduate level. Taking their size into account, a num-ber of them have ranked high among American institutions in their relative production of scholars (Knapp and Greenbaum, 1953) and scientists (Knapp and Goodrich, 1952). These col-leges, because they are small and self-contained, tend to become desirable communities of faculty and students—communities in which the chances of individual participation in educative activi-ties are greater than in larger institutions. The small colleges should be fully utilized in our scheme of higher education.

Smallness in size for an educational institution is not in itself a virtue. The course offerings may be very restricted. There is, in theory, an optimal size for assuring reasonable cov-erage of an area of knowledge and good operating efficiency. But a controlling principle should be the attainment of educa-tional effectiveness, and that can be measured only in the achievements of individuals. One way to achieve optimal size, and avoid the massing of students, is to decentralize the pro-grams.

A major step was taken in this direction with the found-ing of the public community college movement. The communi-ty colleges care for the educational needs of a few million stu-dents for the beginning years of college and for vocational train-ing. They are widely distributed and are situated near the homes of the students. In the populous metropolitan areas, they are usually subdivided into a number of campuses. The work of

creating hundreds of these local colleges deserves much commendation. Some of them have become congested with students
and have severe problems in reaching the individual within the
mass. The movement, however, is in an early stage of development. Decentralization is proceeding. The education of the individual, as elsewhere, needs to be given better attention.

Another of the efforts being made to overcome the tread-
mill effect of college programs has been to permit students to
plan studies of their own. As one option, the student may select
a topic or problem, outline a plan of study, and submit it for
approval. The college appoints a professor to counsel with the
student and later to evaluate his achievement. Ordinarily the
college will have established some criteria as to what may be accepted as an independent study.

A variant in individual studies has been called the honors
program (Cohen, 1965). In this plan, students who have superior academic achievement and potential are accepted. The honors students are given freedom from prescribed courses and procedures, and are invited to seminars arranged for their participation. The aims are to avoid having the student with high potential held back by the slower pace of his classmates and, of
course, to give him the opportunity to proceed at his own pace
and in the depth of penetration in knowledge of which he is
capable. Unfortunately, honors programs have been deteriorat-
ing, because non-honors students think that they should have
similar privileges, and because the institutions cannot nourish
the programs sufficiently. When this happens, we fail to help
students of high ability to achieve in relation to that ability.

A few colleges use a plan that educates on the basis of a
contract with each student. The procedure for implementing
this idea was discussed in Chapter Nine. The principle involved
is a good one—that the individual advances from where he is at a
pace of which he is capable.

Ordinarily, established departments or disciplines define
the requirements for a major concentration within generalized
criteria approved by the faculty. The result is often a tightly
knit schedule of courses. These requirements should be more
flexible than they usually are. Doubtless the existing procedure

meets the needs of most students, because they desire to graduate as a major in economics, or psychology, or physics. The faculty in each case is competent to describe what constitutes good preparation. The standard plan satisfies the requirements of those students who will go on to graduate school, because these subjects conform to the specializations of the graduate schools. However, one of the most serious criticisms of the present-day college concerns the effect of departmentalization on the in-depth studies of students. Of course, it is possible for a faculty to identify the criteria by which a study in depth shall be judged, and then to permit the student by petition to create a concentration of studies for himself—as described in Chapter Nine. A few colleges have adopted this provision. Colleges that have programs that involve personal experience—off-campus work, community studies, study abroad—recognize the principle of individualization; the essence of experience is that it happens to an individual.

As a college devises plans by which to educate the individual within the mass, it should develop a set of principles of education by which to guide the efforts. We suggest the following as guidelines:

(1) A college or university should be more than a composite of experts, however learned they may be. It should be a community of people, some more knowledgeable than others, gathered together to learn.

(2) Each young man or woman between the ages of seventeen and twenty-two needs to feel a sense of belonging. Belonging means, among other things, developing loyalties to something bigger than oneself.

(3) Each student needs recognition for his individual merit, both to do him justice—because if education occurs at all it must occur within him—and to lift his spirit. He should feel that he is something more to the professor than one face in a sea of faces. A pat on the back is more conducive to motivation, effort, and learning than is a sharp word. But the pat cannot be given unless the student is a personality to the professor. Nor is it apt to be deserved unless the professor is stimulating the student to learn.

(4) The differences among individuals increase as age increases, and this is true from earliest childhood. Learning differs for individuals, and so we need to diversify our programs and our methods of education. The occupational and interest outlets for educated persons also become more varied as society becomes more complex, and this too requires diversity of preparation.

(5) Education is a process of passing wisdom from generation to generation. The means is not a funnel through which is poured information from an older mouth into a young ear. Bridges of intercommunication and interaction must be built—as many as possible. Learning does not become wisdom until it has been tested and tempered by experience; hence, outlets for experience need to be provided.

(6) It is the individual who learns. Learning does not take place unless the individual is educated. We should not overlook the creative nature of the college experience.

In conforming with these principles, the colleges and universities can take many precautions to insure that they will educate soundly and thus avoid frustrating their students. First, they should maintain integrity in education. They can review their purposes and potential clientele (consistent with legal or other authorization) and define their role. They can determine their optimum size and select their students accordingly (unless compelled otherwise by law).

They can also emphasize skillful and colorful teaching. The more students we get, the more important this becomes. The need to handle larger groups in the classroom does not justify a shift wholly to mass lecturing. Lectures, yes, but followed through with opportunities for discussion, individual projects and experiences, and other forms of participation.

The colleges need to make certain that they are doing an adequate job of counseling the young people. The student should be assisted in defining his interests and in getting a good understanding of his aptitudes and achievements and of the opportunities before him. Counseling, based on objective data, is one way to individualize.

Counseling includes lending a guiding hand to the youth

leaders who emerge within the group. What kind of training shall we give them while they are experiencing this leadership? We do not underrate the difficulty of the task—the tact, the right degree of permissiveness, the person-to-person relationship, the perpetually open door for consultations, the need to overcome hostility in some students, the mulling over of mistakes to extract the lessons from them, the relating of general education to the art of living—but is not this, too, teaching of a significant sort? Growth in social attitudes and vision and in the ability to assume initiative and to carry responsibility should be among the primary educational aims.

We also need to do a better job of general education. General education is the flux that helps to weld the diverse programs together; it is the cultural background required by everyone for common citizenship; it provides perspective in working toward evolutionary progress; it is the proving ground of ideas and values that enable intelligent men to communicate with one another and to work together.

Finally, let us think twice before we lose or adulterate the community life that has been such a unique characteristic of our colleges. The small institutions should reinforce this goal, for informal relations and personal contact are their forte. At the larger ones, we can make certain that faces also have names; we can reorganize our rigidly arranged recitation halls to facilitate group interplay; we can skillfully guide extracurricular activities to make them socially congenial and educative; we can revise our libraries to bring the books close to the students who use them so that they can help themselves; we can subdivide college units as they become large. Colleges that have large numbers of commuting students need to give special attention to the planning of student centers and the organization of student activities. No amount of administrative mechanics will do the whole job, however. What is desired is a contagion of spirit that pervades the atmosphere.

The issue before us—shall we educate the mass of youth by mass education methods—is serious and requires the attention both of the educator and of those who finance education. We Americans are efficiency-minded and economy-minded. It would be easy to persuade ourselves that, because we have found mass production methods efficient and economical in industry, we should resort to them in higher education. But the human being is not raw material to be processed, and the education of each individual is an experience that is unique to him.

Intellectual Freedom

★★
★★

Many college professors prize academic freedom above every
other consideration (Hofstadter and Metzger, 1955). In a broader sense, all faculty value and support intellectual freedom. Students, too, crave the freedom to be articulate about their beliefs. However, intellectual freedom, including academic freedom, in the colleges and universities is under continuous attack.
The onslaughts in the late sixties were emotional and persistent.
During the sessions of 1968 to 1970, the dockets of the state
legislatures were flooded with bills to curb the freedom of the
public institutions; proposals for financial aid to students at
either public or private colleges often carried stipulations about
student behavior.

Intellectual freedom in the United States is in some degree of peril, as evidenced by the growth of agencies for the sur-
veillance of individuals and by the "enemies lists" compiled at
the White House. Because the public mood has permitted this to
happen, it may be contended that the colleges and universities
must behave in circumspect ways if they want to survive within
a social milieu that puts a premium upon conformance to the
views of those in authority. Trends toward authoritarianism in

167

America present issues that are too broad for discussion here. However, the institutions of higher education face a deep-seated issue—how to preserve their freedoms within a society that is not wholly free.

Freedoms within higher education include the broad concept of intellectual freedom, and also the specific provision for academic freedom. Intellectual freedom includes the rights to speak and to assemble, an aspect of civil liberties guaranteed by our constitution. Intellectual freedom also involves intellectual integrity—the discipline that an individual imposes upon himself in making his utterances and writings conform to his knowledge and beliefs. On the campus, intellectual freedom becomes an issue as faculty or students express unorthodox opinions, or agitate or demonstrate in behalf of some political cause, and exterior forces endeavor to suppress these activities.

Academic freedom has a narrower connotation than intellectual freedom. It is a policy that protects a faculty member in his search for truth, and in teaching or disseminating his findings irrespective of their conformance or nonconformance with prevailing information and beliefs. The essence of academic freedom is that the teacher or researcher is protected in his employment. An instructor who has tenure cannot be disciplined or dismissed without cause, and the cause must be substantiated to the satisfaction of his professional peers. The cause may not be mere eccentricity of opinion.

Cases of academic freedom are often difficult to adjudicate. For example, in 1972 a professor at Stanford University, distinguished in his own field of scholarship, made a study outside of that discipline in which he claimed to find evidence that Blacks have lower intellectual potential than Whites. He submitted for approval a course of study in which the issue and his findings would be discussed. The request aroused emotional opposition. Nevertheless, the administration supported the right of the professor to have his request considered through the established procedures for approving courses of study.

The history of an earlier case at Stanford University is also instructive. At that time, 1900, Edward A. Ross, a young instructor at Stanford, was fired. Ross, an economist by training, was interested in the public issues of the time and published some essays in which he analyzed them. He was, for instance, concerned about the growth of big business in California and about the manner in which many companies had accumulated their wealth and power. During the McKinley-Bryan presidential campaign, widespread use had been made of a pamphlet Ross had written entitled "Honest Dollars." Mrs. Leland Stanford, who possessed more diamonds than most of the queens of Europe, was still the financial angel of the university. She wrote to President David Starr Jordan demanding that Ross be dismissed. He was dismissed. Ross subsequently became employed by the University of Wisconsin, where he was a leader in establishing the new discipline of sociology. While at Wisconsin he was harassed for his unorthodox teaching; in 1910 he was censored by the regents of the university for his book, *Sin and Society,* and in 1935 he was investigated by the state legislature for alleged communistic activities. But there is an interesting sequel in this case. In 1958, the University of Wisconsin named a building the Edward Alsworth Ross House. A memorial plaque was placed in the lobby with an inscription that cites his distinguished contributions to knowledge. It reads in part as follows: "Out of the University of Wisconsin tradition of scholarly attainment through freedom to inquire, Edward Alsworth Ross emerges a giant figure . . . wherever men live together and ponder shared problems, the majestic thought of this great educator attends."

In 1876, Thomas Huxley gave an address on the new biology at Johns Hopkins University. This new university intended to emphasize teaching and research in biology, and so the professors were eager to hear the distinguished interpreter of the new Darwinian theory. The subject of evolution was highly emotional and controversial at that time, and newspaper reporters from New York and elsewhere descended on the scene of the address. Pandemonium ensued. President Gilman later said, "We have sowed the wind and were to reap the whirlwind." Among the charges made against the university was that it had failed to open the meeting with prayer, and hence that it had excluded God. In retrospect, we must bear in mind that until that time the colleges had been under the domination of clergy, and that people in general were well indoctrinated with the biblical story of the creation. Although the story of the creation is still accepted by people of fundamentalist beliefs, the colleges today are free to teach the theory of evolution.

The Ross and Huxley cases show that what is highly controversial at one point in time may differ from what is controversial at another time. Our insights into the history of man and the characteristics of his society have been greatly enlarged because Johns Hopkins and Wisconsin dared to withstand hostile public opinion.

There is a basic reason why there is tension between the academic community and the general community. Kenneth Boulding has described the tension as a clash between the folk culture and the super culture (Boulding 1968, pp. 135-141). People have in common beliefs that are representative of their stage of learning and of the mores of their environment. This type of common denominator enables people to associate together and maintain a government. It is a key to stability, and people in general do not like instability. So people have a protective attitude toward the customs of their community.

A college or university, on the other hand, has the special role of inquiring into the validity of all beliefs and of searching for new perspectives and fresh knowledge. The more controversial an issue is, the stronger is the duty of the college to examine the issue in the effort to find answers that can be substantiated by research. A college originates in the need of the exterior community for education, and for men who are trained in the professions and supplied with the most accurate information and the best skills attainable. The educational program should be based on good scholarship that is the result of critical inquiry. As a result, the college drifts apart from its general community, and becomes a super culture. It would fail in its mission if it did not do so. This difference in outlook and mission between the college and the community is always present. How, then, can the college remain sufficiently in harmony with its environment to draw from the environment the support it must have, and at the same time pursue the goals for which it was created?

Pressures and Limiting Factors

One of the difficulties for the educational institution arises because controversy makes news. It did in the day of Huxley a century ago. Today, with television and radio as well as the newspaper, communication to the general public about unorthodox views or political demonstrations is almost instantaneous. It is also massive and can incite massive reactions. Any threat of change produces feelings of insecurity in the general community.

The personnel of a college are seldom in full agreement about the best policy for the institution to follow. College professors experience firsthand the changes that are occurring in their fields of study; and many of them think they have an obligation to help eradicate general social ills. Students become socially conscious as they explore knowledge that is new to them and as they discuss social issues; many feel compelled to join in social action. Within any college, however, there will be opposed views. One view is that the college personnel should use their superior knowledge and skills to effect desirable change. The other view is that a college must maintain objectivity, for otherwise it will lose its ability to examine methodically any hypothesis that is posed; also if it takes sides on political issues, it will run the risk of landing on the losing side and have its resources trimmed.

The best answer seems to be to maintain a twofold policy. One policy involves the adoption of a dynamic program for action when the subject is nonpolitical—for example, the promotion of artificial insemination as a means of improving livestock. The other policy is to assure security of position to faculty who, in their role as citizens, engage in political controversy.

This does not mean that the institution should abstain from endeavoring to improve the environment in which it works. But when it does this, it should make approaches from several directions, and it should move deliberately over a period of years. By avoiding sporadic and impetuous actions, it can succeed within the limits of the amount of friction that can be tolerated. The people began to tolerate the teaching of evolution after they had begun to understand the theory and the evidence in support of it. As the fruits of actions demonstrate their merit, the change will gain acceptance by the people. For example, some colleges disregarded the established customs when they first permitted Black and White students to room together in a dormitory; at first they encountered public hostility, but by the 1970s this practice no longer aroused general opposition.

Another problem for the college arises because participation in policy formation and decision-making has become more diffused than it had been. On the campus, the tradition that the scholars determine what and how to teach has changed. The participation of college students and general employees has to a degree diluted the academic tradition. The nonscholar tends to confuse civil rights with academic freedom. And the civil rights concept is often diffused by issues relating to salaries, office space, and employees' benefits. The professionally prepared teacher usually has an understanding of and commitment to academic freedom. He has a special interest in standing guard over academic freedom; but it is in the interest of everyone to maintain civil rights within the institution.

A very alarming trend is shaping up off campus—the trend toward transferring the administration of the public colleges and universities to a central office controlled by the executive of the state. One of the most detrimental consequences is the manipulation of academic decisions by state officials. The result is that effectual control of academic matters is put in the hands of a nonacademic, politically oriented state employee. One is reminded of Thorstein Veblen's pert remark: "Plato's classic scheme of folly, which would have the philosophers take over the management of affairs, has been turned on its head; the men of affairs have taken over the direction of the pursuit of knowledge." Manipulation also results from the creation of a single, politically appointed board of control, with an executive officer who is empowered to administer the several institutions. This creates another tier of decision-makers, which increases the complexity enormously. It places the power in the hands of bureaucrats in an office remote from the campus and devoid of contact with the academic personnel. It provides the governor with an easy means of making decisions respecting education and enforcing them through an officer whose tenure is subject to the governor's day-to-day pleasure. The danger to the college from politicization is much greater from this source than from the political activities of students or faculty.

The risk to a scholar who disseminates unpopular findings is great, because the power of the state, when concentrated, can easily overwhelm protective measures taken by the man's academic peers. This, of course, is one of the developments that is causing college teachers to affiliate with large-scale pressure organizations. It is not clear yet, however, whether unions will protect academic freedom. They are taking their lead from the labor field, and so the steps for self-protection tend to be for self-benefits rather than to maintain academic freedom.

Admittedly, the state has a functional role in higher education in that it must determine public policy. This can best be done through an agency for overall planning and coordination—a subject that is discussed in Chapter Fifteen. But the state should not administer the individual institutions—as though they were highways. To do so subverts the professional character of higher education. The long-run interests of society require that intellectual freedom on the campuses be maintained.

In maintaining intellectual and academic freedom, the heart of the problem for the colleges is the need for funds. For the public institutions, funds must come primarily from the public appropriating bodies; for the private colleges, support for the educational program must come from private donors. The focus of the problem lies with the wealthy donor and the politically minded legislator and governor.

The requirements for funds have risen greatly, and so the colleges have become much more dependent on donors and appropriators than formerly. This has affected freedoms on the campus. It has tied the hands of administrators in a manner unsuspected by students and faculty. Administrators have felt obligated to press for resources with which to accommodate the burgeoning enrollments and to keep pace with expanding needs for scientific equipment, laboratories, books, and salaries.

The legislators and the governor are elected by the people

and must stand for reelection. Thus, they are influenced by or represent the folk culture, and there are limits to the support they can give to the super culture. They have come to tolerate eccentricities, because they have got used to eccentric behavior on a campus. They take most scientific publications in their stride because they respect scholarship even if they do not understand it fully. However, they object violently to violence when it tears down the structure that the tax funds have provided. They react sympathetically to pressures from citizens—by mail, telephone, or interview—who feel that their rights or their security are being undermined by students or by faculty actions.

The wealthy donors of funds have similar views. Some may be hostile toward attacks on the system because people of wealth are part of the establishment. On the other hand, many persons with philanthropic interests are individuals of large goodwill who take a long-range view of the social value of the colleges. A private college has some advantage because it can recruit this type of trustee.

The college must have funds to survive and grow; the public must provide the funds. The aim of policy formation on both sides must be to create a viable relationship. In part, this means that the institution and its personnel must behave as persons of reason and seekers of the best answers to problems; in part, it means that the people of the community must be kept educated about the social value of maintaining intellectual freedom and academic freedom.

Student Freedom

The college has an especially difficult problem in maintaining freedom for its students. For one thing, the tradition in the American college has been one of paternalistic protection and guidance of the students. The colleges, so many of which earlier were residential, had assumed an obligation to develop the moral character of the individual student as well as his intellectual abilities. Students were subject to discipline, and this was generally regarded as an internal affair for the college. Thus the concept of *in loco parentis* became institutional policy. All of this has faded away. But many parents and citizens continue to hold the institution responsible for the behavior of their children. The institution, on its part, has lost much of its power to discipline.

When a college desires to discipline a student, it can no longer act arbitrarily. Through a gradual evolution of legal opinion, the courts have begun to apply the principles of civil rights to students. Institutions are now required to use due process in administering discipline. This is, of course, a decided protection of the intellectual freedom of the student and of his right to assemble and engage in peaceful demonstrations.

Many colleges and universities are acting consistently with principles enunciated in a white paper on students' rights prepared in 1967. The organizations that were involved in writing the statement were the Association of American Colleges, the National Association of Student Personnel Administrators, the National Association of Women Deans and Counselors, the American Association of University Professors, and the U.S. National Student Association. The procedural standards for cases involving proposed discipline are as follows (*AAUP Bulletin*, 1968): In all situations procedural fair play requires that the student be informed of the nature of the charges against him, that he be given a fair opportunity to refute them, that the institution not be arbitrary in its actions, and that there be provision for appeal of a decision. These procedures resemble those earlier adopted for use in cases where faculty were being disciplined, and they are consistent with the requirements laid down by the courts.

During the late 1960s, students engaged in protests, demonstrations, disruptions, and strikes. They wanted to stimulate social action, to have greater voice in decision-making, and to protest social ills such as the Vietnam War and racism. They succeeded in getting the voting age lowered to eighteen, in gaining admittance to decision-making councils of the institutions, and in arousing public sensitivity to a number of social problems. Thus their activism produced some positive results. However, some negative results also ensued. The demonstrations often gave way to violence, which sometimes resulted in serious damage to property and injuries to persons, and this aroused hostility among the public. The use of physical power brought counteracting power, through the use of police, in overwhelming force, and it may have brought police onto the campus as a permanent feature of campus government. It was also observed that, even in the largest demonstrations, the activists were unable to command the support of the majority of students.

The good that was achieved must be weighed against the bad, and this raises another issue—how may the concerns of the students best be addressed? Probably no answer fully meets the need. It should be remembered, however, that a college or university in its essence is an institution of reason. Its method is the rational one. It exists to explore issues and to find answers. It therefore should be actively searching for solutions to grave social issues. It should not permit its inquiries into these subjects to become obscured. It should develop courses of study that are relevant. It should marshall interdisciplinary resources for research and teaching, and thus avoid the tight compartmentalization of knowledge and action that provides only fragmentary results. These actions are necessary to overcome the charges by students that their concerns are neglected, and to demonstrate to those who have become impatient that progress can and is being made. One characteristic of a college is the ability of its personnel to take a long view of the causes of problems and the time and effort it takes to find solutions. Research and reason, rather than revolutionary violence, is the democratic way.

The American Civil Liberties Union has drawn a useful distinction between peaceful and violent demonstrations (ACLU, 1970):

> Picketing, demonstrations, sit-ins, or student strikes provided they are conducted in an orderly and nonobstructive manner, are a legitimate mode of expression, whether politically motivated or directed against the college administration, and should not be prohibited. Demonstrators, however, have no right to deprive others of the opportunity

to speak or be heard; take hostages; physically obstruct the
movement of others; or otherwise disrupt the educational
or institutional processes in a way that interferes with the
safety or freedom of others. Students should be free, and
no special permission be required, to distribute pamphlets
or collect names for petitions concerned with campus or
off-campus issues.

The colleges and universities should permit students to engage
in nonviolent protests and demonstrations; they should also encourage participation in decision-making.

College administrators become impatient with students
who do not conform. Their role would be a more comfortable
one if such students were not admitted or could be dismissed.
There is another, more socially valid, point of view, which suggests that the colleges should educate these students. They may
or may not be right in their beliefs. To throw them out of college is to intensify their beliefs. If they can be trained to become genuine students of the issues that motivate them, they
will in time learn to distinguish the valid from the invalid. It
should always be borne in mind that their original views may
have merit. Research has shown that the activists are among the
students of highest intellectual potential. The combination of
motivation and intelligence is precisely what is needed in setting
the educational ferment to work. The outcome may be the production of effective leaders for social action.

Faculty Freedom

Considering the influence of the folk culture on the actions of elected office holders, and considering the dilemma of
the college administrators who must find a viable means of raising funds for the institution, it is apparent that it is up to the
faculties of colleges and universities to guard and protect their
intellectual and academic freedom. No one else is as motivated
or as competent to do so.

The faculties must organize for this purpose within the
college, and also on an interinstitutional scale. This subject is

treated elsewhere when we discuss organization for collective bargaining. The most important end to be sought, however, is the protection of freedoms. Because of this, it is unfortunate that the collective movement has become one of rivalry for power among competing organizations. It is also a loss when these organizations scramble to produce results in gaining employment benefits in a manner that subordinates the issue—academic freedom—that should be most important.

One organization, however, has been supreme in defending academic freedom—the American Association of University Professors. The feeling of need among university professors for mutuality of protection arose as a direct consequence of Stanford's handling of the Ross case. This case had a strong influence on the founding of the AAUP. The organization has been vigorous, but also judicious, in its investigation of complaints. It has publicized blacklists of unapproved institutions in the belief that well-qualified faculty would not accept employment at a blacklisted institution. Thus, such an institution would be under pressure to adopt a policy of due process.

The AAUP was successful in securing agreement among eighty-two national organizations of colleges and universities to a statement of principles and procedures relating to academic freedom. This statement, called the 1940 Statement of Principles of Academic Freedom and Tenure, was adopted by the faculties and governing boards of hundreds of institutions. The principles laid a firm foundation for freedom in teaching and added a statement of the responsibilities of the teacher in his use of the classroom and in his representation of the college in community activities. The more essential phrases in this statement are summarized as follows (*AAUP Bulletin*, various issues):

> Institutions of higher education are conducted for the common good and not to further the interest of either the individual teacher or the institution as a whole.
>
> The common good depends upon the free search for truth and its free exposition.
>
> Academic freedom . . . carries with it duties correlative with rights.

> Freedom and economic security, hence tenure, are indispensable to the success of an institution.
>
> The teacher is entitled to freedom in the classroom in discussing his subject, but he should be careful not to introduce into his teaching controversial matter which has no relation to his subject.
>
> When he (a teacher) speaks or writes as a citizen, he should be free from institutional censorship or discipline, but his special position in the community imposes special obligations (to be accurate, to exercise appropriate restraint, to show respect for the opinions of others, and to indicate that he is not an institutional spokesman).
>
> After the expiration of a probationary period, teachers or investigators should have permanent or continuous tenure, and their services should be terminated only for adequate cause, except in the case of retirement for age, or under extraordinary circumstances because of financial exigencies.

Although this statement has served as the guideline for many years, it was abandoned in 1971 by one organization, the American Association of State Colleges and Universities. An alternative, though somewhat similar wording was adopted, but the action raises a question as to whether other associations may also abandon the uniform code.

A problem has arisen because of the trend toward the unionization of faculties, and two of the national unions that rival the AAUP—the National Education Association (NEA) and the American Federation of Teachers (AFT)—have not adopted the AAUP statement. They are becoming sufficiently powerful to threaten the status of AAUP as the arbitrator of disputes over academic freedom and tenure.

The problem is a complicated one, because faculties that have become unionized elect a bargaining agent. This agent is usually one of the three organizations mentioned above. In ordinary course, this agent becomes the clearinghouse for all grievances; hence, if the bargaining agent is the NEA, or the AFT, or perhaps a local union, it may claim the right to handle the grievances relating to academic freedom and tenure. There is a distinct risk to the teaching-research faculty in handling the matter this way, a point more fully discussed in Chapter Fourteen.

Coupled with the principles of the AAUP is a statement of procedures for cases involving the proposed disciplining or dismissal of a faculty member. Each institution should have well-defined procedures spelled out in its bylaws and approved by the governing board. Care in the utilization of such procedures is of the greatest importance when academic freedom is involved because of the emotional controversy that usually surrounds such cases.

Most institutions have a policy of tenure for faculty, the tenure to become effective after a trial period (Blackburn, 1972). Tenure means a commitment on the part of the institution that provides reasonable security in position for the teacher. It is this security against being fired that gives genuine meaning to academic freedom—freedom to do research and to speak, irrespective of the popularity or unpopularity of what is said or published. In practice, the privilege of tenure has been considerably adulterated, because institutions and legislative bodies have yielded to the demands of pressure groups to define tenure as simply the right to job continuity. Thus, incompetents get frozen into jobs irrespective of whether they are seekers after truth.

The difference in situation between individuals who do not have tenure and those who do should be clearly understood. In most instances, before tenure the institution retains the right at the close of any contract period to make a change in personnel, irrespective of the reasons for doing so. This is a trial period for the individual and for the college. Each is free to discontinue the relationship at the end of any given period of employment. When the contract has expired, there is no obligation to continue beyond such a period until a new contract has been agreed upon.

The period preceding tenure should be long enough to establish bases for an evaluation, and short enough to assure that the evaluation will be made and conclusions about future employment reached. Three to five years is a reasonable period on the college level; seven years is advocated by the AAUP as the limit for year-to-year contracts. The burden of proof is on the teacher to demonstrate during this period his qualifications for retention within the faculty—although it might equally be argued that it is up to the institution to demonstrate its worth as a place where the faculty member desires to remain. This statement does not imply that arbitrary dismissal is permissible. This might violate the immediate contract or place a serious taint on the professional career of the individual. There is a need here for the use of objective procedures just as in other cases, but the clearance of the individual does not replace the need to negotiate a new contract.

After a person has been given tenure, however, the burden of proof shifts. The institution has made a judgment about the qualifications of the teacher and has, in effect, given him assurance of a long-term relationship. If the institution initiates action, it must justify that action; it must make direct charges as to the nature of the causes, give the faculty member an opportunity to defend himself, and hold an orderly hearing before final action is taken.

In most institutions this final action must be taken by the board of governors, because they have the charter authority. The judgment to be made, however, is one that is peculiarly within the competence of the members of the profession, rather than of a lay board. The wise board, therefore, will defer to the judgment of the committee of professors that has examined the case. It is the function of the administrative officers to see that these procedures are carried out and that the case has been fully investigated. If the board should find itself in disagreement with the recommendations of the faculty, action should not be precipitate, but the case should be further reheard in an effort to arrive at an agreed upon basis for action.

Two tests concerning the maintenance of intellectual freedom and integrity may be applied to the actions of the individual. One relates to the responsibility to the institution and to the group. It is one thing for a professor of sociology to examine with his students the institutions of our time to evaluate their strengths and weaknesses as a part of our organized society. It is quite another for a professor of sociology to use the classroom relationship with students to advocate dogma without critical evaluation. To do so shows lack of personal responsibility and violates the code of academic freedom.

The other test is whether a scholar retains his own intellectual integrity; the very purpose of academic freedom is to assure that intellectual integrity may prevail. If he becomes subjected to outside pressures that force him to align all of his teachings with dogma that controverts critical inquiry, he may have lost his own intellectual integrity and hence his right to support from his professional colleagues. It does not make good sense to employ, in the name of academic freedom, persons who, if they had the power, would destroy that freedom.

The remedy for subversion is not loyalty oaths. Taking the oath does not disturb the person who is the real menace; but it does create a problem for the person who is conscientious about the principles of freedom. Those who would undermine our society may go scot-free, while the most determined defenders of freedom and the best informed advocates of social change may have to undergo a grueling experience while jeopardizing their value in the eyes of society. Even worse, if our government resorts to police state measures, we set in motion a process of suspicions, charges, and check-ups that gnaws at the foundations of freedom.

University faculties are generally composed of men of the best historical and ethical perspective and of the highest professional standards that can be assembled in any body. Furthermore, they are committed to a long-standing ideal of self-government. The safest course for society, in protecting itself against subversives in the colleges, is to leave this responsibility squarely on the faculties themselves.

One question has arisen respecting the extent to which the professor has need to express his own opinions or convictions in the classroom. Must he be completely objective at all times and never let his personal views show? We think this is not intended. Anyone who has made the study of his subject that the teacher-scholar is presumed to have made must necessarily have convictions about it. Convictions based on this study and research are valuable to students and to colleagues. Presumably such a person is the best possible one to express convictions, because he has had the best possible opportunity to formulate them. Furthermore, it is essential to genuine success in teaching that an individual let his enthusiasms and beliefs show in his presentations.

The difference between this use of the classroom and an abuse of it is sometimes subtle but is highly important. In essence, it means that the teacher, as a student of his subject, must make certain that his conduct permits the members of his class also to be students of the subject. The student must be free from the necessity of having to subscribe to the beliefs of the instructors. While he accepts the knowledge of the professor for what it is worth, the student must also have the opportunity to consider other sources of wisdom on the subject and to formulate his own beliefs in an objective fashion.

Maintaining a Policy

Institutions vary in their ability to withstand assaults on their freedom. Colleges that have governing boards and administrators who are weak supporters of intellectual freedom, are apt to be troubled as are colleges that have inadequate funding. The situation that can exist when an institution has both substantial resources and skillful leadership can be shown by an example. Harvard University was attacked by a prominent alumnus for retaining two faculty members who had engaged in activities of which the alumnus did not approve. He threatened to withdraw his financial support if the university did not dismiss the men. The president wisely arranged for another, equally prominent alumnus to answer the complaint (*Harvard Alumni Bulletin,* June 25, 1949, pp. 729-736). The answer was a strong defense of Harvard in refusing to take precipitate action. Many precedents and statements of policy by Harvard were quoted. Harvard would not be Harvard, but would become some other kind of institution, if it took the actions desired by the other alumnus. After an exchange of letters, the complaining alumnus partially retreated, and Harvard stood firm for academic freedom.

Are the institutions in America in danger of losing their

intellectual freedom? In spite of the risks to freedom in this country, we should not become pessimistic. Here, as in Britain, we have been building a tradition in support of freedom that will be difficult to undermine. We do need continually to renew our faith and support of the principles of civil liberties, so that we shall not be tempted to resort to totalitarian methods in the effort to preserve democratic ones. We should also recognize that as long as Harvard, Chicago, Michigan, California at Berkeley, Oberlin, and Antioch—to mention a select few—maintain vigorous policies on the freedoms, we shall have models toward which all colleges and universities may work.

We should ponder the significance to our culture of having a heritage that supports freedoms. This culture has been influenced by the Judeo-Christian emphasis on the individual, his personal qualities and merit. This emphasis stems in part from a thousand years of gradual development of the concept of civil liberties. Its basic ideal is a democracy in which individual and social rights are harmonized. It has fostered the discovery of fresh knowledge. It has assumed that insights into the nature of things change and that new perspectives on life will displace established beliefs. Within this culture, in spite of sporadic difficulties, higher education has been nourished and continues to thrive.

In view of the social role of the institutions of higher education to explore, advance, and disseminate knowledge, it is incumbent on them to look beyond the immediate problems caused by attacks on their freedom and to insist on the social necessity of protecting academic freedom and maintaining intellectual freedom. Assuming that an educational institution has a conviction about intellectual freedom, it should have a policy that enunciates that conviction. The institutions of higher education function as the vanguard of a free society.

Leadership
and Participation

"Being president of a college or university is undoubtedly one of the most difficult jobs in America." Thus John A. Garraty, a historian, begins his review of *Between Harvard and America; the Educational Leadership of Charles W. Eliot* (*New York Times Book Review*, Nov. 19, 1972, p. 64). "Like a second lieutenant of infantry leading his platoon into a guerilla-infested jungle, a president must be prepared for attack from any quarter: from unruly student commandos, from entrenched faculties sensitive to the slightest invasion of their privileges and immunities, from cumbersome university bureaucracies, from old alumni reliving adolescent fantasies, from Neanderthal trustees or Philistine legislators."

Harvard, under Charles W. Eliot, was carried skillfully through a period of profound change, and America's oldest college, two and a half centuries after its founding, became its greatest university. Among the distinguished universities of the United States, if not of the world, are relatively young ones, such as Chicago, Cornell, Johns Hopkins, and Stanford. Each of them came to the fore rapidly under strong leadership. Among the colleges of liberal arts, Antioch, Reed, and Swarthmore, each under fresh direction and stimulation, rose quickly to rank among the highest in the undergraduate production of future scholars and scientists. Some of the public universities, including California, Michigan, Minnesota, and Wisconsin, under imaginative and foresightful leadership, not only enlarged the functions of the public university but came to parallel the leading private universities in the quality of their teaching and research, including that at the most advanced levels. That there is a relationship between clarity of purpose and vigorous leadership, on the one hand, and institutional vitality and excellence of achievement, on the other, can hardly be doubted (Stone and DeNevi, 1971).

The problem of leadership in a college or university will be better understood if consideration is given to the essential nature of these institutions. A college or university has a dual nature. On the one hand, it is an educational institution composed of professionals whose mode of working together resembles that of a large legal firm or medical clinic rather than that of a governmental agency or a business enterprise. Its structure is horizontal; its activities decentralized; and its aim is effective education and research.

As an operating organization, on the other hand, it resembles any other large enterprise in its need for organization and management. Some of the operations are concerned with housing, food services, offices, equipment, heat, light, a time schedule, housekeeping, and other services. Composed of people working toward certain objectives, the institution employs various organizational devices for efficient operation and for implementation of policy and program.

Colleges do not produce products that can be sold on the market. The principal services, teaching and research, are both intangible. The students, who are recipients of the educational services, actively participate in the teaching-learning process, although they are not paid because they are not employees. Instead, they pay fees for instruction, but they are not employers of the faculty. The students maintain their free will, and when they leave the organized group, they are free to dispose of their own services as they wish. The education that is imparted by the faculty or absorbed by the students differs from individual to individual. Thus, there can be no standardization of product. Although devices are used to test achievement, the results of such tests are at best only indicative of individual growth. There is no absolute measure.

The traditional research function can be described with similar implications. Pure research is inquiry directed toward solving a problem or testing a hypothesis. The findings may be either positive or negative, and either may be valuable. Undertaken for the sake of the discovery of knowledge, research of this type cannot well be prosecuted with time clock procedures. The research worker needs a maximum of personal freedom in the pursuit of his work. Often it is extremely difficult to place a meaningful value on the outcome of his efforts.

A college or university also engages in applied research and in field services. Research and consulting services that are performed under contracts are parallel in nature to those rendered by commercial service organizations. Even here, however, the college is usually motivated by social concerns rather than by a desire for profits, and often the results are intangible.

The educational program of an institution is unique in another respect, and one that is important to the administration of the institution. The college deals with universal questions and controversial problems. The specialists, who compose a college faculty, search for ideas and new knowledge at the boundary of knowledge. A college faculty is an organized group pursuing inquiry into the unknown. A university also studies the whole of human knowledge; the scope of its work is universal.

Collegiate institutions are nonprofit. They are organized by authority of the state as charitable or nonprofit entities. The budgets ordinarily show deficits from operations, until these can be covered by appropriations or gifts.

The dominant employees of a collegiate institution are professional men and women—the faculty. Thus, they are peers of the administrators and not employees in the usual sense.

These professionals are supplemented by service and operating employees, but in practice there is considerable segregation between the two groups. The operating employees clearly exist to facilitate the efforts of the faculty.

A faculty member has a strong orientation outward from the institution. He usually belongs to one or more professional societies that function on a regional, national or international basis. He looks to his academic peers, more than to the governing board, for recognition as a scholar. The college or university encourages him to do this by putting a premium on his productivity in research and writing. His loyalties are divided. In a sense, his security is provided from outside the institution as much as from within, although this outside recognition simultaneously strengthens his position inside the institution.

A college does not have capital, labor, and management in the same sense that a business organization has. The charges for tuition and fees are not related to the market value of the services rendered. The income does not cover the cost of the educational program, although it may cover the cost of auxiliary services. The institution must use persuasion in securing gifts or appropriations of money for ongoing operating and capital needs.

No individual or group of individuals owns the college. It is a public or semipublic institution. A gift or grant of money to a college does not carry with it any right to help determine its policies or to sell an interest in the organization. Except when bonds are issued that require interest payments and amortization, there is no investment of capital, no expectation that one's capital will be conserved and returned. In a commercial, profit-making enterprise, the investment in plant and equipment must be depreciated to make certain that the capital is not dissipated or lost. For its primary needs, a college does not have this problem, because the procedure in renewing the educational plant is to secure additional appropriations or gifts.

Faculty members are employed because of their professional competence. Individually, they know more about their specialization than any other member of the group, including management. They also have a professional interest and pride in the nature and quality of the educational program as a whole. Because of their importance and their professional stake in the program, faculty members have a large sphere of influence in the determination of policy in the institution. Two-way communication between administration and staff is important in any organization, but especially so in an educational institution. There the creative ideas may flow from faculty, from students, or from administrators, or may be the product of interaction among them.

The president functions in a dual capacity. He is the executive officer of the board and of the institution. But he also serves as a member of the faculty and as head of the faculty. Thus, in one respect he is in full command of the organization, subject to direction of the board of control, but in another respect he is one among professional peers serving as the leader of a group. There are many subgroups within a faculty, and so a college is horizontally decentralized to an unusual degree.

Because of the intangible nature of the work of a college, evaluation of effectiveness and efficiency is difficult. For example, unit costs or norms of management have only limited usefulness. Some unit costs can be calculated, but the effectiveness of research and of education takes precedence in measuring the outcome of the work of the institution. The achievement of both effectiveness and efficiency is a desirable goal, but a college should be effective whether or not it achieves high efficiency.

A college or university has a unique relationship with its clientele and with the public. A private enterprise, placing its product on the market, caters to the interests and wishes of its prospective customers. A college, on the other hand, is a public service institution. Its board of control is composed of trustees who represent and are responsible to the public for the conduct of the institution. In addition, there are many diverse groups who feel they have a right to question the conduct of the institution. These include students, parents, alumni, townspeople, church members, legislators, federal agents, officers of foundations, and patriotic societies. It is obvious, therefore, that the educational institution is subject to many pressures.

Finally, a collegiate institution is influenced by tradition, custom, and precedent. Education is one of the oldest of human activities. Universities have existed for many centuries, and some among them are several centuries old. Scholars rely heavily on previous human experience because much of their study is devoted to analysis of it.

Leadership

This description of the distinctive nature of a college or university makes it clear that the principal officers of the institution should have qualifications that are both comprehensive and unique. An experienced businessman is accustomed to aligning operations for profit-making, and so he might place efficiency of operations ahead of effectiveness in education and research. The authoritarianism of a military officer would disqualify him for leading his professional peers. Professors will not and should not take orders in their professional role. Although the president of a university needs to possess political finesse, he or she cannot educate by compromising viewpoints—that is not the route in the search for truth. Several of the essential qualifications for leadership can be identified.

(1) The individual, man or woman, clearly needs to be an educator. Being an educator means having professional insight into the processes of learning, and knowledge of the qualifications needed by the persons who will carry through the educational job. He needs to have the respect and confidence of his associates as an academic colleague, and at the same time he needs to be able to rise above the confines of an academic specialization in favor of the larger purposes of the institution as a whole.

(2) The college executive with imagination can instill vitality into the institution if he is able to propose original solutions to individual and social needs. He should be a keen observer of the educational and social scenes, and a catalyst for the assimilation of ideas and innovative attitudes. And he should be skilled in the dissemination of fresh ideas.

(3) He needs to be an organizer who understands how to

delegate responsibility and authority, how to define the functions of jobs, the interrelationships among jobs and the lines of communication, and how to synthesize the results flowing from the subdivided efforts into an organic whole. In organizing for effective action, it is essential that he understand the role of a group leader.

(4) The administrator needs to be a keen judge of people, and he must know how to recruit and maintain a staff of high quality and motivation. The quality of the results he achieves will depend in considerable degree on the qualities of the individuals chosen for the principal responsibilities and the manner in which they carry out these responsibilities and coordinate their activities.

(5) The administrator of a large and complex enterprise needs to understand communication as the medium for policy formation and implementation. In an educational institution, communication becomes exceedingly complex because of the professional interests and status of the faculty. Students, also, are involved, because they are the consumers of the education. Communication, therefore, must be intercommunication among all parties of interest. An aspect of this is the use of empirical methods for data collection and analysis. Good information is essential as the basis for decisions and for making projections.

(6) The administrator should possess some understanding of finances and especially of the preparation and administration of a budget. Although the staff are principally involved in operations, the degree of their success will depend considerably on the resources available and the skill with which such resources are allocated. The budget is a primary instrument of administrative control. It is the device through which the implementation of plans and program can be effectuated.

(7) Finally, the administrator needs to understand public relations. A college or university depends on its public for students, for resources, and for a congenial environment in which to do productive work. Moreover, the president must be willing and able to communicate to the public the basic principles of intellectual freedom. The president must have political acumen without being a politician.

Because higher education has so essential a role in our society and at our stage of civilization, and because the problems of the future loom so difficult and complex, the colleges and universities need better educational leadership and administrative direction than they have had. We are still in a period of changing conceptions about the nature and scope of higher education, and hence there is unusual need for creative imagination, foresight, and courage in building group morale and in designing and implementing programs. There is also the task of attaining public confidence in the decisions that are made. High dedication of purpose is required, as is a sensitive awareness to the trends in our society that should indicate the future directions of our educational institutions.

Women have deep concerns about education and much wisdom to contribute to policy formation and implementation. They are seriously underrepresented in positions of leadership. Differences in leadership potential are often a matter of personality. The gifted leader has intangible qualities of personality that are not easy to define, and that are especially difficult to acquire when they are absent. The person who possesses these natural qualities, and the essential wisdom, will stand a high chance of success as an administrator; but he is a rare person and is indeed difficult to discover. The prospective leader with the required personal qualities must also have the knowledge and understanding needed to cope with the problems of administering a college. A number of universities have established programs to supply this need. The universities of Michigan, California, and Columbia took the lead in establishing centers for the study of higher education. These centers are researching the problems of higher education and preparing prospective leaders for the colleges and universities.

Participation

In the American scene, the image of the successful organization is the business enterprise. Business is organized to achieve an efficiency of operations that will maximize the profits. Centralized direction and control by a top decision-maker are advantageous. This plan of organization has been carried over into college and university administration. But because of its unique characteristics, a college or university does not achieve the best results in education by the use of authoritarian methods.

The best plan for an educational institution is one that induces participation by the various interest groups. Even in business, participation has a place (Likert, 1961). For example, negotiations are held with labor to define their responsibilities and to determine the incentives that should be awarded them. Labor is more productive when the workers participate in making decisions that affect them. In any organization, the best decisions are usually made in a localized department where the best information and experience exist. To secure these results, the top executive coordinates, approves, and adopts decisions in which others have participated. The head of a college or university can perform best if he views himself as a group leader. The principal groups with which he must work are the trustees, faculty, and students.

Under the American system, an institution of higher education receives a charter from the state government, or it operates under a grant of authority from the legislature. The charter creates a nonprofit corporation and recognizes a board of trustees as the corporate body (Henderson, 1973). Provision is made for continuity in this body through self-perpetuation or through appointments or elections. The charter ordinarily gives to this body sweeping powers for owning property, managing finances and business affairs, and engaging in educational activities. Frequently such charters define to some extent the responsibilities of the faculty of the institution and of the more important officers. It is clear, however, that the legal authority is vested in the governing board, and it is this body that has the final responsibility to the state and hence to the public.

The American arrangement is different from that of many foreign countries, which commonly create a university as a division or agency of a ministry of education and designate the faculty of the institution as the body that operates it. Variations occur when there is a university council that includes delegates from the faculty, representatives of various divisions of the government, and laymen. In some institutions, especially in Latin America, the council includes representatives of the students. It is usually clear, however, that the functioning of the institution is in the hands of the faculty through the dominance of their representation. The American system is a lay board, composed of business leaders, politicians, and professional men and women—many of them lawyers. This method has some advantages, but creates serious problems for the attainment of unity between the board and the faculty about objectives.

The trustees often come to their positions with little knowledge of the institution or of higher education. They need to become educated about and concerned with the basic educational program, because it is their job to see that the institution is adequately nourished and that sufficient provision is made for facilities and staff. Also, trustees are the interface between the college and the public, and they have a responsibility to ease the tensions between the folk culture and the super culture. They should understand the social import of academic freedom and support a clear-cut policy. They must know what the institution is about if they are to do their job intelligently.

One of the dilemmas in organization lies in getting group participation by the trustees. Although they have the final legal authority, they do not have to be arbitrary in exercising it. For example, boards frequently appoint subcommittees and task forces to consider policies and solve problems, and these groups are expected to report their findings and recommendations. These groups should include representatives from other interest groups. Many boards now hold open meetings; these can be used to hear reports, petitions, and complaints. Occasions should be provided at which board members can meet with faculty members, socially and to discuss the policies and problems of the institution. The same procedure can be used with students. Skill in organizing and conducting these meetings is required to insure that while the result is harmony of understanding about the main job of education, the technical prerogatives of each group are not invaded by the others.

As we discuss in Chapters Fourteen and Fifteen, some major issues of higher education concern the governing board—

its composition, its common bias toward the college as a business enterprise, its tendencies toward authoritarianism, its failure to communicate with the people who compose the institution and to involve them sufficiently in decision-making. Some models of governance will be considered. One of them—the group participative model—calls for a governing board that includes as members representative educators and persons who can represent the student view.

It has been said that the faculty is the institution. This is an overstatement, but both by tradition and by the inherent nature of the job to be done, the faculty is responsible for determining the nature and scope of the academic program, implementing the objectives, choosing the content, and making the final judgments about the selection, progression, and graduation of the students. The faculty members of a college are employed because of their professional training and competence for planning the educational program, for teaching, and for research. It is precisely because of their knowledge of educational issues, methods, and materials that they should be involved in academic decisions. If the decisions were made by a committee of the governing board, a state finance officer, or an administrator who was not associated with the faculty, the institutions of higher education would suffer a serious deterioration in the quality of their programs.

Participation by administrators is essential, of course, because funds, space, and equipment are needed. Someone must preside over the operations. Furthermore, assuming that the administrator is also an educator, his leadership of the group is valuable in stimulating the study of educational problems and in coordinating the efforts of the group in finding solutions. An administrator, because of his overview of the program, his conferences with other educators, and perhaps a charismatic personality, is often the primary source of fresh ideas.

Faculty control over the program may lead to introversions that promote the personal interests of the faculty; or their commitment to tradition may make them blind to changing social needs. For example, at Oxford in the nineteenth century, it was the new scientific associations and not the faculty that secured the introduction of science into the college curriculum. Administrative leadership within the faculty, and influences from the outside, are important in keeping faculties attuned to the needs of society. In part, this can be a function of a lay board, or of lay advisory committees.

A faculty ordinarily is much too large to serve as a policy/program forming group. The best solution is to organize a senate, to which the several subfaculties elect representatives. The senate, concerned as it is with all-institutional matters, should include administrative officers and students elected by their respective constituents. This senate should legislate on governance policies that pervade the institution—policies on intellectual freedom and integrity, on the broad allocations of resources and emphases in the programs, and on personnel matters such as the general level of salaries, the criteria for faculty selections and promotions, and provisions for sabbatical leaves and retirement.

Within each college of the institution, it is valuable to have an executive committee of the faculty. Several of the colleges of the University of Michigan have used executive committees for many years and with good success. The dean of the college is a member and presides, and some of the committees include students. In addition to coordinating the other committees of the faculty and facilitating communication between faculty and administration, such a committee may help in making budgetary plans and in working out personnel problems.

When the faculty is organized with a senate or other governing agency that shares in policy formation, departmental subdivisions can devote themselves to such matters as the determination of personnel matters (but not a full determination of them), the procurement of adequate space and facilities, and supervision of various housekeeping details. In curricular matters, however, the department, as a group of faculty with similar interests, may have a special role in planning the major sequences or the graduate program within its area; but this should clearly be within the overall policies as determined by the faculty as a whole. In addition, it is essential that the general education phase of the academic program should come under the ju-

risdiction of the entire faculty rather than being left as the pre-
rogative of the departments that have courses that may be so
labeled.

Faculties ordinarily delegate some of their work to standing committees. These can usually be limited in number and
confined to the following concerns: the curriculum including
general education, admissions, progression and graduation of
students, library and laboratory facilities and their use, and perhaps special events and activities. If faculty members feel the
need of additional committees, they can of course plan what
they want. They can also create task forces to work on special
programs. But there is little need for a multiplication of committees or for filling the agenda of these committees with essentially administrative details. To do so interferes with the effectiveness of the administration, and also with the best use of the
faculty's time and energies.

In a national survey of student opinion about the relative
importance of current issues on the campuses, the issue of student participation in the governance of the institution received
the highest priority (Bayer and Astin, 1971). Student government is not new to the American scene, but the demand by the
students for inclusion on policy-forming boards and committees
is relatively new. In particular, the students have wanted to be
represented when decisions are made about academic policies
and programs and about the institution's positions on public
issues.

A potent argument for participation by students is that it
is essential to the success of democracy to educate young people at early ages in the principles and practices of democratic
methods. In this sense, then, the college, through student participation in government, may become a laboratory which assists in the education of the student. A second reason for involving the students is that they are the consumers of the education.
Although the task of educating is a professional one for the faculty, the students are the individuals who become educated, and
they have some basis for evaluating the results of the program
and effort. They also have ideas about their needs. To the extent that their motivations can be harnessed, the educational

job will be better done. Admitting the students to some cooperative effort in planning the curriculum and in evaluating the teaching also may serve to give the students a better understanding of the objectives behind the program and the reasons for particular methods. Students also criticize objectives and methods and suggest some that are relevant to their interests and needs. A third reason, voiced by some students, is found in democratic theory. According to this theory, the democratic way implies the political right of persons who are affected by decisions to participate in governmental decision-making.

These reasons are persuasive. Students should have a voice in solving the problems of campus life and in planning and conducting the educational program. It is essential that presidents and deans, and the departmental administrators, communicate openly and directly with student leaders. Students want and deserve to have this privilege. It is time consuming; but what is the college about if not the education of the students?

It cannot be emphasized too much that a college or university is a goal-oriented organization. The goals are best identified if there is general participation in formulating them. An important role of the educational leader is to express these goals and to keep them in sight. They should be constantly before the faculty and students, and also before the agencies, public and private, that provide the funds that nourish the institution. Goals, resources, people, programs—these are the elements to which the educator/administrator provides leadership.

★★★★★★★★★★★★★ ★★★★★★★★★★★★★
★★★★★★★★★★★★★ **14** ★★★★★★★★★★★★★

Administration
and Decision-Making

★★
★★

A college or university is organized under authority from the state, with a board of control that possesses the legal authority over the institution. The board employs a chief executive who administers the policies and programs as authorized by the board. By tradition, and sometimes by charter, the faculty have considerable autonomy in planning the academic programs and in their teaching and research. The institution needs funds with which to provide facilities and to operate, and hence is subject to substantial influence from large donors and control by public appropriating and dispensing agencies.

This plan of organization has produced many good results. The institutions of higher education have responded to the demands for more education and have been contributing to the needs of the people and the nation. New types of institutions have been initiated; many colleges and universities have evolved programs of high quality, both in the academic disciplines and for training technicians and professional men and women. But changing economic and social conditions are pressing heavily on this structure of higher education. Many problems of organization and administration need resolution (Carnegie 1973b).

The first is growth in size and complexity. We think of a college as an ivy-clad retreat perched on a hill overlooking a country town. There are a few such colleges left. They should be treasured, because good education can take place when faculty and students share intimately in the search for knowledge and wisdom. However, the institutions with the vast majority of students are becoming huge, and the new ones—of which there are many—are located in the midst of population centers. They contain multiple units and a multitude of programs. Many of these institutions, especially the public ones, are units within a system. The system develops a bureaucracy of administrators, and this leads to complex procedures and much unnecessary duplication in decision-making.

Each campus has an executive officer, and the multicampus system also has a top executive. Each executive, whether president or chancellor, is underpinned by an array of vice presidents or vice chancellors. Down the line—after chancellor, vice chancellor, president and campus vice presidents, comes the officer—the dean—who really has charge of a college unit within the system. But in most large institutions, even the dean has little involvement in the education of students. For each college is compartmentalized into departments. The department has become the operating unit. Its chairman has considerable power, but important recommendations often need to be approved successively by each of the five or more executives on the way to the top of the system structure.

Even this is not the whole story of the complexity of decision-making in today's institutions. The faculty want to be consulted. Students demand to be involved. Interest groups of various types organize into unions or other power blocks, and intervene. Trustees may approve or disapprove. The state finance officer may withhold funds unless he approves an expenditure. An organization that assigns to each respective officer a sphere of authority is essential. But good education does not result when the consideration of educational matters is interminably repeated by pyramided authorities and months pass by before a decision is final.

It also is not good for education when a cabinet of administrative officers makes the decisions about educational policy. The cabinet typically is composed of the president and the several vice presidents. Each of the latter heads up a functional area of administration—academic, student affairs, business and finance, research, and public relations. This is a logical structuring for the delegation of responsibilities by the president. Because of the weight of the load on the president and because his time is limited, he needs to delegate portions of his duties; otherwise he would have even less time for the type of educational leadership that should characterize the presidency. Incidentally, it is sometimes suggested that these vice presidents should be staff rather than line officers, to restore the line of authority from the president direct to each dean who heads a college or other operating unit.

The majority of the men in a college cabinet may be nonacademic. Thus, when the cabinet supersedes the faculty in making policy and planning the longer-run development of the institution, decisions are being made by men who disregard educational principles and human factors when analyzing data. For example, the manager of finances, plant, and nonacademic personnel formerly devoted himself wholly to these service functions. Now, with the title of vice president, he is automatically included in the cabinet and helps to determine academic policy. He may have more influence on academic affairs than all of the professors combined.

In similar manner, the increasing centralization at the state level, or in large systems, causes decisions that affect academic matters to be made by persons far removed, both in their training and in their perceptions, from the places where education occurs.

Increases in size and complexity make communication much more difficult. Good communication within an academic institution is much more important than in other organizations. The reasons are apparent from the earlier discussions of the nature of a college. Because the faculty are professional men and women, it does not suffice in administration to make arbitrary judgments or to issue directives. Communication from the top executive down will not work unless there is complementary communication upward and sideways.

Colleges formerly found it possible to arrive at a consensus of judgments about policy and program. This was ideal, but seldom is possible when aggregations of people are involved. Personal contact is lost. Large groups tend to develop power blocks, each of which maneuvers to dominate discussions and decisions. A frequent result is conflict rather than consensus. When arguments consume much time or result in failures to agree, the door is opened for the growth of power at a higher level in the hierarchy. If academic policy is to remain in the hands of faculty, solutions to the problems of gaining consensus and reducing conflict must be found.

In some other aspects the colleges are losing some of their autonomy. For example, they formerly had substantial authority over their students and faculties. They had the power over admissions, hiring, discipline, and dismissal. They could act in arbitrary ways. But the law is changing that. Laws have been enacted in several states, and by the Congress, that make it illegal to discriminate in admissions or employment on grounds of race, creed, color, sex, or national origin. And federal agencies, when making grants of funds, now have legislative authorization to withhold allocations where it appears that equality of opportunity is not maintained. This brings pressure on the institutions to conform in policies about admissions. Colleges formerly were *in loco parentis* with their students. The courts, however, have been defining the procedures by which the colleges must protect the civil liberties of their students and faculties. The law of tort responsibility has been extended to nonprofit institutions. The rules of the National Labor Relations Board have been applied to agreements for collective bargaining. And colleges and universities must conform to conditions imposed by such governmental agencies as the National Institute for Education in order to obtain grants for research.

The institutions have been pressured—from within as well

as without—to become more and more standardized. Teachers at two-year colleges move into narrowly defined departments that imitate a university structure; faculties at regional colleges work to have the college become a complex university on an elite level and with doctoral programs; professors in professional schools strive to emulate a prestigious model for that particular type of school. Externally, the numerous accrediting agencies and professional organizations develop professional standards and evaluative criteria that demand conformance from the departments and schools, often at the loss of distinctiveness. In allocating funds, state and federal agencies make their judgments on the basis of data that are uniform and formulas that are easy to apply. These pressures take the course of least resistance. It is easier to control and administer institutions that are highly standardized than those that are tailored to meet social and individual needs.

Institutions of higher education obviously should respond to changes in economic and social conditions. They have done so in a big way—quantitatively. That is, they responded energetically when returning veterans applied for admission, and as the rate of college attendance mounted during the 1950s and 1960s. The states and the federal government provided the needed financial support for growth in size. The urgency of quantitative growth has passed. Now the question is whether the institutions of higher education will be equally diligent in refining the quality of their work, meeting the diverse needs in education, and innovating in educational methods. Will legislators, congressmen, and donors of funds recognize and support measures to improve quality and to introduce innovations where needed?

One of the problems of standardization relates to the need of an institution to account for its use of funds. The problem lies in the method of evaluation of the programs. Recently, many universities have been moving toward cost-benefit and other advanced techniques of management (Knowles, 1969). The ease with which data can now be processed, via the computer, makes statistical analyses a logical method. The idea of judging costs by measuring ensuing benefits sounds attractive.

But, as described in Chapter Nine, the intangible nature of education and the results of research make this difficult. Within reason, one can make judgments about the efficiency of a janitor, because both the cost and the benefit can be quantified. But it is not possible to make other than superficial judgments about the quality of a professor's teaching by any quantitative means. The costs may be assembled, but the most important benefits cannot be quantified.

The evaluation of teaching was discussed in Chapter Nine. The evaluation of research can best be made by the peers of the researcher. Cost-benefit data can help identify situations where further evaluations should be made; the more complete evaluation requires judgments based on examination of the quality and significance of an individual's performance, as well as the quantity.

It is essential in college administration that a distinction be maintained between the concept of efficiency and that of effectiveness. A janitor can be judged by his efficiency; a learning experience or the investigation of a hypothesis must be judged by its effectiveness—the degree to which the objectives have been achieved.

Decision-Making

A major problem in administration arises from the inherent characteristics of an organization (Simon 1967; Barnard 1942). These characteristics exist in any organization but are pronounced in a college or university. They raise serious questions about the decision-making process.

At first glance, the organization appears to be what is shown on an organization chart. The chart invariably portrays a pyramid of officers or functional roles that reaches an apex in the executive officer of the governing board. The chart is useful in showing the relationship of the board to the executive officer, and the further delegations of authority by him to subordinate officers. In any organization, it is essential that the top decision-maker delegate substantial decision-making authority, so that he avoids becoming a bottleneck and thus creating delays in action. It is also essential to subdivide the administrative responsibilities by specializations. When men or women by reason of training or experience have special competence in a particular area, and have authority to make decisions, better decisions will be made. For example, the business affairs or the student affairs in a university require as their respective directors persons who have special knowledge of these matters. This plan of administrative structure is necessary for the administrative implementation of policy decisions.

Problems arise when persons who occupy these administrative posts assume that their authority is broader in scope than it should be—when they make program and policy decisions as well as those concerned more immediately with administrative implementation. It should be recognized, of course, that much policy grows out of the way policy is administered, and a succession of administrative decisions can easily determine the nature and extent of a program. The organizational problem is compounded by the difficulty of drawing a clear line between policy for operations and the administration of policy in operations. The busy executive, distraught by the pressures of his office, will frequently get in the habit of relying on precedent, or on his own view of the circumstances surrounding a problem, rather than turning for guidance to the authorities who should be making policy decisions. He may do this in the name of efficiency; but in the long-run this may not produce the most effective results. To understand this point, it is necessary to reflect on the principles that should govern leadership and participation as described in Chapter Thirteen.

It is also essential that the administrators be cognizant of the informal characteristics of an organization. The informal structure is depicted by the way the components of the organization behave, and therefore it may be a more realistic picture of the way many decisions are made and actions taken than is the formal chart. In any case, the informal structure may influence greatly the formal one.

The power structure in an organization may be composed of one or more of four types of power: (1) the power that is recognized as having legitimate authority; (2) the power that is derived by expertness as authority; (3) the power exercised by individuals or groups whom the decision-makers habitually consult or use as referents for opinion; and (4) the power that has accrued to persons, often of charismatic personality, who lead power blocks. Each of these sources of power needs a brief explanation.

Legitimate authority derives from the delegation of authority by those who have the legal power to confer it. This power stems from the governing board, because it is the board that is given the legal authority and responsibility by the state. It is this authority that is usually expressed by an organization chart. However, to be most effective, the authority must be recognized by the members of an organization as being legitimate. This recognition may or may not pervade the organization.

A college or university has innumerable experts. All faculty are experts in their areas of knowledge and in academic traditions and methods. Furthermore, they feel that they are expert in regard to many activities that concern themselves and the students. Any administrative staff will include dozens if not hundreds of specialists, each of whom is an expert on specific kinds of problems. Usually a segment of the staff is expert in defining problems, gathering and processing data relating to them, and presenting possible solutions. All of these experts want to be consulted when a problem involves their sphere of interest. The problem-solving experts are extremely valuable in helping find solutions that are based on data and objective analysis. When any of these experts are consulted, their advice and recommendations may be so influential as to control the decisions.

In similar manner, an administrator often has friends or consultants, or even golf partners, with whom he talks over his problems and his views about solutions for them. These friends or consultants sometimes really determine what the decisions will be. If one looks realistically at the sources of power in an organization, he may find some of them in individuals who possess no legal or delegated authority but who actually exercise substantial leadership in the formation of opinion. They may have charismatic personalities, they may feel a missionary zeal for some cause, or they may be successful in building a power block—a union, for example—that is strong enough to demand participation when decisions are being made.

Another facet of the sociogram of an institution lies in the networks of communication. The actual networks may vary considerably from those depicted by the chart of communication. Messages may flow as shown by the prescribed lines of authority, but the most weighty information and opinion may flow through channels that pass along the views stemming from informal centers of power. The administrator therefore cannot content himself with issuing decisions and instructions. He needs also to collect feedback about how his messages were received and whom they influenced. He needs to keep his ear to the ground to collect information from the informal network.

A realistic approach to decision-making will be based on these aspects of the power structure and the communication network. The meaning is clear: the people whose interests are affected by decisions, and who possess the power to thwart them or to make them effective, must be involved in the decision-making process. Before discussing models of organization, some of which have the aim of recognizing foci of power or of securing participation by parties of interest, it is important to consider a few more problems that relate to administration.

The first of these is concerned with the composition of the governing board and the attitudes that the members bring to their responsibilities. The board derives its authority from the state and presumably represents the interests of the general public. In reality, the members of the board are almost always drawn from narrow segments of the general population, and often their actions suggest that they do not understand the nature of an educational institution. When the extent of the board's power is taken into account, these deficiencies in the board and its behavior are matters of great concern. Consequently, there have been many proposals for the reform of these boards.

The typical board, which is usually composed of older people, males, and persons from the establishment, is not representative either of the people of the state or of educators (Hartnett, 1969, pp. 19-20). In public institutions, the members are often political appointees who respond readily to the dictates of their political supervisors. Sometimes the board includes as ex officio members the governor and other high state officials whose positions put them on both sides of the fence, as advocates and as judges, when proposals are up for consideration.

Reforms have been proposed, including provisions for a distribution of board membership that would insure that all socioeconomic, minority, sex, and age groups are represented and that some members have had experience as educators. Some advocates contend that the board should include representative faculty and students; others say that the desired effect can be achieved by including some educators and some young people as members, and that these persons do not need to come from within the institution. The need is for knowledgeable people, and not necessarily for persons whose self-interest is involved. Lay experience and influence are healthy, both to counterbalance the self-serving actions of the faculty and students and to inject the insights into social needs that are held by people who labor, initiate enterprises, practice in the professions, and conduct the affairs of government. Our view is that the board should always be broadly representative of the public and should include both lay persons and educators, women and men, persons of experience and youth. Other proposed reforms of the board include clarifying its relationship with the faculty, reexamining its role as bridge between the institution and the public, defining more clearly the prerogatives of the members of the board, and providing for the orientation of new members (Henderson, 1973).

In the decision-making process, the president occupies a key role because he derives his authority from the board. He must cultivate the support of the board, so that the members will back him rather than undermine his efforts when the institution is in difficulties. But, as noted above, there are other kinds of power than that exercised by the board within the institution. There are traditions in education. And there are people with interests to protect and advance, and they help determine what actually happens. Thus the effective president will continuously endeavor to get policies defined and to find solutions that will be accepted by trustees, faculty, students, and others.

The faculty, as educators, should participate in decision-making, but they find it difficult to mobilize their opinions toward this end. Formerly, faculties gathered in town-meeting style for discussion of plans, programs, and student progress. They still hold to this tradition to some extent, but attendance is usually small, the agenda are routine, and the discussions are sometimes dominated by power blocks. As a consequence, the departments have grown in strength and faculty unions are gaining in strength. These suborganizations, official and unofficial, have considerable clout in getting their viewpoints considered. But departments cannot and unions often do not speak for the faculty as a whole. The mechanism for doing this is the faculty senate, previously discussed. The senate, in practice, has been successful in some institutions but not in others. There is still much to be learned about how to make a senate the effective spokesman for the faculty—and also for the students, if they are represented through the senate. When the senate and the administrators share their thinking and work closely together, they can accomplish a great deal. If the senate fumbles, or if the administrators fail to collaborate or merely refer to the senate decisions that have already been made, the plan of having a senate will be only partially successful.

Students have been seeking representation in decision-making at all levels. They have been voicing many grievances about the programs offered and the regulations under which they can act. They feel justified in asking for a voice in governance. During the late 1960s, student groups were pressing for privileges within all departments and faculties, and often for a fifty-fifty representation in decision-making votes. These pressures have been moderated, partly because faculties have been responding to student demands. The greatest progress has come at the departmental level where students, formerly excluded, are now attending the departmental meetings—frequently with responsibility as voting members. In some colleges, representatives of the students may attend faculty and senate meetings. In a few cases, students have been appointed to governing boards.

These moves are being made to gain the benefit of student viewpoints. Students are not, however, being given equal power with faculty and with lay trustees. The inclusion of students makes sense because it enables them to express their aspirations, provide information about their felt needs, and state opinions about good and bad features in the educational process. On the other hand, because students lack training and experience and are transient, it would be a serious mistake for them to attempt to make the primary decisions about the academic program and financial matters.

A college is composed of many groups and officials supposedly working harmoniously toward common goals. However, it is also the scene of much conflict that grows out of the many diverse interests in the college and the competition among these interests for opportunity and resources. Goals may be agreed on when they are highly general, but they are difficult to define as applied to specific situations. That the college is in the business of education all may agree, but whether the department of geography should have the same financial support as the department of physics, or whether Black studies should be taught only by Blacks are questions that arouse emotional differences of opinion. However, if the faculty do not make this kind of decision, someone else will. One way in which some of the concerned groups press their views in the midst of this competition and conflict of interest is to unionize.

Collective Bargaining

Faculties are beginning to unionize and engage in collective bargaining. This raises many new problems for management, and also for the faculties.

The unionization of nonacademic employees is not new, and thus administrative officers have gained some experience in negotiating labor contracts and setting up procedures for hearing grievances. Among faculties, the American Federation of Teachers, which is labor affiliated, has had many campus chapters, but until recently they have not attracted sufficiently large memberships to be influential. Now the movement toward collective bargaining by faculties has spread to a large number of public community colleges, to a limited number of state colleges and universities, and to a few prestigious institutions. The trend toward unionization is strong, especially in the states of New York, Michigan, and Hawaii. The reasons are several: faculty fear the consequences to their salaries as appropriations to the institution do not keep pace with inflation; a new generation of teachers believes that adversarial techniques are necessary in dealing with administrators and governing boards; many faculty believe that unionization is necessary to offset the increasing power of state agencies and bureaucratic systems. Some faculty think that unions have helped labor and also public school teachers to gain additional economic benefits and dignity in their occupations. Still another cross section of teachers think that for idealistic reasons they should align themselves with organized labor.

In a way, the American Association of University Professors has been a faculty union, but heretofore it has existed primarily to protect academic freedom and tenure—as noted in Chapter Twelve. It has used investigations, publicity, and blacklisting of institutions to secure redresses of grievances. Recently, and seemingly with some reluctance, it has begun to foster and engage in collective bargaining. It has been compelled to do so because of the dynamic character of its two rivals, the American Federation of Teachers and the National Education Association. Each of the latter has been vigorous in organizing faculties and endeavoring to get chosen as the bargaining agent. Thus, there are now three unions agitating the formerly quiescent waters.

Collective bargaining between faculties and administration is so new that its impact is difficult to evaluate (Carr and VanEyck, 1973). Perhaps it is significant that, as of 1973, no institution that had adopted collective bargaining had yet discarded it. The trend must be recognized and dealt with. However, there is still time to consider the pros and cons of unionization, and to at least attempt to avoid some serious mistakes.

The advantages lie squarely in the economic benefits and in the establishment of more definitive grievance procedures. The economic advantage comes by way of applying strong group pressures on the agencies that allocate the resources to grant appropriate levels of compensation to teachers and staff. As the systems of higher education become more deeply involved in the political struggles for funds, those who seek the appropriations must fight harder for them. For this purpose, aggressive organizations can apply more effective pressures than can individuals. It is less clear that the union can gain better fringe benefits, because faculty have always had liberal vacations, working freedom, sabbatical allowances, and group insurance. With respect to grievances, a union will support the claim of an individual if it comes within the provisions of the formal agreement with the management. It will also demand an appropriate hearing.

Although unions enable faculty members to bring pressures to gain benefits, mainly economic, they also present serious disadvantages. For one thing, labor-management confrontations are adversarial, and the tradition of higher education is one of unity between faculty and the administrator/educator. Unionization tends to displace educational leadership with labor-oriented leadership. Faculty members, although they are employees, certainly have not thought of themselves as labor. Instead, they consider themselves partners in a professional organization.

There are several other problems related to faculty unions for which solutions are not as yet clear:

(1) To be effective, negotiation must involve the party that really supplies the money—for example, the state. In New York, the unions at the state university have been bypassing the university in order to bargain with state officials. Do the colleges really want to open the door to more intervention by state officials?

(2) Unions operate under the one-man-one-vote rule. Should the bargaining unit include all teachers, all researchers, all technical staff, and all employees of the institution? Will academic faculty subscribe to the transfer of power implied by the inclusion of other persons?

(3) Assuming the desirability of maintaining a faculty-dominated senate, what should be the coordination between

senate and union? Will they duplicate one another and become rivals for power?

(4) Faculty are accustomed to receiving selective rewards —special recognitions in rank and salary. Labor unions have pressed for equal pay for equal work. Can these contradictory principles be reconciled?

(5) Because it takes two parties to make an agreement, the negotiations enable management to make demands also. What will the faculty give in exchange for acquiescence to their demands? It seems probable that they will have to make concessions relating to their teaching loads and their freedom from rigid schedules.

(6) What role should students play? They need an effective means to express their interests, but these interests often conflict with those of the faculty. The presence of students at the faculty-administration bargaining table introduces a third adversarial party.

(7) For what reasons are faculty willing to engage in strikes? And can a way be found to excuse the conscientious objector (on the ground that a strike violates the code of the academic profession)?

(8) Collective bargaining is regulated by law and the rules of the National Labor Relations Board. Faculty should be aware that when they unionize, they become subject to these legal restraints.

Will unionization result in greater excellence in teaching and research? This seems improbable if the agreements are comprehensive and cover academic issues. On the other hand, educational improvement is possible if the mobilization of power within the group results in better financial nourishment for the colleges and universities. Because of these considerations, a tentative answer to the issue of unionization is to organize for the purpose of pressing for economic benefits and improved conditions of work, but to protect against union intrusion into the academic sphere. Unions are doubtless here to stay. It is therefore up to the educators to find a viable role for the unions within the colleges and universities.

Possible Models

The administrative problems that have been analyzed above point to the need for a model of organization that takes account of the distinctive nature of educational institutions. As noted above, the structure and methods that have been used are the same as, or adaptations of, those used in business enterprise. The trend is toward the more complete utilization of business philosophy and methodology. This will produce inferior education. In addition, we question whether the consequences of business management are so good for society that all institutions should emulate the practices. American business in the 1970s, with its conglomerates, its plastic products, its offensive advertising, and its hunger for profits, is greatly in need of reorientation to the real needs of people. These assertions are, of course, controversial, and it is not within the scope of this book to analyze what has been happening to American business. But is there any good reason why systems of colleges and universities should be managed like conglomerates? Although models for educational management may be described in various ways, it will define the issue if we suggest three possible models for consideration.

The first model is the authoritarian type. It is essentially a bureaucracy (in Max Weber's terms), with the power vested at the top of a hierarchy of staff, and with delegations of responsibility to various levels of officers, each of whom is subject to directives from his immediate superior. The flow of communication—goals, plans, programs, orders—is primarily downward, although reports are received from below. This model was inherited from the days of kings and is used in business, where the top man is the "boss."

The plan has undergone modification through the introduction of scientific management, which has replaced the boss's intuitive guesses with decisions based on the analysis of data. Modification has been necessitated, in part, by the rising strength of organized labor, which has demanded a voice in determining the conditions of employment. However, the theory remains the same.

A college has a governing board, and often a charter that implies an authoritarian type of administrative structure. The legal structure will be difficult to change, but until that happens the perceptions of what needs to take place within the structure can be modified. However, the trend is in the direction of implementing the authoritarian model even more fully.

A second possible model is of governance as mediation among subgroups. A college encompasses many such groups. Some of them operate as entities and others are composed of cross sections of the personnel of the institution. Each has its own interests and strives to attain sufficient power to accomplish its ends. Thus, much competition and conflict are generated. A relatively new phenomenon for the campus is the use by subgroups of tactics of dissent and disruption. Each group endeavors to impose its will through aggressive, overt actions. Among these activities is the strike.

A *modus vivendi* is obtained through negotiation and agreement. The administrator may be described as the arbitrator and coordinator of these conflicting interests and demands (Kerr, 1963). If the college is conceived of as a loose confederation of groups, each with a degree of autonomy, then a large amount of administrative energy must be devoted to mediation. To some degree this does describe the actual institution and what happens there. For example, when unions exist on the campus, collective bargaining is necessary. But will this type of administration, even in a large, complex university, produce a viable and effective program?

A third possible model may be drawn from recent theory relating to organization (Likert, 1961). It is the group participative plan. The assumptions of this model are that a college or university is an organization with a variety of goals, that it requires reasonable unity as to goals, and that it is composed of professional men and women, and students, who voluntarily associate with each other because of commitment toward the overall goals.

Colleges and universities have a strong tradition of collegial spirit and action. When one looks at the classroom or laboratory where education and research take place, it is clear that the professor must play a strong role in determining goals and methods. It can also be contended that, because the student is the learner, he will do a better job of learning if he helps map out the goals and participates in determining the methods. Hence it can be reasoned that professors, and to a lesser extent students, should have wider participation in determining the overall goals, the program, and the evaluation procedures.

Traditionally and often legally, through provision in the charter, faculty bodies are given much authority over the academic program and over the progression and graduation of students. The academic administrators usually are members of the faculty, and the president or dean presides. These officers have responsibilities of leadership within the faculty and institution.

Student governments exist on most American campuses, but often deal only with somewhat peripheral matters. Difficulties arise because authority has not been sufficiently delegated to enable the student government to assume genuine responsibility. Furthermore, administrators maintain a paternalistic supervision over its activities. The participative plan calls for the direct involvement of students, rather than student involvement through a parallel organization.

The group participative model of governance is in accord with some of the best traditions and expectations in American higher education. The plan implies the formation of an organizational structure through which participation of individuals or of representatives from subgroups may assume genuine responsibility as part of the decision-making process. People like to have the feeling that they belong, that they are essential and important members of a group, that their interests are understood, and that their opinions count. The morale of the total organization depends to a considerable extent on the satisfaction of the members of the organization, and good morale is essential for securing optimal results in education. The group participative theory thus answers some psychological and sociological needs.

When there has been participation in establishing goals, the motivations of those participating will be increased and this will result in greater effectiveness in reaching the goals. This promotes unity concerning goals, avoids misunderstandings, and avoids resistances that occur when intercommunication has not been full and complete. Under the group participative plan, two-way communication is of the essence. Parallel to this is the principle that the best decisions are made at the locale where the best information lies. Thus, the good executive is one who fosters decision-making at lower levels and who works primarily at the policy level. This enables the executive to put emphasis on leadership, as distinguished from management. Still another principle of relevance here is that productivity is superior when roles within an organization are mutually supportive rather than competitive or hostile.

The group participative plan does not involve complete democracy, despite the fact that it is often described as so doing. It is not a plan under which everyone votes on every decision. Instead, in implementing the plan, a method must be found for streamlining the participation in decision-making. This is a problem, because it is difficult to assure genuine representation for all parties. Rensis Likert (1961, pp. 113-115) has suggested that the administrative structure can be woven together through interlinking pins. By this he means that each subgroup shall have a representative in the next higher functional group.

Another way of describing the organizational structure is to think of overlapping circles. The individual circles comprise the governing board, the president, the administrative staff, the faculty or faculty groups, and the student body. The circle implies group interaction and consensus.

Of the three models described, the group participative plan takes the best account of the complexity of individual and group interests. It is the best means of resolving problems that arise because of influences that come from the sociometric pattern, from the processes of informal communication, and through the utilization of different forms of power exercised by individuals and subgroups. The group participation plan is an orderly pattern for the involvement of people in relation to their interests and their abilities to contribute, with all efforts coordinated by the administration and the final power appropriately vested in the governing board.

Interinstitutional
Coordination,
Multicampus Systems

★★
★★

Along with the tremendous growth in enrollments and in numbers of institutions have come many shifts in organization: from
private to public, from rural to urban, from a pattern of decentralization to greater centralization, from unrestricted competition to functional identification and interinstitutional collaboration, from relative autonomy to strong state intervention and
federal influence. Some of the trends of change are a natural
result of the new conditions; but they have brought problems.

The morale of private colleges and universities is low. The
United States had relied heavily on them. In 1784, in New
York, a major decision of public policy was made—to retain
Kings College (Columbia) as a private institution rather than
make it a state college, and to promote the interest of the state
by establishing the Board of Regents of the University of the

State of New York. The latter was to be an affiliating and examining agency under which all colleges would be chartered and supervised—the first of the state planning-coordinating boards. The colleges, however, would possess a high degree of autonomy in operation.

During subsequent decades, the private colleges and universities flourished, in New York and in most other states as well. Prior to 1900, the private colleges enrolled the majority of students. As of 1950, the ratio was about 50 percent private and 50 percent public. But after that date, surging enrollments from the lower socioeconomic segments of the population and rising costs of operations rapidly diminished the relative standing of the private institutions. In 1973 they enrolled only one-fourth of the students.

This shift in the share of the market, and to some extent in prestige, has been difficult for the private colleges to accept. But the shift has really been from elitism in higher education to egalitarianism. It is the public institution, relying much less on tuitions for its income, and with nonrestrictive policies on admissions, that opens its doors wide to the new types of students.

A possible solution to the financial plight of the private colleges would be to make grants of public funds to private institutions. This has been done in several states, and has been justified as an inexpensive way to get additional facilities for the state and to assist the private colleges to use theirs more fully. The federal government has also included the private institutions in some appropriations for facilities, research, and student aid. Some advocates of subsidization from public funds contend that the private colleges render a public service and therefore should receive general support. But this is a controversial point. Moreover, prohibitions in some state constitutions and the federal principle of the separation of church and state make grants of outright subsidies unconstitutional.

Constitutions can be amended. But is it in the interest of the private sector to become dependent on public subsidy? The short-term advantage must be weighted against the long-run effects. Financial dependence seems inevitably to lead to controls that limit freedom. The historic contributions of the private colleges and universities have been great. Such institutions as Harvard, Cornell, Georgetown, Amherst, Bryn Mawr, Reed, and Oberlin have been centers for experimentation in education, excellence in teaching, and the preservation of academic freedom. Innumerable private colleges, many of them small and church related, have maintained environments that have had strong appeal to students and their parents. Much original and outstanding research has taken place at institutions such as Massachusetts Institute of Technology and the University of Chicago. It seems plausible that freedom from governmental controls has been a factor in producing these achievements. In any event the trend among public institutions is toward intervention by politicians, and toward a standardization of organization and of programs. The private institutions, by preserving their independence, can resist these trends. They need a fresh concept of role, in which their freedom is used to produce distinctive achievement. Distinctiveness of goals is much more important to society, to these institutions, and especially to their students, than is mere growth in size. One of the hazards to effective education lies in the trend of too many institutions getting too big.

Trends and Issues

Two developments in public higher education account for much of the huge increase in enrollments. The most dynamic development has been the rise of the public community college. The other has been the establishment of regionally placed colleges and universities with comprehensive programs, many of them outgrowths of teachers' colleges. Advanced degree programs have also multiplied in number and grown in size.

The issue of the role for the community college was debated fiercely at the close of World War II. Leading educators spoke out about maintaining academic standards. The President's Commission on Higher Education, reporting in 1948, recommended, as national policy, a large expansion of the two-year college program. This was to be a means of opening additional opportunities to youth and adults. The commission recommended that the institutions be comprehensive instead of merely giving the first two years of the usual four-year program, and that they be called community colleges instead of junior colleges. In subsequent years the movement developed rapidly. It will continue to do so because it is clear that youth now plan for fourteen years of school, rather than twelve or eight as in earlier generations.

Some revolutionary ideas about higher education have been advocated. One such idea proposes that higher education should not be confined to two-, four-, or seven-year packages, and suggests that instead the college years should be open for alternation between career preparation and employment. Following a period of work, homemaking, or professional practice, the individual should be able to return to college or university for further study. Or perhaps he should do so merely to satisfy the urge for more knowledge—the kind of urge that comes with greater maturity. The public community colleges already have large enrollments in continuing education. Some have opened special programs for the benefit of women who at age thirty or forty become motivated to resume a career or discover fresh intellectual interests. This revolution in the structuring of education presents unusual opportunities for the community colleges because they are so accessible.

The regional state colleges and universities have similar opportunities to serve their regions, but the trend is otherwise. The faculties want to emulate those of prestigious universities, and the boards of these systems generally do not encourage departures from conformity. These institutions face grave issues. Should they continue to develop standardized programs? Or, as an alternative, should they design new programs based on empirical studies of their own regions? And to what extent should they launch graduate programs and engage in research?

State teachers colleges were originally placed so that each would serve a geographical region. This distribution of the training programs was intended to result in more effective staffing of the schools of each area. Later, when the colleges were converted to comprehensive universities, faculty members were recruited who would broaden the scope of the programs. Presidents often were chosen because they were advocates of the traditional liberal arts. Both professors and presidents worked to shed the teachers college image in favor of one that would be respected by the academic profession. One such president expressed pride in the events that were "gradually making people forget the college's proletarian background," and in the fact that the institution was getting away from being a streetcar college. The faculty members were encouraged to publish in order to gain academic recognition, and faculty demanded the right to grant doctoral degrees. One inevitable result was the tightening of the admission requirements, and these became barriers to residents of the community. In one such institution, for example, the percentage of Black students was cut from 12 percent of the student body to 4 percent. The Blacks saw this as a move by the establishment to exclude them from the only low-cost, senior college to which they could commute.

The regional public institutions turned toward ivy-clad seclusion, as another president put it, and thus drifted away from community involvement. The problem is how to reverse these trends. It seems clear that the regional colleges and universities should take account of community interests and needs. It is also manifest that the need for additional advance graduate programs is lacking, as are the monetary resources to support them. The answer lies in identifying the roles of these institutions, and in reorienting their faculties toward fulfilling those roles.

The enrollments at the graduate level show a strong trend upward, and this will continue. However, the number and types of graduate programs should be more carefully planned and controlled. As noted in Chapter Ten, in some fields it would be better for the practitioners and for society to have fewer doctoral programs and more one and two year master's degree curricula. It was also noted that doctoral programs should be high in quality, and the issue is thus raised about the prudent allocation of resources. It is more in the social interest to have programs of high quality than it is to spread the resources among the multitude of schools that apply for them.

This principle also applies to research. Elsewhere we have distinguished between good scholarship as a requisite for good teaching, and research. The implication is that research should be nourished primarily in those centers that are identified as having this function. One trend in organization is for research to become a group endeavor. As a consequence there is emerging a type of institution that is devoted to research. Sometimes it is also engaged in public service, as are the Atomic Energy Commission and the National Aeronautics and Space Administration; and sometimes it is also oriented toward advanced education, as are the Rand Corporation and Rockefeller University. Higher education must determine the recognition that should be given to these institutes, especially for the granting of doctor's degrees. The training received, if directed toward the growth of the individual, could be excellent.

Systems of Institutions

Many colleges and universities have been grouping themselves into consortia as one attempt to solve common problems. An older example is a consortium to raise money, such as the United Negro College Fund. Most of the consortia are composed either of colleges that are similar in type, such as the Associated Colleges of the Midwest, or those in a geographic area, such as the Kansas City Regional Council for Higher Education. These two types have similar purposes—they want to strengthen their images, introduce innovations for which they can secure special funds, exchange personnel, and conduct programs that are more easily financed and managed as cooperative endeavors than as separate ones. For example, the Great Lakes group of twelve liberal arts colleges collaborates in several study-abroad programs, and the Midamerica State Universities Association identifies unusual opportunities on their respective campuses—programs in which students from any of the universities in the association may register.

The idea of collaboration is appealing and superior to competition. The principal drawback is the additional expense. The consortia have been encouraged by special grants from foundations and the federal government. When this support diminishes, some of the organizations may be in a precarious situation. Each college usually makes a contribution to the central fund. Continuance of this item in their budgets will depend on the benefits being derived and the competing pressures from on-campus programs.

The interstate compacts represent another form of collaboration and stimulative leadership. The Southern Regional Education Board, The New England Board of Higher Education, and the Western Interstate Commission for Higher Education are agencies set up by several states in the respective areas to arrange for the sharing of facilities, the joint financing of selected programs, and the study of the educational problems of the geographic area.

System is a new concept among colleges and universities as well as within business and technology. A system is a super organization encompassing more than one operating institution. The consortium is an organizational device through which institutions, for specific purposes, can become a system. The consortium has special value for private institutions because membership is voluntary.

The more common system for public colleges and universities is the multicampus institution. The common types are a county or district public community college with two or more campuses, a university that has expanded beyond its original campus with one or more additional operating units, and a group of institutions that have been placed under a single board of control. Examples of the respective types are: The City Colleges of Chicago; the University of California; and the City University of New York.

The multicampus institution has flowered during the period of rapidly expanding enrollments. To accommodate the growing number of students, public agencies have had to expand the educational facilities at a fast pace. The most expeditious way to do this has been to utilize the know-how and to some extent the resources of established faculties in establishing branches in new geographic areas. A governmental unit such as a county can concentrate the planning and coordination in a single district office as a convenient way to allocate funds and to insure that an overview of needs and problems is maintained. The multicampus organization has been effective in getting these results.

The system with a control board of trustees and a central administration has appealed to the governors of several state because it is a convenient mechanism through which the state can exercise greater control. During the recent expansion of the institutions, requiring huge additional appropriations of funds, it is understandable that the states have wanted to supervise closely the uses to which the money was put. The plan under which a state has a single governing board for the public sector colleges and universities is not new. Indeed, the plan had earlier been tried in a few states, without large success; and there had been a swing away from the idea. But since World War II, the systems plan has been adopted by a large number of the states. As of 1972, twenty-three states had established a single board, and there were thirty-six other major public multicampus systems. For the 450 public four-year colleges and universities in the fifty states, there existed only 164 governing boards (Paltridge, Hurst, and Morgan, 1973).

Is this form of organization a desirable one to maintain? In what form should it be perpetuated? Is there an optimum size, or should the system encompass all of the public colleges and universities within a taxing unit—a county or the state? What impact does a strong, remote, administrative office have on the educational process? What are the respective spheres of authority of the system administrators and of those of the operating campuses? These organizations have been successful and have become quite dynamic. They may be here to stay. Yet, this seems a logical time to analyze their strengths and weaknesses as a means of controlling their future status and further development.

Lee and Bowen (1971), in a major study of multicampus universities made for the Carnegie Commission, said that the principal roles of the central administration relate to specialization, diversification, and cooperation within the system. A central office is able to extend specialized services to campus units because it can mobilize more energy and resources for such purposes than can the separate units. The staff can be especially effective in planning and in allocating resources because they gain a bird's-eye view of needs; they can easily assemble empirically gathered information, and they can rise above the pressures from localized, competitive demands. They can be more objective because their personal interests are not so involved.

A few innovations can be identified that are attributable to the central staff. It is contended by some authors that innovation is more apt to happen through central planning than when new developments are under the more direct control of persons with vested interest in the status quo. Also, a strong board of trustees can insist that the campuses diversify their programs rather than duplicate one another. They have good control potential because they have the power to specify the conditions under which allocated funds may be used. The State University of New York, for example, includes major universities, regional colleges, specialized colleges, and technical institutes; it also has some supervisory authority over the public community colleges in the state.

The multicampus university, as a device for interinstitutional cooperation, functions much as any system would. Continuing education programs, for example, can be planned so that they utilize staff and facilities of all of the campuses, and thereby avoid overlapping and duplication. Many other opportunities exist for collaboration.

A single president or chancellor establishes rapport with the governor, supervises the lobbying activities, and devotes attention to affairs external to the campuses. A resulting benefit is that the administrative head of each campus is thus freed of major external problems and can give better leadership to internal affairs. Presumably this officer can be more of an educator and less of a public relations specialist.

These contentions—some based on verified experience are impressive. Nevertheless, the multicampus institution is controversial. To do their job well during the recent period of expansion, the central offices have grown enormously in personnel and budgets. In one system, it costs more to operate the central office than it does to finance some of the campuses. According to Parkinson's Law, it seems probable that this administrative superstructure will not shrink; instead the members will find things to do. The things that they decide to do will undoubtedly involve decisions over the internal affairs of the respective campus units. This in turn reveals another serious weakness, indeed threat, to education. It is essential in education that the decisions about the teaching and learning be made by those immediately involved. They cannot be as well made by persons who do not themselves teach or confer with students.

The problem of making decisions in a complex superstructure is a grave one. Under ordinary circumstances it takes eighteen months or so to complete a budget. When clearances have to be obtained at several successive levels of authority, the process is greatly complicated and delayed. A budget will not work well when it is handed down in detailed form from a high authority. To be successful in operation, the planning must come up from the operating scene and down from those who know the limits of the resources.

Although a few innovative college units have been initiated by central administrations, the larger job of innovation lies within each campus. There has been much of this, evidenced by the independent study programs, the use of audiovisual aids, the introduction of ethnic studies and women's studies, and the launching of such internal college units as Monteith at Wayne and Residential College at the University of Michigan. But some central offices are more interested in standardization and conformity, and in avoiding public criticism, than they are in innovating. Black studies arose from a ground swell of opinion and in some instances were denied resources by the central office. Requests for innovations are usually appraised not for their merit but as financial expenditures. Furthermore, the paper work that is required when submitting requests for change absorbs an enormous amount of energy that is nonproductive in teaching. The complexity sorely tests the morale of those who are trying to be productive.

Another hazard for the public system lies in the directness of the pipeline to the governor. This has advantages, but if he—or other public officers—want to intervene, whether about finances or about matters of public controversy, they can do so by simply phoning the chancellor of the system. This official, remote from associations with faculty and students, is dependent on the governor, or on a board under the governor's control, for his tenure. The principal hazard, as noted in Chapter Twelve, is to academic freedom. For the centralized office may bring political intervention closer to each campus and to all of the campuses, even though only one has become the center of a controversy.

The principal problem in carrying on effective education is that the central office becomes a super administrative office for the system. This piles administration on administration, in a vertically structured way that is totally unnecessary in education. It also violates a principle of organization of a college or university—namely that the structure should be horizontal and decentralized. When the central office presides over a system that includes both a university of distinction and regional colleges and universities that are ambitious to expand their roles, the program of distinction may decay into mediocrity because of ill-advised policies of sharing resources.

The idea of the multicampus system for public institutions has had considerable political support, because state officials conceive of their relationship to higher education as about the same as their relationship with highways or public welfare. All of these make large demands for funds, and the funds are limited. Some control is necessary, and a system that is directly under the control of the chief executive of the state is easiest to operate. Furthermore, universities become centers of controversy, and moves are made to suppress outbursts that can be politically damaging to the in-group at the state level. Obviously these are problems for which solutions must be found. However, the short-run political interests must be weighed against maintaining the longer-run function of higher education. We should not drift into a state ministry of higher education pattern—the bane of many foreign countries.

In some instances—upstate New York, for example—the

movement for centralized control has been so strong that the state has placed all of the public institutions of higher education under a single governing board with a chief executive office. The single board idea is not new, but the powerful central administrative office is. Other states have created several systems, each one composed of only a few institutions that have common objectives and problems. Illinois is a good illustration. In the public community college field, it is common practice to have a state planning coordinating agency, with certain supervisory powers; but a high degree of autonomy in operations is left to each college, or each county system of colleges. A primary factor in this arrangement is the sharing by the local community in the financing and management of the colleges. The system works well and could serve as a model for senior institutions as well.

It is the role of the state government, as a matter of public policy, to decide what the scope and general composition of higher education should be. It must decide issues, such as the following: Should higher education be open to all youth of appropriate secondary qualifications? Should people be encouraged by the state to continue their education in spite of age? Should colleges be located near the homes of people? Should there be engineering, nurse training, medical, and other schools, and how many of each? What portion of the state's income should be devoted to higher education? These questions are illustrative of the policy decisions that should be made by the political agencies that make the laws and award the appropriations.

The interest of the public, however, is best served when the policy decisions are expressed in general terms—for example, a decision that any person with a high school diploma should have the right to enroll in a college. The determination of how best to educate the student should be made by those who are professionally qualified to do this. The state, therefore, should not intervene in matters of educational policy and program. It is not easy to draw a line between public policy and educational policy, but it must be done.

State Coordinating Councils

It is not possible today for the busy legislators, or the governor, to survey the needs and problems of higher education with sufficient thoroughness and objectivity to make good allocations of resources. They need expert assistance. For this purpose many states have created state coordinating councils or commissions (Berdahl, 1971). Their role is to make recommendations for public policy and to plan and coordinate the general implementation of programs. They endeavor to define and satisfy the needs for higher education, avoid unnecessary duplications, and prepare bases for the objective distribution of funds. These are aspects of the governance of higher education, but not of intervention into the administration of the institutions as long as they function within the approved guidelines that stem from the public policy decisions.

One of the most difficult problems lies in the allocation of functional roles to the individual institutions. Each college or university, each medical or engineering school, accepts a mandate from the state but presently begins to strive to become something larger or different. The control lies in relating the funds to the identified function. This, however, does not work well because of political pressures and lobbying. A board needs to be available to pass judgment on proposed departures from assigned functions.

Another difficult problem is to find a basis for the equitable appropriation of funds. How does the state determine who should get what? The answer is often settled through political lobbying. Some activity of this sort on behalf of the colleges is essential; otherwise the tax revenues would flow into highways, welfare, and so forth. But the coordinating commission exists to develop plans and supporting data as justification for the political actions. The formula is a device for determining the allocations among institutions and for programs. Formulas result from calculations that represent the amount of work done by units and the relative unit cost (Miller, 1964). When formulas are prepared by persons knowledgeable about higher education, they provide an objective basis for primary budgetary allocations. Educators sometimes object strenuously to formulas, but they are definitely superior to the older catch-as-catch-can basis. Formulas pose one danger, however, in that there is a temptation to use them for detailed controls. Used this way, they can be as inhibiting toward good education as are line-item budgets when imposed by a state and controlled by a state department of finance.

The coordinating commissions have a significant job to do, but they have been given wholly inadequate funds with which to function. A state thinks nothing of paying a fee of two percent of the estimated cost of one building to have it planned, but expects all public higher education to be planned and coordinated for less than it costs to plan one building. This weakness in support causes a chain reaction. The leadership is inadequate, the staff insufficient, the prestige low. The universities resist the organization and frequently bypass it. In spite of the merit of the concept, coordinating councils have not been a great success.

The existence of both coordinating councils and multicampus systems leads to confusion of roles and overlapping of activities. The roles of planning and coordinating all of higher education, on the one hand, and of operating the institutions, on the other, should be clarified and kept separated. This calls for a state agency for planning and coordination, advisory to the state government and supervisory over the functional roles of institutions and the uses of funds in carrying out these roles, and also supervisory over institutions that work within the guidelines set by the state but have autonomy in operations. This plan eliminates the multicampus centralized administration. A possible compromise is to have limited subsystems where supplementary planning and coordination would take place relative to sharing resources and responsibilities. The limitation on the type and size of subsystems would be toward getting the optimum advantages from group operations and avoiding the more extreme centralizations of power. The worst solution is to create a single state operating board that displaces both the institutional boards and the planning-coordinating council.

Under the ideal plan, each college or university, or limited subsystem (such as a county system of community colleges), should have its own board of trustees or regents. When an operating board has authority over nine or nineteen or thirty-nine campuses, it cannot properly fulfill its role. The board members have little opportunity to visit individual campuses, to become acquainted with the varying educational objectives, or to make realistic evaluations of the outcomes of the educational effort. In some systems, an attempt is made to secure this result by having local visiting boards or committees that are advisory to the main board. When there are both a super operating board and local boards, the roles of each need to be clearly defined—a virtually impossible task. The local boards supply a need. But if the members take their duties seriously, why should they not serve as the responsible board?

Much of the discussion in this chapter has been concerned with the danger to society that may be brought about through the politicization of the public institutions by state intervention and controls. The solution must be found in properly distinguishing between matters of public policy and those of educational policy. The state has to formulate public policy within the state. But the institutions of higher education should have a large degree of freedom from detailed controls over what they do and how they do it. The Carnegie Commission on Higher Education (1973b) gave much consideration to this problem and proposed the following pattern of distribution of authority between public agencies and academic institutions.

| | INSTITUTIONAL |
| PUBLIC CONTROL | INDEPENDENCE |

Governance

Basic responsibility for law enforcement

Right to insist on political neutrality of institutions of higher education

Right to refuse oaths not required of all citizens in similar circumstances

Duty to appoint trustees of public institutions of higher education (or to select them through popular election)

Right to nonpartisan trustees as recommended by some impartial screening agency, or as confirmed by some branch of the state legislature, or both; or as elected by the public

Right to reports and accountability on matters of public interest

Duty of courts to hear cases alleging denial of general rights of a citizen and of unfair procedures

Financial and Business Affairs

Appropriation of public funds on basis of general formulas that reflect quantity and quality of output

Assignment of all funds to specific purposes

Postaudit, rather than preaudit, of expenditures, of purchases, or of personnel actions

Freedom to make expenditures within budget, to make purchases, and to take personnel actions subject only to postaudit

Examination of effective use of resources on a postaudit basis

Determination of individual work loads and of specific assignments to faculty and staff members

Standards for accounting practices and postaudit of them

General level of salaries

Determination of specific salaries

Appropriation of public funds for buildings on basis of general formulas for building requirements

Design of buildings and assignment of space

Academic and Intellectual Affairs

General policies on student admissions:
  Number of places
  Equality of access
  Academic level of general eligibility among types of institutions

Selection of individual students

General distribution of students by
level of divisions

Policies for equal access to employment for women and for members of minority groups	Academic policies for, and actual selection and promotion of, faculty members
Policies on differentiation of functions among systems of higher education and on specialization by major fields of endeavor among institutions	Approval of individual courses and course content
No right to expect secret research or service from members of institutions of higher education; and no right to prior review before publication of research results; right to patents where appropriate	Policies on and administration of research and service activities
	Determination of grades and issuance of individual degrees
	Selection of academic and administrative leadership
Enforcement of the national Bill of Rights	Policies on academic freedom
Policies on size and rate of growth of campuses	Policies on size and rate of growth of departments, schools, and colleges within budgetary limitations
Establishment of new campuses and other major new endeavors, such as a medical school, and definition of scope.	Academic programs for new campuses and other major new endeavors within general authorization

*INFLUENCE BUT NOT
PUBLIC CONTROL*   *INSTITUTIONAL
                                            INDEPENDENCE*

Academic Affairs—Innovation

Encouragement of innovation through inquiry, recommendation, allocation of special funds, application of general budgetary formulas, starting new institutions	Development of and detailed planning for innovation

Most of the distinctions made in the above analysis are sound. In some instances—innovations for example—the degree of initiative that can and should be taken by the individual institutions is considerably understated.

The federal government has become a major influence on higher education, both public and private. The colleges sought federal aid and the government responded. With aid comes influence and also control over the uses to which the funds are put. As yet the problem is not as aggravated as with the states, because the grants of funds have not been central to the operations of the institutions. The largest and most controversial item is subsidization of research, especially for the military, when accompanied by a stipulation of secrecy. Universities have a social obligation to work in the open and to publish discoveries of knowledge for all to see. One answer is for the institutions to accept grants only when they conform to academic standards for research. Another solution is for the government to avoid tempting the grantees with funds, the use of which violates the essential goals of higher education. In general, the principles that should be maintained in relations with the state should also apply to relations with the federal government.

★★★★★★★★★★★★★★ 16 ★★★★★★★★★★★★★★
★★★★★★★★★★★★★★   ★★★★★★★★★★★★★★

Financial Problems

★★
★★

Increasing enrollments and accelerating costs coupled with lagging incomes have created serious financial problems for higher
education: How much should students pay? How can we assure
financial equality of opportunity? ·How should the financial
plight of the private colleges be handled? Should we expect
large support from private philanthropy? What is the role of the
state and local governments in providing funds, and what limits
do they face? What part in the financing should the federal
government play? How much can the nation afford—or not afford?

In recent years the financial needs have been exaggerated
by the coincidence of several trends. The institutions emerged
after World War II with plants that were deteriorated and to
some extent obsolete. They had had insufficient maintenance
and virtually no renewals during eight years of severe depression
in the country, followed by four years of war. Repairs and
renovations were essential. Student enrollments had been de-
pleted by the enlistment or drafting of the college age youth;
then suddenly they were vastly enlarged by the returning veterans. In the meantime, youth began to apply for admission to

236

college in rapidly increasing numbers. Facilities had to be doubled and trebled in size, and hundreds of new campuses had to be built. After Sputnik, it was necessary to improve greatly the facilities and learning opportunities, and also the research, in the technological areas of knowledge—and these were expensive areas. Faculty salaries had been neglected during the long period of impoverishment and needed to be brought into line with other wage and salary trends. More recently, the huge expenditures in Vietnam, an imbalance in foreign trade, and governmental deficits at home, caused an accelerating inflation in costs and a deflation in the dollar value of many endowments. Of all American institutions and enterprises, the colleges and universities have been most severely affected by these conditions of instability and change.

What is the total annual cost of higher education? The Carnegie Commission on Higher Education (1973c) estimated that for the academic year 1970-1971, the total monetary outlay for the educational and living expenses of students was $22 billion. The economic costs are higher than this figure, which does not include the income students forfeit when they are not employed. If this cost is included, the annual total for that year would have been $39 billion. The commission further estimated that students and their parents provided about one-third of the monetary outlay and sustained approximately two-thirds of the total economic costs.

Tuition

It is difficult for a college to cover its deficits by adjustments in its income. Students come with the expectation of remaining two, four or more years. The tuition that is quoted to students becomes the basis for their own financial planning. Colleges usually reserve the right to change the rate, but they cannot do this quickly, as a supermarket can do on its meat prices. Furthermore, the colleges are reluctant to raise tuition until necessity compels the action. So there is invariably a lag between an increase in the cost per student and an increase in the charge to the student.

How much should the student pay—the full cost? a proportionate cost? Or should higher education be free to him, just as elementary and secondary education are? The people of the United States believe in education. This has been evidenced in many ways: the decision to make public elementary education both compulsory and free; the decision to finance the public high school from public revenues; the provision in state constitutions for a state university, and the declared intention in some states to make attendance at the state university free of cost; various actions of the federal government, including the declaration in the Northwest Ordinance (1787) that "the means of education shall forever be encouraged"; the Morrill Act (1862) giving each state incentives to initiate programs in agriculture and the mechanic arts; the granting of scholarships to the GIs; and the financial assistance given under various acts of Congress, including the Higher Education Act of 1972.

American tradition has favored keeping higher education free, or at least low in cost to the students. The trend toward charging tuition at public institutions is the result of recent political pressures. The state institutions have been gradually falling in line. In a few states, the public community colleges and such local institutions as the City University of New York have displayed considerable reluctance, but the trend of yielding to the pressures is evident throughout the nation.

The question of how much the student can and should pay has been considered by a number of economists who attempt to allocate the benefits of education between the student and society. They arrive at various formulas, which suggests that precise answers cannot be found. The benefits to the student and to society are by no means exclusively economic; furthermore, as the student benefits economically, so also does society, from the added increments from his services. But how does one rationalize cost-sharing when some of the most important benefits are cultural, social, and political, rather than economic? Even in the economic sphere, how does one calculate the value to society of having a reservoir of educated people available for employment? The cost of abrogated income during college attendance? How do you allocate the economic benefits to students, between those who prepare for a career with low income (or perhaps no income, as in the case of many women who marry) and those who anticipate a high income?

What is the social impact of charging high fees? For example, do physicians rationalize high fees for their patients on the ground that the cost of medical training is high? Does the accumulation of debt pressure women to seek employment during the childbearing years? What will higher tuitions do to the egalitarian movement so recently achieved in higher education?

The Carnegie Commission (1973c) analyzed the subject from several angles and recommended that students should pay about one-third of the educational costs, that public institutions should increase their charges somewhat in order to reduce the disparity between the tuitions at public and private colleges, and that tuition charges should relate to the costs at different levels of education. Under this plan, freshmen and sophomores would pay less than juniors and seniors; and graduate or advanced professional students would pay most of all. A subcommittee of the Committee for Economic Development supported the recommendation for higher fees at public institutions.

The recommendations by economists and by business-oriented committees should be scrutinized with caution. National policy should not be dictated by the immediate problems of finance, nor by the competition that the private colleges meet. Policy should be concerned with social values, and these values are more nearly a philosophical matter than an economic one. The focus should be: What is best for society in the long run?

Students have been flocking into the public colleges rather than the private ones, as formerly, because public colleges are less expensive. The tuitions have been low, and in some cases free. The fees for other services have been reasonable. Most populous communities now have a two-year college and many have a four-year college near the homes of the students. It is easy to commute and thus avoid the expenses of living away from home. Students can find part-time work during the school year and employment during the summer. These various factors have been making it possible for students from low income families to attend college—and this is the heart of the egalitarian movement. The low income families are not few in number—in 1971, 6.9 percent of White families and 19.4 percent of non-White families had incomes below $3000 (Economic Report of the President, 1973). Moreover, the median incomes of families —$10,672 for Whites and $6,714 for non-Whites—were not really sufficient to pay for tuition and in-residence expenses for one, two, or three children who are attending college away from home.

A possible plan is to charge a tuition and simultaneously provide scholarship and loan funds for the students. Theoretically this plan would enable the youth with little money to go to college. Federal programs that provide scholarships, access to loans, and money to subsidize work opportunities are essential and certainly help. If they could be stabilized, if Congress appropriated sufficient funds, if the president did not withhold appropriated money, and if the students felt it wise to go heavily into debt, the plan might be a viable one. But these conditions never prevail. Some of the states—New York, for example —make good provision for scholarships. The New York program is excellent, but since its inception in 1912 it has repeatedly fallen seriously below the goals established by the law. The history of scholarship and loan programs does not support the contention that they will effectively offset high tuitions. Furthermore loans, if relied upon heavily, are undesirable, because the burden falls most heavily on those least able to bear it. Nevertheless, as the institutions force the students to bear more of the costs, the state and federal aid programs become vital.

Some advocate a modified plan that would charge students a larger share of the cost, which they would pay during the years in which they earn money. Payments of these costs could be collected with the income tax. The burden could be equalized by having payments relate to income, with insurance coverage for disability or death. It is argued that the parent generation now, through taxes and tuitions, pays for the education of the earners of the future, whereas those future earners should bear the responsibility. However, this is another plan for violating the principle that a nation should educate its people. Should our children be charged in the future for the use they make now of water, the highways, the national parks, and also for elementary and secondary education?

Without thinking too clearly about the consequences, we have drifted into a policy of placing more and more of the burden of financing higher education onto the students. This trend is strongly against the social interest. It should be stopped —now.

Public Funds for Private Colleges

Should private colleges and universities be subsidized by public funds? This is an important issue in higher education. These colleges are severely threatened, because their tuitions have become so high as to narrow their market, their endowments have been adversely affected by inflation, and their annual needs for gifts exceed the abilities of alumni and philanthropists to provide these funds. Many foreign countries, Great Britain, for example, include the private institutions in the grants of funds. Oxford and Cambridge now receive from the government the major portion of the funds required to cover their deficits. In the United States there are some precedents for this policy. In its early history, New York State subsidized several private colleges, but later the constitution was amended to make such action illegal. A recent attempt has been made to resume the policy by making grants relate to the number of degrees awarded. Other states have made grants based upon credit-hour production. These efforts to relate the state funds to the service rendered to students have been designed to avoid the constitutional restrictions. This is a makeshift approach of dubious constitutionality and indicates that our historic policy needs careful reexamination.

States do legitimately encourage private institutions in some ways. The colleges are exempt from taxes on their plants. People may make gifts to them that can be deducted from income when calculating their income tax. Students may use public scholarship money at private colleges. The state and federal governments make money available to build student housing and some other facilities. Research is contracted for with the understanding that the institution may charge a percentage for use of facilities and for overhead. Efforts such as these are in accord with the principle that diversity among institutions is socially desirable. When private colleges possess vitality and freedom, they add an important element in diversity. They also share in providing opportunities for students and thus to some extent relieve the public agencies of this burden.

The essence of the matter lies in the relation of subsidization to control. This subject has been discussed in another context in Chapter Twelve. If the private institutions are to be free from public constraints and are to strive for distinctiveness in programs, they need to guard their independence zealously. It is in the public interest that they do so. The Newman report (1971) describes the trend among our colleges and universities to become more and more homogenized, that is, more and more alike. The private institutions are needed in society, not so much to care for additional students, but to preserve the alternatives in higher education.

Support from Philanthropy

When the majority of our colleges and universities were private, and even later when enrollments at private colleges approximated those in public institutions, higher education was well supported by private gifts and bequests. The institutions were fewer and much smaller, they catered heavily to families of elite status, memorials were highly valued by donors, and memberships on boards of trustees (with accompanying responsibility for finances) were prized for the prestige they afforded. Furthermore, the drain of income and inheritance taxes on wealth was not large because the needs of government to implement social legislation and to maintain an adequate national defense were not great. Donors had the ability to give, and they derived satisfactions from making gifts and bequests to colleges. Large gifts—sufficient in amount to clear a deficit, erect a building, or add a memorial endowment—could be secured from a few donors.

A number of developments changed this situation: the

organization of labor with resulting bargaining strength, the introduction of social security and of various social welfare programs, and the greater taxation of large incomes and estates. These social changes have brought about a greater dispersion of wealth. The needs of the colleges have grown so much that the donations of a few, and the grants from philanthropic foundations, although important, are insufficient. Resort must be had to massive drives for funds. To a degree the institutions, both private and public, have learned how to organize financial development programs. The solicitation of gifts from a vast array of persons, foundations, and corporations is a costly but productive method.

The trend in philanthropic support for higher education is indicated by the gifts and bequests to a sample of fifty institutions (in millions of dollars): 1940-1941, $79; 1950-1951, $110; 1960-1961, $344; 1970-1971, $590. The trend is consistently upward, and the amount has increased sevenfold in thirty years. In 1969-1970, a total of one billion dollars was given to colleges and universities; however, this was only five percent of the total income received by them (American Council on Education, 1973).

These funds come from disposable income. In spite of high income taxes, the total amount of disposable income in the United States keeps rising. In 1972, it was $795.1 billion, twice the amount ten years earlier (Economic Report of the President, 1973). Doubtless disposable income will continue to increase, and as long as it does, gifts and bequests can be obtained. This element in finance is socially desirable, not only because of the money that is obtained for the colleges, but also because it affords an alternative in evaluating the work of the recipients. It is good to have people, independently of government, choosing colleges that they think merit financial support. The private college that can muster a strong appeal may collect many millions of dollars to support its budget—as have Harvard, Stanford, and others. So also can the public universities. But for higher education as a whole, the financial burden has steadily been shifting from philanthropy to public funds.

Responsibility of Local and State Governments

Governments—local, state, and federal—have a duty to provide education, including higher education. The roles of the three levels are reasonably well defined, but constantly seeking adjustment. This is a complex matter of political policy or expediency, tempered by the ability to finance. Roughly speaking, the sphere of responsibility conforms to the spheres of local, state, and national interests.

The public community college is a local institution. People can commute to it each day, and adults may attend. Often the community college is concerned with preparing personnel for employment in local business, industry, and institutions. Many community colleges were initiated by local superintendents of schools or by committees of citizens. The people of the community launched the college, authorized a bond issue for the erection of a plant, and taxed themselves.

In some states, however, the state took the lead in planning a community college system. New York, for example, began with six technical institutes and later added five comprehensive two-year colleges, all paid for by the state. With the reorganization of higher education in New York in 1948, a plan for the statewide development of public community colleges, with geographically contiguous districts, was authorized by the state legislature. A formula for financing the colleges was adopted. Operations were to be shared—one-third was to be paid by local people including students and parents, one-third by the local taxing district, and one-third by the state. The local and state governments were each to provide half of the capital costs. This formula has often been cited as a model for community colleges, and perhaps it is; but it was arrived at as a political compromise between the advocates of full state responsibility and those who proposed that all costs be borne within the local community.

The history of municipal colleges is interesting in that they too, were initiated within the local community. As these colleges grew in size and took on university characteristics, they became too expensive to be supported by local revenues. They

also began to provide services—a medical school, for example—
of significance far beyond the boundaries of the local taxing
district. During the postwar period, when enrollments rose rapidly, these institutions were given state support or were taken
over by the state. Wayne State University in Detroit, for example, began as a two-year college under the board of education,
changed to a municipal university, and finally became a state
university. The City University of New York, the first unit of
which was founded in 1847, did not receive state subsidy until a
century later, in 1948. That subsidy was intended to equalize
state support for teacher training throughout the state, the state
having provided the full cost of operating teachers colleges outside New York City. More recently state support has been extended to the entire university system, and reached 50 percent
of the university's budget in 1973. Because student fees have
been kept low, the money supplied by the city is a staggering
sum. Whether the university should be taken over more fully by
the state is a highly controversial political issue.

The argument for local finance focuses heavily on the
issue of local control. The people who are to be benefited and
taxed should have an influential voice in determining policies. A
sticking point in the New York City controversy, for instance, is
the issue of student tuition. If the state took control, it would
immediately increase the costs to the students, whereas the people of the city have consistently maintained a low-cost policy. A
college that is managed by local people may be more sensitive
to the needs of the community and thus maintain programs that
respond to these needs.

Obviously, the biggest local problem in all communities is
taxes. By custom, education is financed primarily from taxes on
real property. Real estate taxes however, cause the burden to
fall on home owners and do not relate to the flow of wealth. In
addition, local communities vie with one another to attract industry; low taxation is one of the incentives communities offer
when competing for industry. As a result, the revenue that can
be secured from local taxes is limited—when the people begin to
feel oppressed, they reject proposals for increases in levies and
for bond issues. Hence, the ability of government to spend is

limited both by inflexible taxes and by commitments that cannot be changed.

In most states, the public community college districts continue to have some power to levy taxes, but to a restricted degree, with the states bearing an increasing part of the costs. With only a few exceptions, the state carries the primary responsibility for the other institutions of higher education, and to some extent for assistance to financially handicapped students.

The Carnegie Commission in 1973 estimated the respective contributions of the local and state governments to the institutions of higher education as $884 million from the local governments and $6,720 million from the state governments. Thus, the states provide 88.4 percent of these public funds. Obviously, the relative contributions vary from state to state, and in some instances the state's share approaches 100 percent.

What should be the responsibility of the states for higher education? The national governments of some countries control and finance the universities. The American tradition, however, has been to keep the control and hence the financing as close to the people as possible. This policy for elementary and secondary education is so strong that it would be extremely difficult to shift their cost to federal control and finance. As has been shown, in higher education there are areas where the dissemination of knowledge and the promotion of research is of primary national interest. Programs related to national defense, to equalization of opportunity, to maintenance of health, and to those areas such as in nuclear energy where the mobilization of funds must be on an extraordinary scale need and indeed require the support of the nation as a whole.

Thus, it is easier to define the responsibility of a state by first reducing the total cost by what the local and federal governments should or can do. In advancing the public interest, the state does the rest—the state has the essential responsibility for higher education. This is because the state is the public agency that is nearest to the people and has sufficient resources at its command to meet most of the needs of the colleges and universities.

Actually, the demands on the states created by the huge expansion of enrollments during the fifties and sixties seemed almost impossible to meet; yet each year the appropriations have been substantially increased. The institutions complain that their proposals have been reduced, but proposals are always inflated so that, after cuts, a viable budget remains. The facts about the generous actions by the state legislatures and also about the local governments speak for themselves. The trend of support has been (in millions of dollars): 1939-1940, $178; 1949-1950, $562; 1959-1960, $1,541; 1969-1970, $6,563 (American Council on Education, 1973).

It is, of course, easier to convince the state of the need for new buildings than for improvements in salaries or for quality programs; also for freshman-sophomore programs than for more advanced and costly ones. The lobbyists want new buildings for their regional campus, and the voters want their children to be admitted to college. The problem for the near future differs from that of the recent past in that it will be necessary to persuade the state to provide sufficiently for improvements in quality and for new, possibly innovative programs.

Federal Funds

According to the Carnegie Commission (1973c), the federal contribution to the institutions of higher education in 1970-1971, after deducting noneducational expenditures for some research and services, was $1,945 million, as compared with a local and state total of $7,604 million. Thus, of the total of public funds for direct support, the federal government provided 20.3 percent. If the research and services unrelated to the teaching are added, the contribution of the federal government amounted to $3,790 million.

As a matter of fact, however, federal support goes beyond the institutional subsidies and is a mixture of many diverse types. The budgets for the Office of Education, the National Institute of Education, the National Science Foundation, and many other agencies are significant to higher education. Moreover, the government operates institutions of its own such as the military academies, Howard University, and some educational programs in the Department of Agriculture. It has been a major source of financial aid for returning veterans to assist them to go to college, for equalizing opportunity for college students, and for students in fields where shortages of personnel have been predicted. The federal government has been a major help in providing colleges and universities with facilities and equipment during periods of emergency need. Actually, an appropriation bill before Congress will ordinarily include thirty or more categories of proposed activities relating to higher education.

The trend of federal support has been sharply upward, as is shown by the following amounts at ten year intervals (in millions of dollars): 1939-1940, $40; 1949-1950, $527; 1959-1960, $1,041; 1969-1970, $3,451 (American Council on Education, 1973). This trend will probably continue for the foreseeable future, although the scope of support will vary with successive national administrations, depending on their programs for the involvement of the federal government. One reason for the large increase in federal appropriations has been the political attractiveness of providing funds with which to equalize opportunity.

The ability to procure the revenues with which to meet the many needs of our developing society lies more and more with the federal government, which takes primary responsibility for collecting income tax. Thus, as the wealth in the nation increases, the government can channel a portion of it into higher education. As the requirements of the colleges and universities mount, the most feasible source of additional funds continues to be the federal government. It can, and should, supplement the budgets of the states with considerably more than a contribution of 20 percent of the total public funds appropriated for higher education. Or, as an alternative, it should share the federally collected revenue with the states.

There are some areas where the federal government might justifiably assume full responsibility. Medical education is an example. The health of the people is a national problem. Many things make it so—the need for national health services or an insurance program, the need to equalize medical services among various parts of the country and among various socioeconomic groups, the need to produce a sufficient supply of health personnel, the need for programs to train new categories of health services personnel, and so forth. The federal government should also assume complete responsibility for a few national universities. A few major universities function on the national level, but their continuing strength in advanced study and research is threatened by shortages of funds and by local rivalries for funds. The need for a mobilization of large-scale resources behind programs at advanced levels of education, and for concurrent research, is great. Federal subsidy of a few such institutions could assure continuity of high quality and distinctiveness of programs. It is time to develop a system of federal universities.

What should be the respective contribution of each of the sources of income for higher education? The question is controversial and speculative, but the projections made by the Carnegie Commission can be posed for consideration. They are shown in Table 6. Among the principal issues raised by this projection are: Should the federal government take more responsibility than shown? Is too much burden placed upon students and parents? Perceptions will vary, but we think the answer to both questions is "yes."

What Can We Afford?

How much flow of wealth can the nation afford to devote to higher education? Or not afford? The best index of what has happened and what could happen is found in the Gross National Product. The trend of allocation to higher education from the GNP is shown in Table 7.

The trend of increase in emphasis on higher education relative to other uses to which the GNP is put is encouraging. The portion that is now so devoted is materially higher than had been recommended by earlier commissions, such as the President's Commission on Higher Education (1948), and predicted by various authorities (Henderson, 1966). The surge in demand has been greater than had been anticipated, as has the response in finances.

Table 6

The Projected Account for Education for 1983 (in billions of dollars, 1970)

Income source	Public sector	Private sector	Total	Costs borne by		
				Families	Taxpayers	Philanthropists
State and local government	10.1	0.6	10.7		10.7	
Federal government	2.7	0.8	3.5		3.5	
Tuition and fees	6.6	5.1	11.7	11.7		
Endowment income	0.2	0.6	0.8			0.8
Gifts	0.7	1.1	1.8			1.8
Total educational funds of institutions	20.3	8.2	28.5 (100.0%)	11.7 (41.2%)	14.2 (50.0%)	2.6 (8.8%)
Adjustments						
Subsistence				9.5		
Student aid			8.7	−8.5	7.2	0.5
Total monetary outlays on education			37.2 (100.0%)	12.7 (34.1%)	21.4 (57.5%)	3.1 (8.4%)
Forgone income (net of student subsistence)			32.4	32.4		
Total economic cost			69.6 (100.0%)	45.1 (64.8%)	21.4 (30.7%)	3.1 (4.5%)

Source: Carnegie Commission on Higher Education, *Higher Education: Who Pays? Who Benefits? Who Should Pay?* (New York: McGraw-Hill, 1973, p. 180, Table E-1).

Table 7

Total Expenditures for Higher Education
in Relation to Gross National Product

Year	GNP Billions of dollars	GNP Percent devoted to higher education
1930	91.1	0.6
1940	99.7	0.8
1950	284.8	1.0
1960	503.7	1.3
1970	976.4	2.6
1972	1,152.1	2.7

Sources: *Economic Report of the President* (Washington, D.C.: U.S. Government Printing Office, 1973, p. 193); and American Council on Education, *A Fact Book on Higher Education* (Washington, D.C.; 1973, Table 73.103).

The question, however, is not what we have accomplished, but what we can afford. The Carnegie Commission (1972a) has recommended that the relationship be held to 2.7 percent of the GNP. They derived this figure by proposing that the upward drive of costs in higher education be tapered off. This, they said, can be achieved by reducing the normal period at college from four to three years and by reducing the cost per student. They also recommended that the high school take over some of the functions of the first year of college. By these means, they estimated that a saving of $10 billion dollars per year can be effected below what the normal trend of growth would produce by 1980. Suggestions on how to save money deserve consideration, but these particular suggestions would undermine some important aspects of higher education. They are not the best answer, or even a realistic answer, to the overall question. Programs in higher education need enrichment, not curtailment. Knowledge does not remain static; it is constantly enlarged. The scope of education does not lessen; it grows.

Because of the growth in knowledge, perhaps the time in college should be lengthened rather than curtailed. In our technological and increasingly sophisticated society, jobs demand more knowledge and more refined skills as qualifications. The integration of cultural education with vocational education needs to be greater, not less. The extent of unemployment among some categories of youth indicates that perhaps public policy should be to keep young people in college longer. The trend toward lifelong learning—extended degree programs, seminars for executives and professional men, open universities, and so forth—is strong. Although some of these programs are self-financing, the facilities and other forms of subsidy need to be provided.

Each person should devote more time to becoming well educated. The issue is not merely how to reduce costs of operating the colleges, but also how to prepare well-educated men and women. When we put a low limit on expenditures for education, it means that we value other things more. In the United States, we have become accustomed to spending huge sums on the military, on space explorations, and on the development of atomic energy. We devote increasing sums to pensions, veterans benefits, and welfare. We spend readily for drugs, appliances, and travel. Where in the hierarchy of values does higher education belong? As we become better educated and hopefully more cultured, perhaps we will make better value choices.

Higher education is a social investment. Some economists contend that higher education produces human capital (Mushkin, 1962; Schultz, 1963). Much of the growth rate of our industrialized society can be attributed to the education of our people. A college education enhances the earning power of individuals. Educated people lead more satisfying lives, carry out their responsibilities as citizens more intelligently, and are more adaptable in the presence of social change. The research conducted by universities is productive of fresh knowledge that relates to the health, welfare, and happiness of the people. A college or university is an institution in which individuals can strive to reach their highest potential as intelligent beings and as members of a democratic society. Viewed in the light of these contributions, the conclusion must be that we devote too little, rather than too much, of our resources to the institutions of higher learning and to assisting people to get full advantage from the offerings and services of our colleges and universities.

Unresolved Problems

★★
★★

If asked what problems they face, most college presidents would first list insufficient funds and too few students. Both are problems that require adjustment in the management of an institution. They are serious; but the size of the enrollment in a college is not a basic issue in higher education, nor is the balancing of this year's budget. These current concerns point however to other problems that are fundamental.

There is no real shortage of students for postsecondary education. If the goal of lifetime learning, now being advocated, is realized, as it probably will be, total enrollment will rise to new heights. The temporary problem for institutions now is to accommodate themselves to the situation caused by expansion beyond present needs. For example, many private colleges, placing the goal of quantity above quality and distinctiveness, greatly enlarged the scale of their operations, failing to recognize that the new surge of students was coming principally from lower-income and disadvantaged families and that the great bulk of them—for economic reasons—would flow into public community colleges.

The inadequacy of appropriations and of gifts has both

short-run and long-run aspects. In the short run, contractual and tenure obligations incurred during rosier times must be fulfilled. And the pressure caused by inflation must be dealt with. A profit-making enterprise, as noted earlier, can raise its selling prices to keep pace with rising costs. But colleges hesitate to increase charges to students continually. They are concerned about the tendency to make tuition so costly that it seriously discriminates against students from low-income families. Many students, furthermore, have made plans for two, four, or more years based on published tuition charges. Colleges can also not depend on government bodies and contributors of funds, who have their own problems in trying to allocate resources equitably; and proposals to levy new taxes meet great public resistance.

In the long run, funding depends on the relative importance given to higher education by the public. Students recognize the value of colleges and have been flocking in, usually with encouragement from their parents. Financial support of higher education has greatly increased, not only in appropriations of public funds, but also in grants and gifts. Since the mid-1950s, huge sums of money have been poured into new buildings and equipment; innumerable new community college, state college, and university campuses have been built; and large additions to existing institutions have been made. People have been convinced of the merit of higher education, and they have been generous. The problem now is to persuade the public how necessary it is to sustain, improve, and further diversify college programs.

The issue here lies in the area of values, as discussed in Chapter Sixteen. What priority does the public want to give to higher education in relation to conveniences, pleasure activities, space exploration, national defense, and so forth? To resolve the question, they need to see that because economic, social, and cultural values flow from the operation of educational institutions, support of higher education is an investment. They need to be convinced that although the percentage of gross national product devoted to higher education has risen, the allocation is still small in relation to the benefits derived.

As colleges and universities have become increasingly dependent on government bodies for funds, a serious problem has arisen in the move by political leaders to take over their operation. Legislators often demand control, conformity, and efficiency without regard to the nature of higher education. In order to get these results, the state usurps more and more of the operational decision-making—a process highly dangerous to intellectual inquiry and to good education. Decision-making becomes complex and bureaucratic, presidents of the colleges are inhibited in their role as chief executive, and the campus becomes a battleground in a struggle for power. The administration of the system, focused in a central office and removed from direct contact with education, grows ever larger in size and ever costlier to support. In spite of these effects, many states are moving toward the creation of centralized systems, in effect making higher education a department of government. Business and political leaders, usually loud in their denunciation of governmental interference in business, nevertheless vehemently advocate rigid governmental controls in higher education. They fail to perceive that colleges and universities, of all the institutions in society, should have the greatest possible freedom.

Unquestionably, the state has a role in higher education. That role is planning, coordinating, and financing. It should deal with public policy relating to the provision of higher education, but not with educational policy relating to curriculum planning and teaching. The problem arises when the state fails to differentiate between planning and coordinating, on the one hand, and operating on the other. An institution, to have quality and freedom, needs to have its own board, a strong educational leader, and a decision-making process for educational policy that involves faculty, students, and administrators.

The prevailing trend at the state level is especially threatening to intellectual freedom. Because of the differences between the folk culture and the superculture, noted in Chapter Twelve, there is continual tension between higher education and the general public. Fresh ideas and criticisms of established mores are resisted by the public. But many students and faculty today question the values that prevail in our society and feel a duty to do so. Often, the response of the state, when power is highly concentrated, is to suppress utterances which do not accord with prevailing beliefs. Through the organizational device of a controlled, centralized system, the state finds it increasingly easy to penalize the institution that does not conform—a good reason why state planning and coordinating boards should not be turned into ministries of higher education.

Intellectual freedom also needs attention within the colleges. When gangs of students at some universities invaded classrooms to threaten professors who were thought not to be teaching the right viewpoints, faculty members divided ideologically instead of uniting in support of the integrity of the classroom. If intellectual freedom is to prevail—and indeed if the best education in all forms is to be provided—an institution must possess internal unity arrived at through rational discussion. When faculty members polarize over goals, communication decreases or becomes invective; the president, failing to exercise leadership, has not involved faculty members and students sufficiently in a dialogue about educational policies and programs. Organizational structures must be created that involve faculty and students in policy and program determination.

In view of the exterior pressures on the colleges, represented by the growing concentration of power in remote bureaucracies and politically dominated offices, faculty members must organize for self-protection and advancement. It is not only the individual scholar who needs protection today, but equally the whole profession of college teachers. Large-scale organization has thus become necessary, but it is not yet clear which type of organization will prevail—the professional one or the trade union. Labor-oriented unions, more than professional organizations, have sophisticated skills for confronting centralized authority. But although college professors have much in common with labor, they serve society in a uniquely different way.

In addition to defending themselves as scholars, faculty members must be ready to defend and promote the institutions of higher education vigorously. Some of this responsibility for protecting and promoting colleges and universities also belongs to the governing boards. The persons who decorate these boards however conventionally do not have good insights into education. Their interests commonly lie with the taxpayers, and their protective efforts are on behalf of the taxpayers rather than the institutions. It is difficult for the institution, while appealing for funds, to advocate freedom from political and moral restraints. For this reason advocacy of freedoms must come from organizations of individuals—the professors and the governing boards *if* these boards have a good perspective on the relative importance of higher education and their role as advocate.

In order to achieve this perspective, the boards must be reformed. For one thing, their members typically do not represent the public any more than they represent the institution itself. Moreover, they act as though a college were a business enterprise. Colleges are not businesses. (The ways in which they differ were pointed out in Chapter Thirteen.) In essence, colleges convert tangible resources into intangible products, and the organization theory to which many board members are accustomed is inappropriate for this task. To achieve effectiveness in education and research, a college needs to include its professional staff in decision-making and establishment of goals and objectives, with the governing board playing a role also. This process requires communication among all parties from the board to the students. The best model is the group participative one discussed in Chapter Fourteen.

Another basic problem within institutions lies in the character and quality of instruction. Three necessary changes come immediately to mind (and there are many more): increased training in inductive reasoning through problem-solving and in use of the tools of empirical research (so that students can help find solutions to pressing social problems); increased practical experience (so that students will find education relevant and be able to relate theory to practice); and increased training in the use of computers (so that students can study complex problems and gain experience in the interdisciplinary teamwork which computers can facilitate).

Changes in the character of instruction must always be made however in the context of the overall purpose of the institution. In the 1960s, many teachers colleges, which were regionally placed, service-oriented institutions, some with outstanding reputations in their field, shifted emphasis to the liberal arts disciplines, usually with graduate and research programs. The diversification of programs was fine; the attempt to emulate the university, however, distorted seriously the roles of these institutions. Here we have the issue of purpose: Were the colleges to be intellectually elite institutions, or were they established to respond to social need?

Part of the problem arises from the perceptions of faculty. By and large, faculty members are discipline oriented, and their judgments reflect this bias. Furthermore, the incentive to secure recognition by scholarly societies and by the college itself causes faculty members to emphasize research and writing at the expense of undergraduate teaching. But most of them cannot obtain the sought-after prestige, and the result is frustration. We are not condemning research and writing, although we find little genuine evaluation of writing for its quality or its social contribution, but we believe that professors misconceive their basic role. This problem should be attacked by a reassessment of standards by professional bodies and accrediting associations; a reevaluation by colleges of their own work; a revision of the incentives given to faculty; and a change in priorities so that research is given its rightful place, but that teaching and counseling are recognized as the primary functions.

Colleges need to give consideration also to human values, partly because of the rate at which technological progress has been made. The impact of scientific discoveries has been accelerated, but scientists have failed to concern themselves with the total effects on humanity, as illustrated in the prosecution of the Vietnamese war, in the pollution of our environment, and in the growing disparity between the poor and the affluent. Also, in spite of tremendous advances in knowledge about diseases, the health of large segments of our population is seriously deficient when compared with health in other countries that have good medical knowledge. Colleges should emphasize human values also to counteract the overwhelming incentives for material gain in our society. The graduates of our law schools, if those who surrounded President Nixon are examples, have been terribly deficient in ethical training and in sensing the duty of a public servant to the public. When professional schools emphasize financial success rather than human welfare, the effects poison our social fabric.

It is therefore a good sign that within the professions a new school of thought about values is arising. A few medical schools, for example, have established internships in community centers so that students can study social and environmental effects on health. Many medical schools have added the behavioral sciences both as a prerequisite and in their own curricula. Innovations similar in purpose are beginning to be found in such schools as architecture, business administration, and engineering. New programs in architecture give consideration to the environmental impacts of area planning and building design; some business schools analyze the economic consequences of business decisions; progressive schools of engineering emphasize the conservation and management of natural resources rather than their exploitation.

Events of the past few years have raised sharp questions not only about professional education but also about liberal education and its identification with Western culture. We are having to discard the melting pot concept, in which immigrants were converted to the English-Western model. Blacks have made us realize that the melting pot has not applied to them. And it has not applied to Chicanos, Orientals, and American Indians. As a consequence, ethnic studies have now been introduced at several hundred colleges, a remarkable development which has made us increasingly aware of our neglect of non-Western cultures. This neglect is all the more glaring because of the manner in which the United States has moved into the world scene following two world wars.

However, although liberal education can be defined by the Western subject matter taught, it can also be defined by the ultimate product, the cultured, well-educated man. In Chapter Two criteria for a liberal education were proposed: increasing literateness and articulateness; increasing knowledge about oneself, one's physical world, and one's social environment; providing a sense of values—moral, esthetic, religious, and social; and widening horizons through an understanding of the relationship of the part to the whole. These criteria have applicability to all cultures. Using this approach, educators should be able to construct a curriculum and related experiences for students that define problems for study and research and that help students uncover wisdom wherever in the world it might be found. For general education purposes, the cultures of the world can be synthesized and studied. This is the large task that lies ahead for the teachers in liberal education.

Joining the minorities in demanding a fresh approach to their education is the majority group—women. It is no myth that higher education has been male oriented and has discriminated against women. And only recently have the barriers to their employment in male-dominated occupations and professions been partially lowered. Institutions are beginning to revise admission practices and the often unstated requirements for degrees, especially graduate degrees. A number of colleges have also introduced women's studies to give women a new perspective on their identity, role, image, and socialization.

The desires of students have been felt in other areas too. One of the consequences of the rapid growth of the 1960s was that administrative attention became focused on the accommodation of numbers of people in the aggregate. Students had to be housed, registered, and enrolled in classes, and their accumulating credits counted. In the midst of this busywork, students demonstrated their unhappiness with the numbers game, and they also expressed concern with the lack of relevance they sensed in their education.

One result of their demands for relevance is the present tendency to vocationalize higher education. We are apprehensive about this trend because we believe that education needs to deal not solely with preparing people for work but also with facilitating personal growth, appreciation of the environment, analysis of contemporary society, knowledge of various cultures, scientific achievement, and intellectual growth.

While relevance for some students, especially those from low-income families, is equated with a practical education, for many other students relevance means concern with the political, social, economic, and environmental problems that have become so evident. Colleges and universities generally have given insufficient attention to these concerns. Research studies attack the problems, but in fragmented ways. Much university research, in fact, has helped to implement war technology, further the exhaustion of natural resources, and promote the growth of monopolistic power. The institutions have been self-seeking in searching for research grants and timid in promoting intellectual freedom. Research policies need overhauling, reevaluation, and fresh orientation toward the public good.

In the mid-seventies, the pressure of expanding numbers has receded, the computers have cooled down, and the need to submit to activist students has lessened. This, then, is a time for consolidation of gains and reconsideration of programs and of standards. Such reconsideration however should not be based solely on student demands. Egalitarianism, to which we fully subscribe, is sometimes interpreted to mean that the curriculum and teaching must be accommodated to the students' perceptions of their needs. Students are the consumers of education and hence should have a measure of influence in determining program and policy. A good education begins by teaching a student where he is in his educational development and then proceeds to enlarge his abilities, knowledge, and appreciations. At the same time, however, it is a disservice to graduate students who are less than competent in skills, who have only superficial knowledge, or who have experienced little or no growth in personal and social attitudes. All students should be expected to meet identifiable standards of personal development and academic achievement whether the education is practical or theoretical—quality of result applies to both learning to type and learning to think.

The curriculum would be more relevant to students if it focused on the basic issues of our time. Certainly we must cherish and pass along the knowledge and wisdom of the past. But the curriculum need not be devoted fully to the past. Instead the primary orientation needs to be the further development of society and preparation for the future. The aim should be the achievement of a more perfect society. "The good man in the good society" is a trite phrase, but it continues to be the ideal toward which all of higher education—students, faculty, administrators, and trustees—should strive.

Bibliography

AAUP Bulletin, Summer 1968, *54.*

American Civil Liberties Union. *Academic Freedom and Civil Liberties of Students in Colleges and Universities.* New York, 1970.

American Council on Education. *Fact Book on Higher Education.* Loose-leaf reporting series. Washington, D.C., 1973.

American Society for Engineering Education. "Final Report: Goals of Engineering Education." *Journal of Engineerng Education,* Jan. 1968, *58* (5), 373-443.

Anderson, C. A., Bowman, M. J., and Tinto, V. *Where Colleges Are and Who Attends: Effects of Accessibility on College Attendance.* New York: McGraw-Hill, 1972.

Armytage, W. H. G. *Civic Universities: Aspects of a British Tradition.* London: Ernest Benn, 1955.

Ashby, E. "The Case for Ivory Towers." In A. D. Henderson (Ed.), *Higher Education in Tomorrow's World.* Ann Arbor: University of Michigan, 1968.

Astin, A. W. *College Dropouts: A National Profile.* Washington, D.C.: American Council on Education, 1972.

Axelrod, J. *The University Teacher as Artist.* San Francisco: Jossey-Bass, 1973.

Axt, R. G., and Sprague, H. T. (Eds.) *College Self-Study.* Boulder, Colo.: Western Interstate Commission for Higher Education, 1960.

Bantock, G. H. *Culture, Industrialization, and Education.* London: Routledge and Kegan Paul, 1968.

Barnard, C. I. *The Functions of the Executive.* Cambridge, Mass.: Harvard University Press, 1938.

Bayer, A. E., and Astin, A. W. "Campus Unrest, 1970-1971: Was It Really All That Quiet?" *Educational Record,* Fall 1971, 309.

Bayer, A. E., Royer, J. T., and Webb, R. M. *Four Years after College Entry.* Washington, D.C.: American Council on Education, 1973.

Bell, D. *The Reforming of General Education.* New York: Columbia University Press, 1966.

Bennis, W. B. *Changing Organizations.* New York: McGraw-Hill, 1967.

Berdahl, R. O. *Statewide Coordination of Higher Education.* Washington, D.C.: American Council on Education, 1971.

Blackburn, R. T. *Tenure: Aspects of Job Security on the Changing Campus.* Atlanta: Southern Regional Education Board, 1972.

Boulding, K. E. "The Role of the University in the Development of a World Community." In A. D. Henderson (Ed.), *Higher Education in Tomorrow's World.* Ann Arbor: University of Michigan, 1968.

Brubacher, J. S. *The University . . . Its Identity Crisis.* New Britain, Conn.: Central Connecticut State College, 1972.

Brubacher, J. S., and Rudy, W. *Higher Education in Transition.* New York: Harper and Row, 1968.

Carnegie Commission on Higher Education. *The Open Door Colleges: Policies for Community Colleges.* New York: McGraw-Hill, 1970.

Carnegie Commission on Higher Education. *Less Time, More Options: Education Beyond the High School.* New York: McGraw-Hill, 1971a.

Carnegie Commission on Higher Education. *New Students and New Places: Policies for the Future Growth and Development of American Higher Education.* New York: McGraw-Hill, 1971b.

Carnegie Commission on Higher Education. *The More Effective Use of Resources: An Imperative for Higher Education.* New York: McGraw-Hill, 1972a.

Carnegie Commission on Higher Education. *Reform on Campus: Changing Students, Changing Academic Programs.* New York: McGraw-Hill, 1972b.

Carnegie Commission on Higher Education. *College Graduates and Jobs: Adjusting to a New Labor Market Situation.* New York: McGraw-Hill, 1973a.

Carnegie Commission on Higher Education. *Governance of Higher Education: Six Priority Problems.* New York: McGraw-Hill, 1973b.

Carnegie Commission on Higher Education. *Higher Education: Who Pays? Who Benefits? Who Should Pay?* New York: McGraw-Hill, 1973c.

Carnegie Commission on Higher Education. *Priorities for Action: Final Report.* New York: McGraw-Hill, 1973d.

Carnegie Commission on Higher Education. *Toward a Learning Society.* New York: McGraw-Hill, 1973e.

Carr, R. K. and VanEyck, D. K. *Collective Bargaining Comes to the Campus.* Washington: American Council on Education, 1973.

Cheek, K. V., Jr. "The Black College in a Multiracial Society." In D. W. Vermilye (Ed.), *The Expanded Campus: Current Issues in Higher Education 1972.* San Francisco: Jossey-Bass, 1972.

Cohen, J. W. (Ed.) *The Superior Student in American Higher Education.* New York: McGraw-Hill, 1965.

Cohen, M., and March, J. *Leadership and Ambiguity: The American College President.* New York: McGraw-Hill, 1974.

Commission on Financing Higher Education. *Nature and Needs of Higher Education.* New York: Columbia University Press, 1952.

Corson, J. J. *Governance of Colleges and Universities.* New York: McGraw-Hill, 1960.

Cross, K. P. *Beyond the Open Door.* San Francisco: Jossey-Bass, 1971.

Cross, K. P. *New Students and New Needs in Higher Education.* Berkeley: Center for Research and Development in Higher Education, University of California, 1972.

Curti, M., and Nash, R. *Philanthropy in the Shaping of American Higher Education.* New Brunswick, N.J.: Rutgers University Press, 1965.

Daedalus. "Students and Politics." Winter 1968.

Darley, J. G. *Promise and Performance.* Berkeley: Center for Research and Development in Higher Education, University of California, 1962.

Dewey, J. *Democracy and Education.* New York: Macmillan, 1916.

Dewey, J. *Experience and Education.* New York: Macmillan, 1950.

Donaldson, R. S. *Fortifying Higher Education: A Story of College Self-Studies.* New York: Fund for the Advancement of Education, 1959.

Dressel, P. L. *College and University Curriculum.* Berkeley: McCutchan, 1968.

Dressel, P. L., and Faricy, W. H. *Return to Responsibility: Constraints on Autonomy in Higher Education.* San Francisco: Jossey-Bass, 1972.

Dressel, P. L., and others. *The Confidence Crisis: An Analysis of University Departments.* San Francisco: Jossey-Bass, 1970.

Duryea, E. D., Fisk, R. S., and Associates. *Faculty Unions and Collective Bargaining.* San Francisco: Jossey-Bass, 1973.

Eckert, R. "Ways of Evaluating College Teaching." *School and Society,* Feb. 4, 1950, 65-69.

Economic Report of the President. Washington, D.C.: United States Government Printing Office, 1973.

Eddy, E. D., Jr. *Colleges for Our Land and Time.* New York: Harper and Row, 1957.

Erikson, Erik. *Identity: Youth and Crisis.* New York: W. W. Norton, 1968.

Eurich, A. C. (Ed.) *Campus 1980.* New York: Delacorte Press, 1968.

Flexner, A. *Medical Education in the United States and Canada.* New York: The Carnegie Foundation for the Advancement of Teaching, 1910.

Flexner, A. *Universities: American, English, German.* London: Oxford University Press, 1930.

Flexner, H. "General Education and Academic Innovation." *Journal of Research and Development in Education,* Fall 1972, 46-57.

Folger, J. K., Astin, H. S., and Bayer, A. E. *Human Resources and Higher Education: Staff Report of the Commission on Human Resources and Advanced Education.* New York: Russell Sage Foundation, 1970.

Gaff, J. G., and Associates. *The Cluster College.* San Francisco: Jossey-Bass, 1970.

Greene, T. M., and others. *Liberal Education Reexamined.* New York: Harper and Row, 1943.

Harcleroad, F. F. (Ed.) *Issues of the Seventies: The Future of Higher Education.* San Francisco: Jossey-Bass, 1970.

Harcleroad, F. F., Molen, A. T., Jr., and Rayman, J. R. *The Regional State Colleges and Universities Enter the 1970s.* Iowa City: ACT Publications, 1973.

Harris, N. C. *Developments in Technical and Vocational Education.* Washington, D.C.: U.S. Department of Health, Education and Welfare, 1969.

Hartnett, R. T. *College and University Trustees: Their Backgrounds, Roles, and Educational Attitudes.* Princeton: Educational Testing Service, 1969.

Harvard Alumni Bulletin. "Freedom at Harvard." June 25, 1949, pp. 729-736.

Harvard Committee. *General Education in a Free Society.* Cambridge: Harvard University Press, 1945.

Heiss, A. M. *Challenges to Graduate Schools.* San Francisco: Jossey-Bass, 1970.

Henderson, A. D. "The Administrator/Student Conflict." *Administrative Law Review,* Nov. 1968, *21* (1).

Henderson, A. D. "The Economic Aspects." In McGrath, E. J. (Ed.), *Universal Higher Education.* New York: McGraw-Hill, 1966.

Henderson, A. D. "An Educator's View of the Goals Report." *Journal of Engineering Education,* Sept. 1968, 25-50.

Henderson, A. D. (Ed.) *Higher Education in Tomorrow's World.* Ann Arbor: University of Michigan, 1968.

Henderson, A. D. *The Innovative Spirit.* San Francisco: Jossey-Bass, 1970.

Henderson, A. D. *The Role of the Governing Board.* Washington, D.C.: Association of Governing Boards of Universities and Colleges, 1973.

Hodgkinson, H. L. *Institutions in Transition.* Berkeley: Carnegie Commission on Higher Education, 1970.

Hofstadter, R., and Metzger, W. P. *The Development of Academic Freedom in the United States.* New York: Columbia University Press, 1955.

Hofstadter, R., and Smith, W. (Eds.) *American Higher Education: A Documentary History.* 2 vols. Chicago: University of Chicago Press, 1961.

Houle, C. O. *The Design of Education.* San Francisco: Jossey-Bass, 1972.

Hutchins, R. M. *Conflict in Education in a Democratic Society.* New York: Harper and Row, 1953.

Janssen, P. A. "Higher Education and the Black American." *The Chronicle of Higher Education,* May 30, 1972, 1-2.

Jellema, W. W. (Ed.) *Efficient College Management.* San Francisco: Jossey-Bass, 1972.

Jencks, C., and Riesman, D. *The Academic Revolution.* Garden City, N.Y.: Doubleday, 1968.

Jordan, D. S. *The Voice of the Scholar.* San Francisco: Paul Elder, 1903.

Justman, J., and Mais, W. H. *College Teaching: Its Practice and Potential.* New York: Harper and Row, 1965.

Kallen, H. M. *The Education of Free Men.* New York: Farrar and Straus, 1950.

Katz, J. and others. *No Time for Youth.* San Francisco: Jossey-Bass, 1968.

Katz, J. "The Challenge to 'Body Knowledge' Learning from Person-Centered Advocates." *Liberal Education,* May 1972, 142.

Keeton, M. T. "Alternative Pathways to Liberal Education." In McGrath, E. J., *Prospect for Renewal.* San Francisco: Jossey-Bass, 1972.

Keeton, M. T. *Models and Mavericks.* New York: McGraw-Hill, 1971.

Kellogg, C. E., and Knapp, D. C. *The College of Agriculture: Science in the Public Service.* New York: McGraw-Hill, 1966.

Keniston, K. *The Uncommitted: Alienated Youth in American Society.* New York: Harcourt, Brace, and World, 1965.

Kerr, C. *The Uses of the University.* Cambridge: Harvard University Press, 1963.

Knapp, R. H., and Goodrich, H. B. *Origins of American Scientists.* Chicago: University of Chicago Press, 1952.

Knapp, R. H., and Greenbaum, J. J. *The Younger American Scholar: His Collegiate Origins.* Chicago: University of Chicago Press, 1953.

Knowles, A. S. (Ed.) *Handbook of College and University Administrators.* New York: McGraw-Hill, 1969.

Knowles, A. S., & Associates. *Handbook of Cooperative Education.* San Francisco: Jossey-Bass, 1971.

Ladd, E., and Lipset, S. M. *Professors, Unions, and American Higher Education.* New York: McGraw-Hill, 1973.

Lee, C. B. T. (Ed.) *Improving College Teaching.* Washington, D.C.: American Council on Education, 1967.

Lee, E. C., and Bowen, F. M. *The Multicampus University.* New York: McGraw-Hill, 1971.

Leonard, E. A. *Origins of Personnel Services in American Higher Education.* Minneapolis: University of Minnesota Press, 1956.

Likert, R. *The Human Organization: Its Management and Value.* New York: McGraw-Hill, 1967.

Likert, R. *New Patterns of Management.* New York: McGraw-Hill, 1961.

McConnell, T. R., and Mortimer, K. *The Faculty in University Governance.* Berkeley: Center for Research and Development in Higher Education, University of California, 1971.

McGrath, E. J., and Johnson, J. T. *The Changing Mission of Home Economics.* New York: Columbia University, Teachers College, 1968.

McKeachie, W. J. *Teaching Tips: A Guidebook for the Beginning College Teacher.* Lexington, Mass.: D. C. Heath, 1969.

Martin, E. D. *The Meaning of a Liberal Education.* New York: W. W. Norton, 1926.

Martin, W. B. *Conformity: Standards and Change in Higher Education.* San Francisco: Jossey-Bass, 1969.

Mayhew, L. B. *Colleges Today and Tomorrow.* San Francisco: Jossey-Bass, 1969.

Mayhew, L. B. *Reform in Graduate Education.* Atlanta, Southern Regional Education Board, 1972.

Medsker, L. L., and Tillery, D. *Breaking the Access Barriers: A Profile of Two-Year Colleges.* New York: McGraw-Hill, 1971.

Miller, J. L., Jr. *State Budgeting for Higher Education: The Use of Formulas and Cost Analysis.* Ann Arbor: University of Michigan, Institute for Public Administration, 1964.

Miller, R. I. *Evaluating Faculty Performance.* San Francisco: Jossey-Bass, 1972.

Moberly, W. H. *Crisis in the University.* New York: Macmillan, 1949.

Monroe, C. R. *Profile of the Community College.* San Francisco: Jossey-Bass, 1972.

Moore, R. S. *Consortiums in American Higher Education, 1965-1966.* Washington, D.C.: U.S. Department of Health, Education and Welfare, 1968.

Moos, M., and Rourke, F. E. *The Campus and the State.* Baltimore: The Johns Hopkins Press, 1959.

Mushkin, S. J. *Economics of Higher Education.* Washington, D.C.: U.S. Government Printing Office, 1962.

Naughton, E. A. "What You See Is What You Get: Black Student/White Campus." In Vermilye, D. W. (Ed.), *The Expanded Campus, Current Issues in Higher Education.* San Francisco: Jossey-Bass, 1972.

Newcomb, T. M., and Feldman, K. A. *The Impact of College on Students.* 2 vols. San Francisco: Jossey-Bass, 1969.

Newman, F. *Report on Higher Education.* Washington, D.C.: U.S. Government Printing Office, 1971.

Newman, J. H. *The Idea of a University.* New York: American Press, 1941.

Orlans, H. (Ed.) *Science Policy and the University.* Washington, D.C.: The Brookings Institute, 1968.

Ortega y Gasset, J. *Mission of the University.* Princeton: Princeton University Press, 1944.

Packer, H. L., and Ehrlich, T. *New Directions in Legal Education.* New York: McGraw-Hill, 1972.

Paltridge, J. G., Hurst, J., and Morgan, A. *Boards of Trustees: Their Decision Patterns.* Berkeley: Center for Research and Development in Higher Education, University of California, 1973.

Panos, R. I., and Astin, A. W. "Attrition among College Students." *American Education Research Journal,* 1968, 5 (1).

Paulsen, F. *German Universities: Their Character and Historical Development.* Translated by Edward D. Perry. New York: Macmillan, 1895.

Perkins, J. A. (Ed.) *The University As an Organization.* New York: McGraw-Hill, 1973.

Peterson, R. E. *American College and University Enrollment Trends in 1971.* New York: McGraw-Hill, 1972.

President's Committee on Education Beyond the High School. *Second Report to the President.* Also the *Summary Report.* Washington, D.C.: U.S. Government Printing Office, 1957.

President's Commission on Higher Education. *Report, Vols. I, II, III, IV, V, VI.* Washington, D.C.: U.S. Government Printing Office, 1947-1948.

Riesman, D., and Stadtman, V. A. *Academic Transformation.* New York: McGraw-Hill, 1973.

Robbins, Lord, Committee on Higher Education. *Higher Education Report.* London: HMSO, 1963.

Robinson, L. H. *The Emergence of Women's Courses in Higher Education.* Washington, D.C.: ERIC Clearinghouse on Higher Education, n.d.

Robinson, L. H. *The Status of Academic Women.* Washington, D.C.: ERIC Clearinghouse on Higher Education, 1971.

Rourke, F. E., and Brooks, G. E. (Eds.) *The Managerial Revolution in Higher Education.* Baltimore: Johns Hopkins Press, 1966.

Sanford, N. (Ed.) *The American College: A Psychological and Social Interpretation of the Higher Learning.* New York: John Wiley, 1962.

Schmidt, G. P. *The Liberal Arts College.* New Brunswick, N.J.: Rutgers University Press, 1957.

Schultz, T. W. *The Economic Values of Education.* New York: Columbia University Press, 1963.

Selden, W. *Accreditation: A Struggle over Standards in Higher Education.* New York: Harper and Row, 1960.

Sewell, W. H., and Shah, V. P. "Socioeconomic Status, Intelligence, and the Attainment of Higher Education." *Sociology of Education,* Winter 1967, *40* (13).

Simon, H. A. *Administrative Behavior.* (2nd ed.) New York: Free Press, 1967.

Singer, M. B. In Ward, F. C. (Ed.), *The Idea and Practice of General Education.* Chicago: University of Chicago Press, 1950.

Smith, B. L., and Associates. *The Tenure Debate.* San Francisco: Jossey-Bass, 1973.

Spaeth, J. L., and Greeley, A. M. *Recent Alumni and Higher Education: A Survey of College Graduates.* New York: McGraw-Hill, 1970.

Spurr, S. *Academic Degree Structures: Innovative Approaches.* New York: McGraw-Hill, 1970.

Stone, J. C., and DeNevi, D. P. *Portraits of the American University, 1890-1910.* San Francisco: Jossey-Bass, 1971.

Stuart, C. E. v. School District No. 1 of the Village of Kalamazoo, et al., 30 Mich. 69 (July 21, 1874).

Taubman, P., and Wales, T. *Mental Ability and Higher Educational Attainment in the Twentieth Century.* New York: McGraw-Hill, 1972.

Time. "Less School—More Work." August 27, 1973, p. 54.

Trent, J. W., and Medsker, L. L. *Beyond High School: A Study of 10,000 High School Graduates.* Berkeley: University of California, Center for Research and Development in Higher Education, 1967.

Tyler, R. W. *Basic Principles of Curriculum and Instruction.* Chicago: University of Chicago Press, 1950.

U.S. Department of Labor, Bureau of Labor Statistics. *Employment of Recent College Graduates.* Washington, D.C.: U.S. Government Printing Office, 1973.

Van Doren, M. *Liberal Education.* New York: Holt, 1944.

Watkins, B. T. "Student Demands for 'Practical' Education Are Forcing Major Changes in Curricula." *The Chronicle of Higher Education,* Nov. 26, 1973, p. 2.

Williams, H. *Planning for Effective Resource Allocation in Universities.* Washington, D.C.: American Council on Education, 1966.

Williamson, E. G. *Student Personnel Services in Colleges and Universities.* New York: McGraw-Hill, 1961.

Wolfle, D. *The Home of Science: The Role of the University.* New York: McGraw-Hill, 1972.

Woody, T. *A History of Women's Education in the United States.* 2 vols. New York: The Science Press, 1929.

Bibliographical References

The following publications include comprehensive and recent bibliographies on the problems, policies and projections in higher education:

Henderson, A. D. *Training University Administrators: A Programme Guide.* Paris: UNESCO, 1970.

Newman, F. *Report on Higher Education.* Washington, D.C.: U.S. Department of Health, Education and Welfare, 1971.

Carnegie Commission on Higher Education. *Priorities for Action: Final Report,* Appendix A, 191-192; Appendix B, 193-200. New York: McGraw-Hill, 1973.

Index